Workshop
Schwerpunkte:
Lesen, Hören, Sprechen, Schreiben, Wortschatz und Grammatik

Reading workshop
Schwerpunkt Leseverständnis: Geschichten und Sachtexte passend zum Unit-Thema

Speaking workshop
Schwerpunkt: monologisches und dialogisches Sprechen

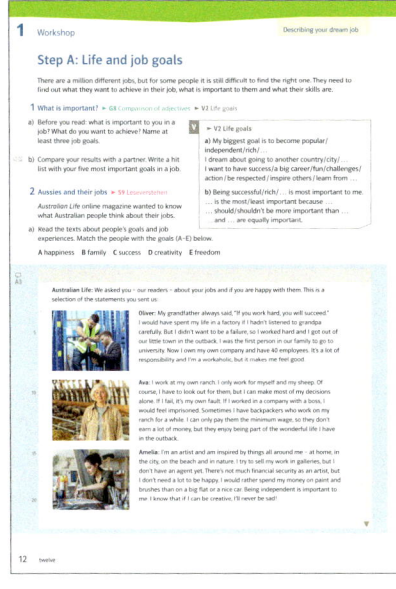
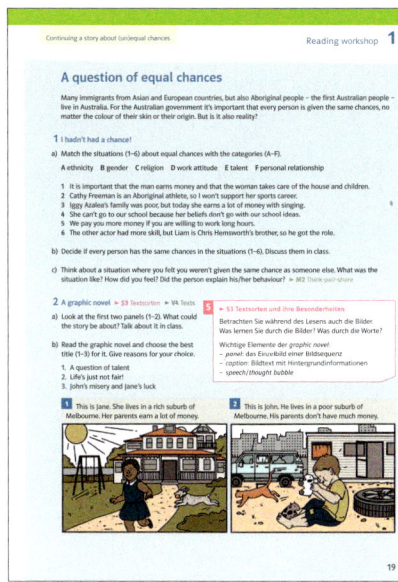
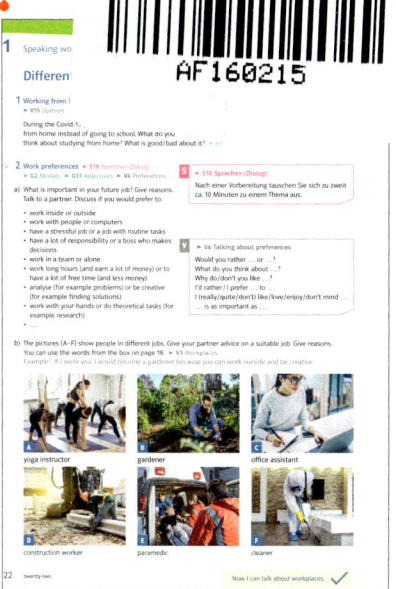

Video lounge
Video oder Videorecherche zum Thema der Unit mit Übungen

Check out
Übungen zur Prüfungsvorbereitung

Symbole

► H1		Verweis auf leichtere Übung / Aufgabe (Niveau A1+)
► S1		Verweis auf Skill
► G1		Verweis auf Grammatik
► M1		Verweis auf Methode
► V1		Verweis auf Vokabular
🚩		Interkulturelle Informationen
💬 A1		Verweis auf Audio-Track A1 (online)
🎬 V1		Verweis auf Video V1 (online)
🎬 VG1		Verweis auf den Grammatik-Erklärfilm passend zum Grammatikthema (online)
👥		Partnerarbeit
👥👥		Gruppenarbeit
🌐 dp78ec		Auf den Starter-Seiten im Buch finden Sie Gateway-Codes. Diese führen zu allen Audios (als Download oder zum Streamen), Vokabellernlisten und weiteren Zusatzmaterialien im Internet. Geben Sie den Code in das Suchfeld auf www.klett.de ein.

Gateway Upgrade BW
Englisch für die Berufsfachschule

1. Auflage   1 5 4 3 2 1 | 25 24 23 22 21

Alle Drucke dieser Auflage sind unverändert und können im Unterricht nebeneinander und können im Unterricht nebeneinander verwendet werden. Die letzte Zahl bezeichnet das Jahr des Druckes.
Das Werk und seine Teile sind urheberrechtlich geschützt. Das gleiche gilt für die Software und das Begleitmaterial. Jede Nutzung in anderen als den gesetzlich zugelassenen oder in den Lizenzbestimmungen (CD/DVD) genannten Fällen bedarf der vorherigen schriftlichen Einwilligung des Verlages. Hinweis § 60a UrhG: Weder das Werk noch seine Teile dürfen ohne eine solche Einwilligung eingescannt und in ein Netzwerk eingestellt werden. Dies gilt auch für Intranets von Schulen und sonstigen Bildungseinrichtungen. Fotomechanische oder andere Wiedergabeverfahren nur mit Genehmigung des Verlages.

Hinweis: Die Mediencodes enthalten zusätzliche Unterrichtsmaterialien, die der Verlag in eigener Verantwortung zur Verfügung stellt.

© Ernst Klett Verlag GmbH, Stuttgart 2021. Alle Rechte vorbehalten. www.klett.de
Das vorliegende Material dient ausschließlich gemäß § 60b UrhG dem Einsatz im Unterricht an Schulen.

Herausgeber: Dr. Frank Haß, Kirchberg
Autorinnen: Jennifer Baer-Engel, Göppingen; Dagmar Taylor, Edinburgh (UK); Anja Treinies, Düsseldorf; Christine Vincent, Gainesville (FL); sowie: Gerlind Becker, Berlin; Daniella Suillivan, Berlin
Beratung: Luise Buschmann, Sigmaringen; Katja Eberhard, Ludwigshafen; Maike Hoff, Tübingen; Jürgen Schmid, Albstadt

Entstanden in Zusammenarbeit mit dem Projektteam des Verlages.

Externe Redaktion: Birgit Ahlemeyer (Vokabular), Neuruppin; Lektorat editoria: Cornelia Schaller, Fellbach; Christine Vincent, Gainesville (FL), USA
Gestaltung: KOMA AMOK, Stuttgart
Umschlaggestaltung: KOMA AMOK, Stuttgart
Titelbilder: Getty Images Plus, München; E+/Rocky89; stock.adobe.com, Dublin; by-studio
Illustrationen: Julia Bernhard, Berlin; Christian Dekelver, Weinstadt; Peer Kramer, Düsseldorf
Satz: graphitecture book & edition
Repro: Schwabenrepro GmbH, Fellbach
Druck: PASSAVIA Druckservice GmbH & Co. KG, Passau

Printed in Germany
ISBN 978-3-12-809300-0

Gateway Upgrade BW

Englisch für die Berufsfachschule

Herausgeber:
Dr. Frank Haß

Ernst Klett Verlag
Stuttgart · Leipzig · Dortmund

Inhalt

	Themen	Kompetenzen	Seite

Unit 1: Australia: endless options?

Starter Creating a poster about your rights and obligations	Rights and obligations **S1** Informationen beschaffen **S10** Hörverstehen **S11** Visualisierung Your turn My rights and obligations	**IK:** Rechte und Pflichten in Australien ab 18 **KK:** Hören / Telefonat **MK:** Online-Recherche	10
Workshop Describing your dream job	Step A: Life and job goals **S9** Leseverstehen **S19** Wortarten erkennen und bilden **G16** Conditional clauses **V2** Life goals Step B: Job skills and workplaces **S13** Bildbeschreibung **S10** Hörverstehen **V3** Workplaces, jobs and tasks Your turn The perfect job for me!	**KK:** Lesen / Online posts **KK:** Quiz / eigene Fähigkeiten **KK:** Hören / Jobs **KK:** Sprechen / sich einigen	12
Reading workshop Continuing a story about (un)equal chances	A question of equal chances **S3** Textsorten und ihre Besonderheiten **S13** Bildbeschreibung **S15** Fortsetzung einer Geschichte **V5** Writing a story Your turn How their lives continue	**KK:** Lesen / Graphic novel **KK:** Schreiben / Fortsetzung einer Geschichte	19
Speaking workshop Talking about workplaces	Different workplaces **S18** Sprechen (Monolog/Dialog) **V6** Talking about preferences	**KK:** Sprechen / Monolog; Dialog	22
Video lounge	Meet the experts: Talking about jobs **S5** Hörsehverstehen **V3** Workplaces, jobs and tasks	**MK:** Hörsehverstehen / Tutorial	23
Check out Preparing for a test	Check out: Australia	**KK:** Hören / Radiosendung **KK:** Lesen / Zeitungsartikel **KK:** Schreiben / Fortsetzung einer Geschichte	24

S = Skills **G** = Grammatik **V** = Vokabular
IK = Interkulturelle Kompetenz **KK** = Kommunikative Kompetenzen **MK** = Medienkompetenz

	Themen	Kompetenzen	Seite

Unit 2: Working in Ireland

Starter Writing a comment about working abroad	And then I moved to Ireland **S6** Einen Kommentar schreiben **S10** Hörverstehen **S13** Bildbeschreibung **V7** Giving a recommendation **V9** Writing a comment Your turn Should I stay or should I go?	**IK:** Irland **KK:** Hören / Aussagen über den Umzug nach und einen Job in Irland **KK:** Schreiben / Kommentar	28
Workshop Writing a job application	Step A: Job adverts **S9** Leseverstehen **V10** Analysing job adverts Step B: Applying for a job **S20** Bewerbung **S21** Lebenslauf **V12** Analysing cartoons **V13** CV **V14** Writing a letter of application Your turn My application	**KK:** Lesen / Stellenanzeigen **KK:** Lesen / Lebenslauf **KK:** Lesen / Bewerbung **IK:** Lebenslauf **IK:** Bewerbung **KK:** Schreiben / Lebenslauf; Bewerbung	30
Reading workshop Writing a dialogue between two fictional characters	Returning to Dublin **S9** Leseverstehen **S13** Bildbeschreibung **S15** Fortsetzung einer Geschichte **S17** Mediation **V5** Writing a story Your turn A conversation with Jerry	**IK:** Dublin im Wandel der Zeit **KK:** Lesen / Romanauszug **KK:** Schreiben / fiktiver Dialog	36
Video lounge	Meet the experts: Doing a good job interview **S5** Hörsehverstehen	**MK:** Hörsehverstehen / Tutorial	40
Speaking workshop Acting out a job interview	Job interviews **S10** Hörverstehen **S18** Sprechen (Dialog/Rollenspiel) **V15** Doing a job interview	**IK:** Vorstellungsgespräch **KK:** Hören / Vorstellungsgespräch **KK:** Sprechen / Dialog	41
Check out Preparing for a test	Check out: Ireland	**KK:** Hören / Vorstellungsgespräch **KK:** Lesen / Zeitungsartikel **KK:** Schreiben / Empfehlung; Bewerbung	42

S = Skills   **G** = Grammatik   **V** = Vokabular
IK = Interkulturelle Kompetenz   **KK** = Kommunikative Kompetenzen   **MK** = Medienkompetenz

Inhalt

	Themen	Kompetenzen	Seite

Unit 3: Multicultural South Africa

Starter
Preparing and doing an interview

Rainbow nation
S10 Hörverstehen
S22 Ein Interview führen
V17 Multiculturalism
V18 Doing an interview
<mark>Your turn</mark> An interview with a famous person

IK: Kulturen in Südafrika
KK: Hören / Interviews
MK: Sprechen / Ein Interview führen

46

Workshop
Writing the story behind a picture

Step A: South Africa in pictures
S13 Bildbeschreibung
G19 Adverbs and sequence of adverbs
Step B: The story behind the picture
S9 Leseverstehen
S15 Eine Geschichte zu einem Bild schreiben
G20 Conjunctions and adverbial clauses
V5 Writing a story
<mark>Your turn</mark> The story behind the picture

IK: Geschichte Südafrikas
IK: Soweto Uprising
KK: Lesen / Zeitstrahl; Bildbeschreibung; Geschichte eines Fotos
KK: Sprechen / Bildbeschreibung
KK: Schreiben / Geschichte zu einem Foto

48

Reading workshop
Planning and promoting an event against racism

The Big Five Marathon
S9 Leseverstehen
S4 Eine Präsentation halten
S11 Visualisierung
S19 Wortarten erkennen und bilden
V19 Animals
V22 Sensations
<mark>Your turn</mark> No racism

IK: Natur Südafrikas
KK: Lesen / Erfahrungsbericht
MK: eine Veranstaltung planen

54

Speaking workshop
Talking about and suggesting free-time activities

Free-time activities
S18 Sprechen (Monolog/Dialog)
V21 Free time
V23 Making suggestions

KK: Sprechen / Freizeitaktivitäten
KK: Sprechen / Monolog; Dialog

59

Video lounge

Discovering South Africa
S1 Informationen beschaffen
S5 Hörsehverstehen
V24 Talking about locations

MK: Hörsehverstehen / Internetrecherche

58

Check out
Preparing for a test

Check out: South Africa

KK: Hören / Radiosendung
KK: Lesen / Wikitext
KK: Schreiben / Kommentar; Geschichte zu einem Foto

60

S = Skills   **G** = Grammatik   **V** = Vokabular
IK = Interkulturelle Kompetenz   **KK** = Kommunikative Kompetenzen   **MK** = Medienkompetenz

	Themen	Kompetenzen	Seite
Unit 4: Digital Hong Kong			
Starter Recommending a selfie spot	**Discovering the city** **S10** Hörverstehen **S3** Textsorten und ihre Besonderheiten **V23** Sightseeing **V7** Recommendation Your turn A recommendation	**IK:** Hongkongs Selfiespots **KK:** Hören / Radiosendung **KK:** Schreiben / Empfehlung	64
Workshop Creating a poster about media addiction	**Step A: Media habits** **S7** Sammeln und ordnen **S10** Hörverstehen **S25** Media **V25** Talking about media habits **Step B: Media usage in Hong Kong** **S9** Leseverstehen **S2** Diagramme analysieren **V25** Media **V26** Talking about media habits **V27** Analysing charts **V28** Feelings **G4/G1** The passive voice I+II **Step C: Am I addicted to my phone?** **S11** Visualisierung **S17** Mediation Your turn A poster about media addiction	**KK:** Hören / Radiosendung **KK:** Sprechen / Diagramme analysieren **KK:** Lesen / Onlinekommentare; Test **MK:** Schreiben / Poster	66
Reading workshop Writing a profile of your favourite influencer	**Living for the likes** **S1** Informationen beschaffen **S9** Leseverstehen Your turn My favourite influencer	**IK:** eine chinesische Influencerin **KK:** Lesen / Zeitungsartikel **KK:** Schreiben / Profil	73
Video lounge	**Meet the experts: Talking about contracts** **S5** Hörsehverstehen **S12** Eine E-Mail schreiben **V29** Writing an email	**MK:** Hörsehverstehen / Tutorial **KK:** Schreiben / E-Mail	76
Speaking workshop Talking about and discussing mobile phone habits	**How important is your mobile phone?** **S18** Sprechen (Monolog/Dialog) **V30** Asking for help	**KK:** Sprechen / Monolog; Dialog	77
Check out Preparing for a test	**Check out: Hong Kong**	**KK:** Hören / Sprachnachrichten **KK:** Lesen / Kurzgeschichte **KK:** Schreiben / Geschichte zu einem Foto; E-Mail	78

S = Skills   **G** = Grammatik   **V** = Vokabular
IK = Interkulturelle Kompetenz   **KK** = Kommunikative Kompetenzen   **MK** = Medienkompetenz

Inhalt

	Themen		Seite
Unit 5: Green California?			
Starter Writing a wiki entry about an aspect of California	High tech meets agriculture **S3** Textsorten und ihre Besonderheiten **S7** Sammeln und ordnen **S10** Hörverstehen Your turn A wiki entry	**IK:** Kalifornien **KK:** Hören / Podcast **KK:** Schreiben / Wikieintrag	82
Workshop Having a debate about a zero-waste snack shop	Step A: Waste not, want not **S9** Leseverstehen **S17** Mediation **G25** Infinitive and participle constructions instead of subordinate clauses **S12** Eine E-Mail schreiben **V31** Food Step B: Shopping and packaging **S10** Hörverstehen **S18** Sprechen (Diskussion/Debatte) **V32** Packaging and material Your turn Organising and having a debate	**IK:** Müllvermeidung **KK:** Lesen / Zeitungsartikel **KK:** Schreiben / E-Mail **KK:** Hören / Radiosendung **KK:** Sprechen / Debatte	84
Reading corner Writing a blog post about your ideal school	My ideal school **S9** Leseverstehen **S8** Einen Blogpost schreiben **V33** School Your turn My ideal school	**IK:** Waldorfschulen im Silicon Valley **KK:** Lesen / Blog **KK:** Schreiben / Blogpost	91
Speaking workshop Having a conversation in a diner	Talking about food **S18** Sprechen (Monolog/Dialog) **V34** In a restaurant	**KK:** Sprechen / Monolog; Dialog	95
Video lounge	Californian national parks **S5** Hörsehverstehen **S4** Eine Präsentation halten **V1** Giving a presentation	**IK:** Nationalparks in Kalifornien **MK:** Hörsehverstehen / Internetrecherche **MK:** Präsentation	94
Check out Preparing for a test	Check out: California	**KK:** Hören / Wettervorhersagen **KK:** Lesen / Zeitungsartikel **KK:** Schreiben / Kommentar; Bewerbung; Blogpost	96
Advanced texts	Lesetexte auf höherem Niveau		100
Helping hand	Parallelaufgaben zu den Units 1–5 auf leichterem Niveau		110
Mediation	Sprachmittlungsaufgaben zu den Units 1–5		124
Skills	Tipps und Strategien zu verschiedenen Fertigkeiten		129
Grammar	Grammatik-Wiederholung mit Übungen		158
	List of irregular verbs		186
Methods	Unterrichtsmethoden		187
Solutions	Lösungen		190
Vocabulary	Wortschatz: Word banks (Funktions- und Themenwortschatz)		193
	Dictionary (Wörterbuch Englisch-Deutsch)		210
Weltkarte	Markierung der Länder und Regionen zu den Units		222

S = Skills   **G** = Grammatik   **V** = Vokabular
IK = Interkulturelle Kompetenz   **KK** = Kommunikative Kompetenzen   **MK** = Medienkompetenz

Gateway-Materialien online

Alle Audios, Videos und Vokabellisten zu Gateway stehen Ihnen auf www.klett.de kostenlos zur Verfügung. Am Anfang jeder Unit finden Sie einen Online-Code. Geben Sie diesen auf www.klett.de in das Suchfeld oben ein, um direkt zu Ihren Materialien zu gelangen.

Klett

Code hier eingeben — Weiter

Geben Sie hier Ihren Lehrwerks-Code oder Online-Link ein und springen Sie direkt zu Ihren Materialien.
Die Mediencodes enthalten zusätzliche Unterrichtsmaterialien, die der Verlag in eigener Verantwortung zur Verfügung stellt.

Gateway Foundation
Englisch für die Berufsfachschule
2. Lernjahr Ausgabe Baden-Württemberg ab 2021

Schülerbuch
978-3-12-809300-0

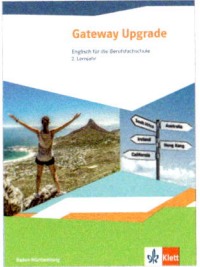

Audios zum Anhören

Track 1 — Track 2 — Track 3

Audios zum Download

Download Audio-Dateien

Download Audio-Dateien Gateway Foundation (ZIP, 12.03 MB)

Vokabellernliste (als pdf und editierbare Word-Datei)

Grammatik-Erklärfilme

Mit Hilfe von Grammatik-Erklärfilmen und interaktiven Übungen können grammatische Phänomene wiederholt und gefestigt werden.
Die Filme und Übungen finden Sie unter dem **Online-Code g36zt9** auf www.klett.de.

– Present tenses	GV1 Simple present, present progressive GV2 Questions and negative sentences
– Past tenses	GV3 Simple past, past progressive GV4 Present perfect, simple past GV5 Past perfect
– Future tenses	GV6 Will-future, going-to-future
– Nouns and articles	GV7 Plural GV8 Genitive GV9 Articles
– Pronouns	GV10 Pronouns
– Quantities	GV11 Much, many GV12 Some, any
– Adjectives and adverbs	GV13 Adjectives, adverbs GV14 Comparison of adjectives, adverbs GV15 Word order
– Modals	GV16 Modal auxiliaries
– Relative clauses	GV17 Relative clauses: who, which, whose
– Conditional clauses	GV18 If-clauses
– Gerund	GV19 The gerund
– Passive voice	GV20 The passive: present, past, future
– Reported speech	GV21, 22, 23 Reported speech

sq6bi9

1 Australia: endless options?

Rights and obligations

In this unit you will:
- create a poster about your rights and obligations.
- describe your dream job.
- continue a story about (un)equal chances.
- talk about workplaces.

Australia is the country of many people's dreams: you can visit lots of interesting places, see kangaroos and koalas and have a lot of adventures. That's why many people want to live there, so they apply for a job. However, if you want to live in Australia, you must follow its rules too.

A

D

B

C

E

1 What can you do in Australia?

a) Look at the pictures (A–E). Match the places with them: farm, Bondi Beach, Sydney, Uluru and Great Barrier Reef. What can you do and see in Australia? Do you know of any other activities or places there? Talk to a partner. You can research online.

b) What can you do and see in Australia? Do you know of other activities or places in Australia? Talk to a partner. When you turn 18 in Australia, you have to pay attention because some rules and rights change at this age. Match the pictures (A–E) with the rights and obligations (1–5).

Turning 18 in Australia

1. You can change your name and get married without anyone's permission.
2. You are allowed to sign a work contract. Be careful: there is a minimum wage your employer has to pay you and you have to pay tax.
3. You can buy alcohol, but you aren't allowed to drink it in all places. If you are caught drinking, you have to pay a fine.
4. You can be held responsible for any agreement you make (for example, if you borrow money, rent a flat, book an adventure trip or sign any contract).
5. You can have a permanent driving licence.

Starter 1

2 Young Aussies

A1 a) Listen to Georgina (age 17) and her cousin Peter (age 22) on the phone. Where are they from?

b) Listen again. What rights and obligations are they talking about? Copy and fill in the table. ► H1 ► S10 Hörverstehen

	rights	obligations
Georgina	…	…
Peter	…	…

c) Read the statements of young Australian adults. Add the rights and obligations they mention to the table from a).

A2

Lilith: When you turn 18, you don't need your parents' permission any more. That's why I got a tattoo and didn't tell them. But I had to pay for it myself. And I married my boyfriend because my parents didn't allow it before. I heard in some countries you have to attend school until you are 18. Here in Australia, it's only until 16. That's also when I started working full time.

Delilah: In Australia, after your 18th birthday you can go to bars and nightclubs and stay there 24 hours if you want. But the most important thing when I turned 18 was being able to vote. If you don't vote, you can get a fine. So it's a right and an obligation. I can go to peaceful demonstrations and others have to respect my rights, beliefs and opinions and I have to respect theirs.

Edan: At 18, I could finally get a credit card. I made some mistakes and spent too much money. Now I have debts to pay! I thought about stealing the money but in Australia you can go to prison from the age of 10 for criminal actions. So I decided it's better to earn the money with a real job. Now I have learnt how to deal with my money responsibly.

d) Add the missing rights and obligations from the flyer in ex. 1 to your table from a).

3 Your turn My rights and obligations ► S11 Visualisierung ► V1 Presentation

a) What are your rights and obligations in Germany at age 16 and 18? Think about voting, alcohol, work, contracts, driving etc. Make notes. You can research online. ► S1 Informationen

b) In small groups, make a poster about young adults' rights and obligations in Germany.

c) Present your results in class.
► S4 Präsentation ► M11 Gallery walk
► V1 Presentation

d) Vote in class: which group should present their poster in your school?

S ► S11 Visualisierung
- Planen Sie den Aufbau des Posters: Wo soll man zuerst hinschauen? Welche Information ist wichtig?
- Verwenden Sie Bild- und Schriftgrößen, die man gut erkennen bzw. lesen kann.
- Begrenzen Sie die Textmenge. Verwenden Sie kurze Sätze und Schlagwörter.
- Nutzen Sie den verfügbaren Platz.

V In Germany you must / are required to / …
It is your obligation to protect / follow / listen to …
Contracts must be fulfilled / completed by …
You have the right to …
Workers are allowed free time / equal pay / holidays …
Everyone is allowed to …
You can demand / ask for / …

Now I can create a poster about my rights and obligations.

1 Workshop

Describing your dream job

Step A: Life and job goals

There are a million different jobs, but for some people it is still difficult to find the right one. They need to find out what they want to achieve in their job, what is important to them and what their skills are.

1 What is important? ▶ G8 Comparison of adjectives ▶ V2 Life goals

a) Before you read: what is important to you in a job? What do you want to achieve? Name at least three job goals.

b) Compare your results with a partner. Write a hit list with your five most important goals in a job.

> **▶ V2 Life goals**
>
> a) My biggest goal is to become popular/independent/rich/…
> I dream about going to another country/city/…
> I want to have success/a big career/fun/challenges/action/be respected/inspire others/learn from …
>
> b) Being successful/rich/… is most important to me.
> … is the most/least important because …
> … should/shouldn't be more important than …
> … and … are equally important.

2 Aussies and their jobs ▶ S9 Leseverstehen

Australian Life online magazine wanted to know what Australian people think about their jobs.

a) Read the texts about people's goals and job experiences. Match the people with the goals (A–E) below.

A happiness   B family   C success   D creativity   E freedom

Australian Life: We asked you – our readers – about your jobs and if you are happy with them. This is a selection of the statements you sent us:

Oliver: My grandfather always said, "If you work hard, you will succeed." I would have spent my life in a factory if I hadn't listened to grandpa carefully. But I didn't want to be a failure, so I worked hard and I got out of our little town in the outback. I was the first person in our family to go to university. Now I own my own company and have 40 employees. It's a lot of responsibility and I'm a workaholic, but it makes me feel good.

Ava: I work at my own ranch. I only work for myself and my sheep. Of course, I have to look out for them, but I can make most of my decisions alone. If I fail, it's my own fault. If I worked in a company with a boss, I would feel imprisoned. Sometimes I have backpackers who work on my ranch for a while. I can only pay them the minimum wage, so they don't earn a lot of money, but they enjoy being part of the wonderful life I have in the outback.

Amelia: I'm an artist and am inspired by things all around me – at home, in the city, on the beach and in nature. I try to sell my work in galleries, but I don't have an agent yet. There's not much financial security as an artist, but I don't need a lot to be happy. I would rather spend my money on paint and brushes than on a big flat or a nice car. Being independent is important to me. I know that if I can be creative, I'll never be sad!

Jack: It took me a long time to find a job I enjoyed. After school, I had a lot of unskilled jobs, like fruit-picking. It's hard work and the pay is low. You have to move to wherever the work is. After about two years of doing that, I started a job training programme and soon I'll be a plumber. If I had continued as an unskilled worker, I would have been unhappy for the rest of my life. Plus it's bad for your health and there's no job security. You only get paid when you work and there aren't any benefits like health insurance or paid holidays.

Marli: I'm a real Australian as I'm from an Aboriginal family, still I think I have different goals compared to white Australians. When I was a young girl, I was taken away from my home because the government didn't think my parents were taking good care of me. Today I have a big family of my own – five kids! I chose to be a stay-at-home mum; that was my goal. Having time with my children is much more important to me than a career and a lot of money. If I didn't have my big family, I would feel lost.

b) Read again. Are the statements true or false? Correct the false ones.

1. Oliver is working in his own company.
2. It's important to Ava to make her own decisions.
3. Ava sometimes invites Australian guests on her farm.
4. Amelia thinks you can only find art in nature.
5. Amelia doesn't spend much money on her flat.
6. Jack believes he will be unhappy for the rest of his life.
7. Marli's children grow up in another family.
8. Marli works in her own household.

c) Which person is described here: Oliver, Ava, Amelia, Jack or Marli?

1. doesn't want to be a worker in a factory.
2. is a skilled worker now.
3. lives in the outback.
4. didn't grow up with her family.
5. is a creative person.
6. went to university.
7. is inspired by her environment.
8. thinks a career isn't so important.

d) Look at your hit list from ex. 1b) again. Do you want to add any new goals?
Rank your new list from most important (1) to least important (5) in your job. Then discuss your goals in class.

3 Focus on words

a) Find a word or phrase from the texts in ex. 2a) which means the opposite.

1. success ↔ ■ (lines 3–9)
2. free ↔ ■ (lines 10–15)
3. terrible ↔ ■ (lines 10–15)
4. trained ↔ ■ (lines 22–29)
5. disadvantage ↔ ■ (lines 22–29)
6. to feel at home ↔ ■ (lines 30–37)

b) Explain these words and phrases. Write complete sentences.

1. workaholic (line 8)   2. artist (line 16)   3. be inspired by (line 16)   4. goal (line 31)

1 Workshop

4 The parts of speech ▶ S19 Wortarten
▶ G13, G14, G15, G17 Parts of speech

▶ S19 Wortarten

noun = *Hauptwort*
verb = *Tunwort*
adjective = *Wie-Wort, das ein Nomen näher beschreibt*
adverb = *Umstandswort, das z.B. ein Verb näher beschreibt*
preposition = *Verhältniswort*
pronouns – *Fürwort (Personalpronomen, Besitzwörter, etc.)*
article – *Artikel*: the, a

a) Sort the underlined words from Oliver's text on page 12 into the right category.

> My grandfather always said, "If you work hard, you will succeed." I would have spent my life in a factory if I hadn't listened to grandpa carefully. But I didn't want to be a failure, so I worked hard and I got out of our little town in the outback. I was the first person in our family to go to university. Now I own my own company and have 40 employees. It's a lot of responsibility and I'm a workaholic, but it makes me feel good.

noun	verb	adjective	adverb	preposition	pronoun
grandfather	work	little	hard	in	my
…	…	…	…	…	…

b) Copy the table and complete it with words from the same word families. Work with a dictionary.

	noun	adjective	verb
1.	success	■	■
2.	■	failing	■
3.	■	■	to decide
4.	■	inspirational	■
5.	creativity/■	■	■

c) Complete the text. Use words from the table in b). ▶ H1

I couldn't find any job that interested me. Then one of my teachers ■ (1) me to ■ (2) my dream job. After I had made the ■ (3) to try, I was sure that I could be ■ (4). I've always been happiest when I can be ■ (5) – with wood, paint and paper. So when I was done with school, I ■ (6) to open a shop filled with my own ■ (7) – paintings, furniture and books. The first six months were difficult and I was sure I was going to ■ (8). But now people tell me that the shop is very ■ (9) for them and I even offer art classes in the evening. They're a huge ■ (10)!

▶ S19 Wortarten

Achten Sie beim Einsetzen verschiedener Wortarten in einen Lückentext auf die Position und die umgebenden Wörter:
- Vor einem Nomen steht meist ein Artikel oder ein Adjektiv.
- Ein Adjektiv steht immer bei einem Nomen.
- Jeder Satz verfügt über ein Verb.

d) Complete the sentences with the correct prepositions.
▶ G15 Prepositions ▶ H1

1. My goal at the moment is to succeed ■ school.
2. I want a job where I can take care ■ other people.
3. My decision is based ■ my experience during my internship.
4. I've been inspired ■ my mother who is a nurse.
5. I wish I had listened ■ my own feelings sooner.
6. It's important to spend time ■ big decisions like this.

Workshop 1

G ▶ G16 CONDITIONAL CLAUSES

GV18

a) Match the sentence parts from the texts on pages 12–13.

1 If you work hard,
2 If I worked in a company with a boss,
3 If I had continued as an unskilled worker,

A I would have been unhappy for the rest of my life.
B you will succeed.
C I would feel imprisoned.

b) Complete the table with the correct tense. Use the words from the word bank.

| past perfect | simple past | would + have + past participle | will-future | would + infinitive |

Type I

	if-clause	main clause
TENSE	simple present	■
USE	it is very possible that this condition will happen	

Type II

	if-clause	main clause
TENSE	■	■
USE	you doubt that the condition can happen	

Type III

	if-clause	main clause
TENSE	■	■
USE	you know this condition isn't possible because it is in the past	

5 Focus on grammar ▶ G16 ▶ G5 Simple Past ▶ G6 Past Perfect ▶ G7 Will-Future

a) Finish the sentences. Use conditional clauses type I.

1. If Oliver goes back to the outback, he ■.
2. You won't fail if you ■.
3. I will work as a surfing instructor if ■.

b) Finish the sentences. Use conditional clauses type II.

1. If I didn't finish school, ■.
2. If Ava didn't take care of her sheep, ■.
3. You wouldn't inspire other people if ■.

c) Finish the sentences. Use conditional clauses type III.

1. If you hadn't listened to your teacher, ■.
2. I would have made a different decision if ■.
3. If Marli had stayed with her family when she was young, ■.

d) Finish the sentences. Use conditional clauses types I–III.
   Example: If the sun shines later on, I will buy some ice cream.

1. If I had won the lottery last year, ■.
2. If I were in Australia for a year, ■.
3. If the sun shines later on, ■.

1 Workshop

Step B: Job skills and workplaces

To choose the right job, you need to find out about your personal skills. The workplaces might play a role for your choice too.

6 The skill for success

a) You need special words and phrases to describe skills. Match the English words (1–20) with their German translations (A–T).

> 1 **take care of sb** | 2 creative | 3 motivated | 4 flexible | 5 friendly | 6 be good with numbers | 7 hard-working | 8 helpful | 9 well-organised | 10 patient | 11 polite | 12 practical | 13 reliable | 14 strong | 15 punctual | 16 a fast worker | 17 be good at languages | 18 have an eye for detail | 19 be good with computers | 20 a team player
>
> **A** pünktlich | **B** gut organisiert | **C** höflich | **D** hilfsbereit | **E** gut rechnen können | **F** stark | **G** praktisch | **H** freundlich | **I** schnell arbeiten | **J** flexibel | **K** fleißig | **L** teamfähig | **M** sich um jemanden kümmern | **N** motiviert | **O** gut mit Computern umgehen können | **P** geduldig | **Q** ein Auge fürs Detail haben | **R** gut in Sprachen sein | **S** zuverlässig | **T** kreativ

b) Which skills are important in these jobs? Write down at least three skills for each job. You can use the list from a) and a dictionary.

waitress	chef	train driver	hairdresser	accountant	electrician	security guard
friendly	…	…	…	…	…	…

c) Compare your table with a partner. Do you agree on the skills for each job?

7 What are your special skills?

a) What are you good at? Write down three skills that make you special. Use ideas from ex. 6a).

b) Do the quiz and find out more about your personal skills.

FINDING YOUR SKILLS

Are you unsure about the right job for you? Well, maybe it could help to take a look at what type of person you are:
Are you creative, practical, flexible, well-organised …?
What are your special skills?
This quiz can help you to find out!

1. On holiday …
A you always go to the same place. Last year was great. Why go somewhere new?
B you like to discover new places or do challenging activities.
C a fun time with friends is the most important thing for you.

2. Your bike breaks down.
A Oil on your hands? Yuk! You take your bike to a shop so they can repair it.
B You find the problem, get out your tools and repair it.
C You ask a friend to help you to repair it.

Workshop **1**

3. **Two of your friends have a problem.**
   A You decide it's better to keep out of it.
   B You think about it and suggest a practical solution.
   C You offer to listen to each friend, and then try to find a solution together.

4. **Your room is . . .**
   A always well-organised. Looking for things is such a waste of time and drives you crazy!
   B is quite full, but not really a mess.
   C your castle. OK, it's not very tidy but it's a cool place to hang out with friends.

5. **Your group wants to plan a surprise party for a friend.**
   A You make a 'to do' list for each one of you and send it to everyone via text message.
   B You offer to supply your music box and to put a playlist together.
   C You make the decorations and the party invitations.

6. **You plan to watch a film in the afternoon, but the weather is great and your friend suggests hanging out in the park or at a café.**
   A You're not happy about a change in plans.
   B You're fine with that, but want to do something outdoors and not just sit around.
   C It's a great idea and you suggest texting a few more friends and meeting up together.

c) Check your results on page 192.
- Are you happy with them? Why or why not?
- Did you learn something new about yourself?

Discuss with a partner.

8 Where do they work? ▶ **V3** Workplaces

Now that you know about your personal skills, let's have a closer look at different jobs.

a) Describe the pictures (A–F). Where are the people? What's their job? What are they doing? Take notes.
   ▶ **S13** Bildbeschreibung   ▶ **G1** Present tenses   ▶ **G17** Articles   ▶ **V11** Pictures

flight attendant   hairdresser   mechanic   nurse   receptionist   shop assistant

A

B

C

D

E

F

1 Workshop

b) Copy the table and listen to six people talking about their jobs. Match the statements (1–6) with the photos (A–F). Then fill in the jobs and workplaces. ▶ S10 Hörverstehen

	job	workplace	positive	negative
Statement 1	Photo A: hairdresser	…	…	…
…	…	…	…	…

c) Listen again. Which positive aspects about their jobs do the speakers mention? Which negative ones? Add them to the table from b). ▶ H1 ▶ S10 Hörverstehen

d) Talk about the jobs with a partner. What do you think: which job is the hardest/easiest/most fun/most stressful/…? ▶ G8 Comparison of adjectives

9 What do they do at work? ▶ V3 Workplaces

a) Which tasks do you have to do in a job? Match the verbs (1–19) with the nouns (A–U). Sometimes a noun may be used more than once.

1 talk to | 2 help | 3 cut | 4 colour | 5 create | 6 change | 7 repair | 8 get to know | 9 serve | 10 welcome | 11 offer | 12 take | 13 answer | 14 give | 15 bring | 16 show | 17 clean | 18 decorate | 19 unpack

A tyres | B cars | C to look their best | D something to drink | E the jackets | F new things | G the shop | H lunch | I phone calls | J the windows | K customers | L packages | M food and drinks | N patients | O a special style | P hair | Q advice | R medicine | S guests | T the temperature | U passengers

b) Match the tasks from a) with the pictures from ex. 8.
Example: hairdresser – talk to customers

10 Your turn The perfect job for me! ▶ S16 Schreibstil ▶ V2 Workplaces

a) What's your dream job? Look at the results from ex. 7b) and the different jobs from ex. 8. Give at least three reasons why this job is perfect for you.

b) Describe your dream job, its workplace and tasks. Write about 100 words.

c) Exchange your ideas about your dream job with at least three partners. Do they agree with your choice? Do they recommend a different job? Take turns.
▶ M1 Milling around
Example:
A: What's the perfect job for you?
B: Electrician would be the perfect job for me because I like practical tasks and I don't like sitting in an office.
A: I agree. That's a great job for you./I disagree because …

Speaker A:
I'm good with numbers/with computers/at languages/at cooking.
I'm flexible/polite/hard-working/strong/patient/well-organised/reliable.
I have good know-how in …

Speaker B:
Good idea!/Great!
I agree/disagree because …
I think (that) …
But a/an … must have good marks/be good with computers/…
Wouldn't you prefer working in an office/outside/with people …?

Now I can describe my dream job. ✓

Continuing a story about (un)equal chances

Reading workshop 1

A question of equal chances

Many immigrants from Asian and European countries, but also Aboriginal people – the first Australian people – live in Australia. For the Australian government it's important that every person is given the same chances, no matter the colour of their skin or their origin. But is it also reality?

1 I hadn't had a chance!

a) Match the situations (1–6) about equal chances with the categories (A–F).

A ethnicity **B** gender **C** religion **D** work attitude **E** talent **F** personal relationship

1. It is important that the man earns money and that the woman takes care of the house and children.
2. Cathy Freeman is an Aboriginal athlete, so I won't support her sports career.
3. Iggy Azalea's family was poor, but today she earns a lot of money with singing.
4. She can't go to our school because her beliefs don't go with our school ideas.
5. We pay you more money if you are willing to work long hours.
6. The other actor had more skill, but Liam is Chris Hemsworth's brother, so he got the role.

b) Decide if every person has the same chances in the situations (1–6). Discuss them in class.

c) Think about a situation where you felt you weren't given the same chance as someone else. What was the situation like? How did you feel? Did the person explain his/her behaviour? ▶ **M2** Think-pair-share

2 A graphic novel ▶ **S3** Textsorten ▶ **V4** Texts

a) Look at the first two panels (1–2). What could the story be about? Talk about it in class.

b) Read the graphic novel and choose the best title (1–3) for it. Give reasons for your choice.

1. A question of talent
2. Life's just not fair!
3. John's misery and Jane's luck

S ▶ **S3 Textsorten und ihre Besonderheiten**

Betrachten Sie während des Lesens auch die Bilder. Was lernen Sie durch die Bilder? Was durch die Worte?

Wichtige Elemente der *graphic novel*:
– *panel*: das Einzelbild einer Bildsequenz
– *caption*: Bildtext mit Hintergrundinformationen
– *speech/thought bubble*

1 This is Jane. She lives in a rich suburb of Melbourne. Her parents earn a lot of money.

2 This is John. He lives in a poor suburb of Melbourne. His parents don't have much money.

1 Reading workshop

Jane's parents would do anything for her. They help her with her homework, but expect good marks.

John's parents have to work to support their kids. They are proud of John who helps a lot.

Jane goes to a school with great equipment and many interesting clubs.

At John's school, the classes are big and they don't have a lot of money for new equipment or clubs.

After school, Jane goes to university. Her parents pay the fees, so she has a lot of free time.

After school, John goes to university too. To pay the fees, he works at a construction site.

Jane has finished university with good marks and starts working in an office.

John works even more, so he hasn't got much time to study.

Reading workshop 1

c) Choose a panel of the graphic novel and describe it to a partner: what do you learn about Jane or John? Only use the visuals, not the caption. Your partner tries to guess the right panel. Take turns.
▶ **S13** Bildbeschreibung ▶ **V11** Pictures

d) Read the graphic novel again. Answer the questions in complete sentences.

1. Where does Jane grow up?
2. How does John's school work?
3. Why does Jane have a lot of free time at university?
4. What does John's father tell him?

3 Two different lives

a) Copy the table. Make notes on the positive and negative aspects of life for each character.
▶ **H1** ▶ **G21** Quantifiers

 About 3.4 million of the 25 million Australian people live under the poverty line (2020). The Aboriginal people are often affected. It's a result of colonisation and having to live on the edge of society. The white working class can also be poor.

	positive aspects	negative aspects
John	…	parents don't have much money, …
Jane	goes to a great school, …	…

b) Match the adjectives from the word bank with Jane or John. Give reasons. ▶ **G13** Adjectives and adverbs

`successful` `humble` `confident` `lucky` `hard-working` `selfish` `sad` `independent`

c) Describe and compare their lives. What is the same? What is different? ▶ **H1**
Example: While Jane's parents help with the homework, John's parents … However, both parents …

d) Can you imagine this story happening in Germany too? Give reasons. ▶ **M15** Round robin

4 Your turn — How their lives continue **S15** Geschichte (Fortsetzung) ▶ **G7** Future tenses ▶ **G20** Conjunctions
▶ **V5** Story

a) Continue the story about Jane or John's life. Write about 160 words by answering the following questions:

1. What do you think are Jane and John's dreams for the future?
2. What steps will they have to take to make their dreams come true?
3. What will their future lives look like 10 years from now?

V
He/She decides to … because he/she is good at …
His/Her experience with … prepared him/her for / made him/her realise that …
He/She always wanted to …, so he/she is going to …
He/She could already …, so it will be easy to …

S ▶ **S15** Eine Geschichte schreiben (Fortsetzung)
- Nennen Sie Gründe für Geschehnisse in Ihrer Geschichte.
- Verwenden Sie Details (z. B. Ortsbeschreibungen) und Adjektive. So wird Ihre Geschichte lebendig und interessant.
- Beschreiben Sie die Gefühle der Personen.
- Beziehen Sie sich auf Inhalte der *graphic novel*.

b) Read your story to a small group. Give feedback to each other.
▶ **M8** Writers' conference

 Now I can continue a story about (un)equal chances.

1 Speaking workshop

Talking about workplaces

Different workplaces

1 Working from home ▶ **S18** Sprechen (Monolog)
▶ **V15** Opinion

During the Covid-19 pandemic many students studied from home instead of going to school. What do you think about studying from home? What is good/bad about it? ▶ **H1**

S ▶ **S18 Sprechen (Monolog)**

Während des monologischen Sprechens, sprechen Sie spontan über ein Alltagsthema (z. B. Ihre Vorlieben, Meinung und Erfahrungen).

2 Work preferences ▶ **S18** Sprechen (Dialog)
▶ **G2** Modals ▶ **G13** Adjectives ▶ **V6** Preferences

a) What is important in your future job? Give reasons. Talk to a partner. Discuss if you would prefer to:

- work inside or outside
- work with people or computers
- have a stressful job or a job with routine tasks
- have a lot of responsibility or a boss who makes decisions
- work in a team or alone
- work long hours (and earn a lot of money) or to have a lot of free time (and less money)
- analyse (for example problems) or be creative (for example finding solutions)
- work with your hands or do theoretical tasks (for example research)
- …

S ▶ **S18 Sprechen (Dialog)**

Nach einer Vorbereitung tauschen Sie sich zu zweit ca. 10 Minuten zu einem Thema aus.

V ▶ **V6 Talking about preferences**

Would you rather … or …?
What do you think about …?
Why do/don't you like …?
I'd rather / I prefer … to …
I (really/quite/don't) like/love/enjoy/don't mind …
… is as important as …

b) The pictures (A–F) show people in different jobs. Give your partner advice on a suitable job. Give reasons. You can use the words from the box on page 18. ▶ **V3** Workplaces
Example: If I were you, I would become a gardener because you can work outside and be creative.

A
yoga instructor

B
gardener

C
office assistant

D
construction worker

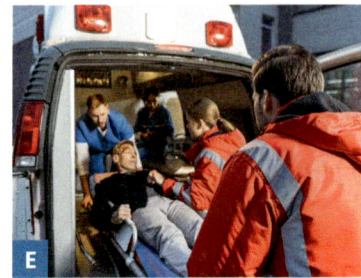

E
paramedic

F
cleaner

22 twenty-two

Now I can talk about workplaces.

Video lounge 1

Meet the experts: Talking about jobs

There are lots of jobs to choose from and you have to do different tasks in each of them.

1 My work experience ▶ V3 Workplaces

a) Before you watch: which jobs have you had so far? Name the job (or internship) and describe your workplace and your tasks. Talk to a partner.

b) Compare your work experiences in class. ▶ M12 Double circle

2 Jobs, tasks and challenges ▶ S5 Hörsehverstehen ▶ V3 Workplaces

a) Watch the tutorial. Which jobs does Emily talk about?

1. barkeeper
2. sales assistant
3. hairdresser
4. personal assistant
5. electrician
6. bus driver
7. waiter / waitress
8. car mechanic

b) Watch the tutorial again. Complete the tasks with the missing information.

1. changing tyres and ■ broken parts
2. ■ electronic systems in a car
3. cutting and ■ hair
4. helping ■ find a new style
5. putting ■ onto shelves
6. laying cables on a ■ site
7. checking electrical ■ in an office
8. ■ orders and clearing tables

3 Interesting workplaces ▶ V3 Workplaces

a) Hairdressers mostly work in salons and sales assistants often work in shopping centres. But there are also unusual workplaces. Collect ideas with a partner.
Example: A hairdresser can work on a big cruise ship.

b) Someone offers you a job that you don't really like, but it's in a super cool workplace. Where would it be? Do you take it? Why or why not? Discuss in class.

1 Check out

Check out: Australia

1 Listening

a) Listen to the radio programme. Are the statements true or false?

1. Noah is taking part in a work training programme.
2. Noah's only goal was to earn money to travel.
3. Noah's stay in Australia was great because now he knows what he wants to do in the future.
4. Noah lived with an Australian family and took care of their children.
5. In the future, Noah wants to become an event planner because he likes to organise.

b) Listen again. Choose the correct answer.

1. Why is Noah on the radio show?
   a) He talks about tourists and their impressions of Australia.
   b) He talks about his worst work experience.
   c) He talks about his work experiences during a work and travel programme.

2. When did Noah arrive in Australia?
   a) ten months ago
   b) four weeks ago
   c) one year ago

3. Why do young people from Europe like work and travel programmes in Australia?
   a) There are more jobs available than anywhere else in the world.
   b) Life in Australia is less expensive than in Europe.
   c) They help you to afford a longer stay in the country.

4. What were Noah's personal goals for his trip to Australia?
   a) He wanted to explore all of Australia.
   b) He wanted to try different jobs and become more fluent in English.
   c) He wanted to finally learn English.

5. How did Noah get along with his English in the beginning?
   a) His English wasn't perfect, but he had to use it.
   b) People often didn't understand him.
   c) He found it more difficult to learn English in Australia than in Germany.

6. Which job tasks didn't Noah try in Australia?
   a) picking fruit
   b) working in a hotel
   c) taking care of children

7. Where does Noah want to work in the future?
   a) in a hotel
   b) in a café
   c) on a farm

Check out 1

2 Reading

a) Read the article. Put the topics (A–G) in the order they appear in the article. There are two more than you need.

A The history of commercial indigenous food
B Lowanna's school education
C Skills and qualities to run your own business
D What makes Lowanna's company special
E Lowanna's family background
F Introducing Lowanna and her company

Lowanna's success story

19 March 20...
by Ava Brown

ESPERANCE, AUSTRALIA - "I believe that protecting the Aboriginal culture and running an innovative business at the same time doesn't cause a conflict. In fact, it's often a huge success." Lowanna is a 32-year-old Aboriginal woman who has founded her own business. Her company produces healthy snacks and smoothies with traditional indigenous ingredients. However, her path to success hasn't always been easy.

Lowanna was born in a small Aboriginal community in Western Australia. As a result of Australia's past and today's politics, the indigenous peoples are facing some serious problems such as health issues, alcoholism and many young people committing suicide. "My family story is rather sad too. My mum died when I was a little child and after that my dad started drinking. So my grandma took care of me most of the time. She taught me about our culture, our traditions and our land – and most importantly, we prepared traditional meals together every day. Thanks to her, I became interested in traditional ingredients and eating habits in general."

The idea of using native ingredients commercially isn't a new one. Since the 1970s, non-indigenous Australians have become interested in growing and eating native plants, seeds, meat and insects. They were known under the name of 'bush tucker', also called 'bushfood' today. In the 1980s, indigenous food found its way into gourmet restaurants, and there have been TV programmes on bush tucker. So what makes Lowanna's business special?

"We use traditional ingredients in a more modern way. Our eating habits have changed over the years and my company has a solution for it. We believe

that even if we don't have time to sit down for a meal, our food can still be healthy. Another point is that people today are more interested in where their food comes from. All our products are organic and the ingredients are grown by indigenous producers. Did you know that commercial native Australian food has been produced mainly by non-native Australians? We wanted to change that and have discovered that it's been appreciated by our customers – both native and non-native."

Of course, you need more than a good knowledge of food to found and run your own business. We asked Lowanna which qualities and skills it takes. "Well, in the beginning you need to be creative and have the right idea at the right time, but that isn't enough. You must always stay motivated, even if things get difficult. Some people think that working life is more relaxed when you're your own boss, but the opposite is true. You need to be a hard-working person as you often have to work long hours. You must be ready to be responsible for many things as different jobs must be done and workers must be paid. But if you follow your dream, you'll be happy." (476 words)

1 Check out

b) Read the article on page 25 again. Are the statements true or false? Correct the false ones.

1. Lowanna thinks that tradition and innovation can't go hand in hand.
2. Lowanna's company is a hotel.
3. Her father died when she was a child.
4. Lowanna's grandmother prepared a lot of traditional meals with her.
5. Non-native Australians also produce indigenous food.

c) Complete the sentences with the missing information from the article.

1. Australia's indigenous peoples are facing problems, for example …
2. 'Bushfood' is a name for food with …
3. Lowanna's products are all …

d) Fassen Sie auf Deutsch zusammen, welche Qualitäten ein/e erfolgreiche/r Unternehmer/in laut Lowanna haben muss.

3 Writing

a) Write a comment about the pros and cons of living and working in another country like Australia after school. Write about 100 words.

b) Choose one of the tasks (1–2). Write about 160 words.

1. Finish the story about Tara and her problem at work.

    Tara had been working in an office in Sydney for seven years. The job was OK and she earned good money, but over the years Tara was becoming more and more unhappy. She felt like something was missing in her life and she decided to …

2. Uluru, a mountain in the middle of Australia, is very important to the Aboriginal people. Tourists were climbing Uluru for a long time, but now it's forbidden. Write a report about it. Use the information from the notes below.

late 1930s: visitors began climbing Uluru
1964: 1st section of climb chain finished → more safety
1985: Uluru-Kata Tjuta National Park given back to Anangu people (original owners)
Aboriginals allowed people to climb, but didn't like it.
Reason: Uluru is a sacred place
1990s: 'Please don't climb' signs installed; visitors learnt about Anangu culture
→ fewer visitors climbed rock
2017: park's management decides to ban climbing Uluru
26 October 2019: Uluru climb closed

Check out 1

4 Use of language

a) Find words or phrases in the article on page 25 which mean more or less the same (=), or the opposite (↔).

1. to think = ■ (lines 2–10)
2. company = ■ (lines 2–10)
3. native = ■ (lines 11–24)
4. solutions ↔ ■ (lines 11–24)
5. old-fashioned ↔ ■ (lines 35–48)
6. stressful ↔ ■ (lines 49–62)

b) Explain one of these words from the article. Write complete sentences.

1. ingredients (line 10)
2. traditional (line 23)
3. eating habit (lines 24–25)

c) Write two questions to Lowanna about her business. Use different question forms or tenses.

d) Change the category of these words. The categories are given in brackets. You can find the missing words in the article on page 25.

1. belief (noun) – ■ (verb) (lines 3–11)
2. innovation (noun) – ■ (adjective) (lines 3–11)
3. successful (adjective) – ■ (noun) (lines 3–11)
4. production (noun) – ■ (verb) (lines 36–49)
5. health (noun) – ■ (adjective) (lines 36–49)
6. difference (noun) – ■ (adjective) (lines 50–63)

e) The parts **in bold** have been changed in text B. Complete text B with the correct words. You need to change the categories of the words in text A.

Text A:
Lowanna: "Well, in the beginning you need to **have creativity** and the right idea at the right time, but that isn't enough. You must always **stay motivated**, even if **things get difficult**. However, then you'll **have success** or you'll learn which **improvements** you'll need next time."

Text B:
Lowanna: "Well, in the beginning you need to **be** ■ (1) and have the right idea at the right time, but that isn't enough. You must always **hold onto your** ■ (2), even if **you're facing some** ■ (3). However, then you'll **be** ■ (4) or you'll learn what you'll need to ■ (5) next time."

f) Complete the sentences with the correct verb forms. Use conditional clauses types I–III.

1. If I ■ (be) 18 now, I would get a tattoo – but I'll have to wait another year.
2. If my boyfriend ■ (not ask) me to marry him, I will ask him!
3. She wouldn't have had to pay debts if she ■ (use) her credit card responsibly.
4. If he had voted, ■ (not get) a fine.
5. Workers ■ (not earn) more than the minimum wage if they work on this farm.
6. I never go to nightclubs. If I went to a nightclub, I ■ (not have) any fun.

g) Finish the following sentences. Use conditional clauses types I–III.

1. My family would go to Australia if …
2. I will go outside if …
3. If I won the lottery, I …
4. My parents wouldn't have met if …
5. If Lowanna hadn't worked so hard, …
6. If my mum asks me about my grades, …

🌐 dp78ec

2 Working in Ireland

And then I moved to Ireland

In this unit you will:
- write a comment about working abroad.
- write a job application.
- write a dialogue between two fictional characters.
- act out a job interview.

Amazing landscape with green grass, rocky coastlines, sheep and cheerful people – you can find that everywhere on the Emerald Isle. So many tourists come to visit the castles, drink a pint at a local pub, listen to traditional music, go hiking or celebrate Irish events. Some people even decide to stay and look for a job.

A

B

C

D

E

1 Highlights of Ireland

a) Look at the pictures (A–E) for a photo contest about "Irish highlights". Describe the pictures to a partner. Use the words from the word bank. Take turns. ▶ **S15** Bildbeschreibung ▶ **G22** Plural

| cliffs | Saint Patrick's Day | sheep | to visit | pint | old castle |

| cathedral | pub | to drink | fishing boat | to celebrate |

| lush green | to go hiking | music | famous | traditional |

V ▶ **V7 Giving a recommendation**
I think you need to / have to / should …
I recommend to …
My recommendation would be …
It is a good idea to …
My advice is (to) …
Make sure you (don't) …

b) What would you recommend to visit, try or do in Ireland? Write one sentence for each picture. ▶ **H2** ▶ **G2** Modals ▶ **V7** Recommendation
What would you recommend a person who wants to visit Germany?
▶ **M5** Round robin

28 twenty-eight

Starter 2

2 People's experiences ▶ S10 Hörverstehen

a) Do you know anybody who moved to another country for work? Talk to a partner.

b) Listen to the people talking about moving to and working in Ireland. Match the pictures (A–D) with the speakers (Matthias, Amir, Miyu, Eva).

A

B

C

D

c) Copy the table. Then listen again. What's their job? Where do they come from? What was the reason for moving to Ireland? Complete the table with the information.

speaker	job	original country	reason for moving to Ireland
Matthias	…	Germany	…
Amir	IT specialist	…	…

d) Listen again. What are the pros and cons of working in another country? Discuss in class and make a list.
▶ H2 ▶ S18 Sprechen (Diskussion) ▶ V8 Discussion

3 Your turn — Should I stay or should I go? ▶ S6 Kommentar ▶ V9 Comment

a) Choose one or two arguments for and one or two against working abroad. Look at the list from ex. 2d).

b) Write a comment. Would you like to work abroad or not? Use the arguments from a).
Write about 100 words. ▶ S16 Schreibstil

V ▶ V9 Writing a comment
The question is: should …?
Firstly/secondly …
Moreover, … | Either … or …. | Not only … but also … | On the other hand, …
In my opinion … | If you ask me, …
I agree/disagree with/that … | I think/believe …
My conclusion is … | To sum up, … | All in all, …

S ▶ S6 Einen Kommentar schreiben
1. *Introduction*: Führen Sie das Thema mit einer Frage, einem Zitat oder einer eigenen Beobachtung ein. Dann benennen Sie das konkrete Thema, welches Sie diskutieren werden.
2. *Main part*: Stellen Sie die Pro- und Kontra-argumente vor und geben Sie Beispiele. Beginnen Sie mit der Gruppe von Argumenten (Pro oder Kontra), welche nicht mit Ihrer Meinung übereinstimmen.
3. *Conclusion*: Fassen Sie die wichtigsten Argumente nochmals zusammen und nennen Sie anschließend Ihre eigene Meinung.

c) Exchange your comment with a partner. Give each other feedback. ▶ M7 Peer correction ▶ M10 Tip-top

Now I can write a comment about working abroad. ✓

2 Workshop

Writing a job application

Step A: Job adverts

You finally decide that you want to work in Ireland after school. You want to apply for a job, but first you need to check some job adverts to find a job which suits you.

1 What's important in a job?

a) What is important to you when looking for a job? Make a ranking based on the following aspects:
▶ **V10** Job adverts

position (apprenticeship, internship, …) | **type of contract** (permanent, fixed-term, …) | **tasks** (answer the phone, …) | **requirements** (driving licence, …) | **working hours** (full-/part-time, shifts, …) | **salary** (per hour/month, …) | **benefits** (near your home, free public transport, cafeteria, retirement plan, …)

b) Discuss your ranking with a partner.
Example: A high salary is important to me because I want to buy a car.
I don't care about the tasks.

2 What's the job about? ▶ **S9** Leseverstehen

a) Read the job adverts. Match the headings (1–3) with the job adverts (A–C).

1 retail assistant 2 electrician (apprenticeship) 3 office assistant

 The Irish grade system is based on letters (A–F). 'A' means 'excellent' and 'F' means 'failed'.

A **OXF Pipeline Construction** has a vacant position in Galway, Ireland. In our team, you will learn on the job through firsthand experience and make money at the same time!

YOU …are interested in construction.
…are strong enough to carry heavy material and tools.
… are not afraid to work in dark, narrow spaces like tunnels.
… are a quick learner.
… have a driving licence.

Apply today for an apprenticeship with a fixed-term contract!
Give us a call: 202-555-0171

B **Hi-Media**, a German tech firm based in Limerick, is looking for assistants to support management.
Your **responsibilities**: greet and direct visitors, answer calls, plan meetings, prepare and check documents.

Our ideal candidate:
• has basic computer skills,
• is very polite,
• knows how to dress formally,
• has strong communication skills (at least grade B in English and German),
• can do multi-tasking,
• is willing to travel from time to time,
• is looking for a permanent job.

Apply online: www.wilkinsrecycling…ie

C **WE WANT YOU AT WANDERLUST OUTDOOR SHOP**

Do you have a passion for outdoor sports? Become a part of **WANDERLUST**!

In our bike section, you will help our customers find exactly what they are looking for. That's why you should have great communication skills (English and another language), should be interested in (free ride) bikes and hiking, and have basic technical know-how (at least grade C in maths). We're open until 10 p.m. → minimum age = 18. We can offer you a contract for one year.

To apply, please come to the store and bring your CV, or write an email.

Address:
WANDERLUST OUTDOOR SHOP,
41 Drury St
D02 Dublin
mswhite@wanderlust…ie

b) Read the adverts again. Copy the table and complete it. ▶ H2 ▶ V10 Job adverts

job	requirements	interests	type of contract
apprentice electrician	strong, …	construction	…
office assistant	…	…	…
retail assistant	…	…	…

3 Who gets the job?

a) Unfortunately the three jobs in ex. 2 aren't available any more. But can you find out who got the job? Read the CVs (1–3). Match each candidate with a job from ex. 2a). Give reasons for your choice.

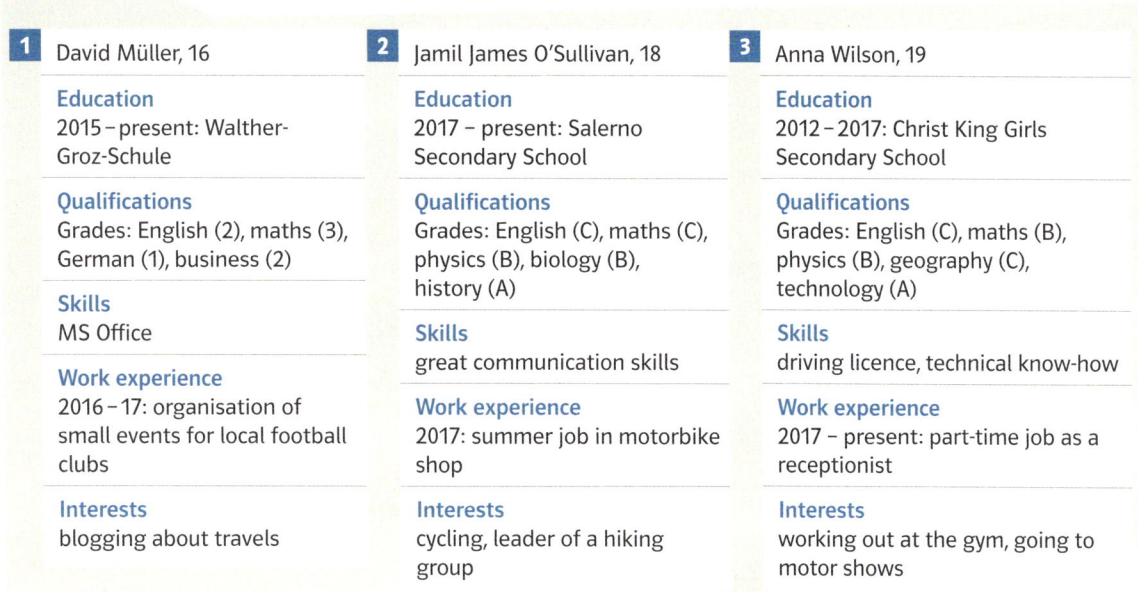

1 David Müller, 16

Education
2015 – present: Walther-Groz-Schule

Qualifications
Grades: English (2), maths (3), German (1), business (2)

Skills
MS Office

Work experience
2016 – 17: organisation of small events for local football clubs

Interests
blogging about travels

2 Jamil James O'Sullivan, 18

Education
2017 – present: Salerno Secondary School

Qualifications
Grades: English (C), maths (C), physics (B), biology (B), history (A)

Skills
great communication skills

Work experience
2017: summer job in motorbike shop

Interests
cycling, leader of a hiking group

3 Anna Wilson, 19

Education
2012 – 2017: Christ King Girls Secondary School

Qualifications
Grades: English (C), maths (B), physics (B), geography (C), technology (A)

Skills
driving licence, technical know-how

Work experience
2017 – present: part-time job as a receptionist

Interests
working out at the gym, going to motor shows

b) Compare your results with a partner. Do you agree with each other?
Example:
A: I think Jamil got the job as a retail assistant because …
B: Yes, I agree with you, but maybe he could also work as a … now because …

After primary school, Irish pupils go to Junior Cycle for three years. They can choose different subjects, but maths, English, history, geography and politics are a must. They finish it with the Junior Certificate which can be compared to "Mittlere Reife" in Germany.

4 Different job adverts ▶ S9 Leseverstehen ▶ V10 Job adverts

a) In groups of four choose one of the job adverts on page 32. Read your advert carefully. Take notes on these aspects:

1. job title/position
2. tasks
3. requirements
4. working hours
5. type of contract
6. way to apply
7. salary
8. benefits

b) Present your results to the class. The others take notes.
▶ S4 Präsentation ▶ V1 Presentation

▶ V10 Analysing job adverts

My advert is for the job as …
The tasks/working hours are …
The contract is permanent/for one year.
The salary is … per month.
You can apply via email/letter/phone/job agency.

2 Workshop

c) Which of these job adverts matches your ranking from ex. 1a) best? Would you apply? Give reasons.
▶ M2 Think-pair-share
Example: I would apply for the job as a nursery assistant because the contract is permanent which gives me security.

A Six-month HOTEL INTERNSHIP in small hotel in Cork

Duties:
Work at reception and help guests check in. Check that rooms are ready.
Help guests with questions about the city and our hotel.

Requirements:
Candidates must be at least 18 years old. Experience in hotel work isn't required.
The intern must be polite, well-organised and motivated to learn.
The intern also has to speak English and another language.

Benefits:
Free bed and board and a bus ticket for the region.
Shift work: 7 a.m. to 3 p.m. / 3 p.m. to 11 p.m.

Go to www.hosteledi…ie to apply.

B We are a company of accountants in Dublin looking for an

OFFICE ASSISTANT

motivated to learn new skills. The assistant works in reception and also helps with general office tasks. He/She needs to have good communication and computer skills (MS Office). Being polite and wearing suitable clothing are a must!

There is a permanent contract for the right candidate after three months' probation. €15,00 an hour during probation, then 20% more + paid holidays.

Contact margaret@west…ie to apply.

C  We have a vacant position in Kildare County for a full-time, fixed-term

PLUMBING APPRENTICESHIP

We are looking for people who are interested in helping plumbers with repairs and installations.

Requirements: Candidates need to be fit and willing to work on construction sites. They need to be reliable and have an eye for detail. Driving licence is a must!

Salary: €13,000 a year.

Working hours: 40 h a week. We also work evenings, weekends and holidays.
We offer full on the job training. This is a great career opportunity, not just a job.

Call Adrian on 02 3636 1234.

D   Happy Toddlers Wexford is looking for

NURSERY ASSISTANTS

Tasks:
– Take care of children (ages: 1–5).
– Plan and be part of daily activities.
– Make sure play areas are clean and safe.
– Speak English, German and another foreign language.

Apply to manager@happytoddlers…ie

The ideal candidate is friendly, patient and doesn't mind working in a loud environment. He or she is able to communicate well with children from many different countries.
We offer on the job training and €11,00 an hour. You get free meals (breakfast and lunch).
This is a permanent, full-time (9 to 5) position.

Workshop **2**

Step B: Applying for a job

To successfully apply for a job, most employers want a written application with a letter and a CV.

5 A cartoon ▶ S15 Bildbeschreibung (Cartoon) ▶ V12 Cartoon ▶ G1 Present tenses

a) Describe the cartoon. Who is in it? Where is the person? What is he/she doing? What is he/she talking about? Talk to a partner.

> **V** ▶ **V12 Analysing a cartoon**
>
> a) The person is sitting/writing/talking about …
>   The speech/thought bubble/caption says …
> b) The cartoon shows/presents/criticises …
>   The cartoon illustrates the topic/the problem that …
>   The cartoon is making fun of …
> c) I like/don't like the cartoon because …
>   I think the cartoon is funny/silly because …
>   I agree/disagree with the message because …

Speech bubble: Hi, Mom! D'you remember in which grade I was given an award for my excellent performance of the song about little ducks?

b) Explain the message of the cartoon. What does the author want to say? Which topic does the cartoon present?

c) Do you know any other pieces of advice or rules for writing a CV? Collect your ideas in class. ▶ **M5** Round robin

d) Give your opinion: do you like the cartoon? Give reasons.

6 Laura's letter of application ▶ S20 Bewerbung

a) Your friend, Laura, also wrote a letter of application to apply for one of the jobs in ex. 2a). Read her letter of application. Which job did she apply for? Write a complete sentence.

> **A7**
>
> Dear Ms White,
>
> I would like to apply for the retail assistant position advertised on your company website. My experience and skills qualify me well for the job. I am an 18-year-old student doing a business course at a college in Dublin. At the moment, I have a part-time job in a local supermarket.
>
> 5 My passion for outdoor sports and my experience in retail make me an ideal candidate for the retail assistant position at Wanderlust Outdoor Shop. From experience, I know that being friendly and helpful to customers is very important. Also, I am used to working in a team at a busy workplace. In my free time, I like riding my mountain bike in the forests nearby. If my bike breaks down, I always fix it myself. Of course I am willing to pass on my know-how to customers at Wanderlust and I am
> 10 motivated to learn even more about bikes.
>
> Please find attached my CV. I would welcome the opportunity to train in your company and look forward to hearing from you.
>
> Yours sincerely
> Laura Mendes

2 Workshop

b) Read Laura's email again. Answer the questions in full sentences. ▶ H2

1. Which school does Laura go to?
2. What is she doing at school?
3. What experience does she have?
4. Which skills and interests qualify her for the job?
5. Which document did Laura add to her application?

c) How do you say it in English? Translate the following sentences. Laura's email on page 33 can help you. ▶ H2
▶ G14 Pronouns ▶ G17 Articles ▶ V14 Letter of application

1. Ich möchte mich auf die Stelle als … bewerben.
2. Meine Fähigkeiten qualifizieren mich für die Stelle.
3. Meinen Lebenslauf lege ich bei / hänge ich an.
4. Ich würde mich über die Möglichkeit freuen, für Ihre Firma zu arbeiten.
5. Ich freue mich darauf, von Ihnen zu hören.

7 Laura's CV ▶ S21 Lebenslauf

a) Before you read: decide which categories you should include in a CV.

A education history B family C interests
D personal data E profile F qualifications G references
H religion I skills J work experience

 Laura's CV is in the Irish format. Every country has its own format. Do you know the differences between Laura's CV and a German one?

b) Read the CV and check if you were right. Match the correct categories from a) with the parts of the CV (1–8).

Name: Laura Mendes Address: 128 Caple Street, Dundrum, Dublin 88 Phone: 077 7295 1576 Email: lmendes@online…ie Date of birth: 12 July 20…	1
(…): I just finished college. I am a motivated team player with a passion for music and nature. I am good at communication (in different languages) and always helpful.	2
(…): 2020 – now: Part-time job in a garden centre	3
(…): 2019 – 2021: Art & Design course at ELT college, Dublin 2014 – 2019: Hillside Secondary School, Dublin	4
(…): Grades in Junior Certificate: English (A), maths (B), German (C), French (C), history (B)	5
(…): Very good communication skills (English, Irish Gaelic, German and French) and great at working on my own. Good at gardening and fixing cars.	6
(…): outdoor sports – especially running and hiking, video games	7
(…): These are available upon request.	8

c) Laura made six mistakes in her CV. Read her letter of application on p. 33 again. Compare it with her CV. Find the mistakes and correct them.

 In Ireland there are two official languages: English and Irish Gaelic. Most Irish people spoke Irish until the 19th century. Today it is taught in school again.

Workshop 2

8 Your turn — My application

You want to reach the next step: being invited to the job interview. Write your own job application.

a) Write your own CV.
   ▶ **S21** Lebenslauf   ▶ **V13** Writing a CV

b) Read the job adverts on pages 30 and 32 again. Choose a job that you like. What are the company's requirements and offers? Take notes. ▶ **V10** Job adverts

c) Read the job advert for your favourite job again. Why are you a great candidate for it? Compare the company's requirements with your skills, experiences and strengths.

d) Write a letter of application. Write about 160 words.
   ▶ **S20** Bewerbung
   ▶ **V14** Letter of application

S ▶ **S21 Einen Lebenslauf schreiben**

Denken Sie daran, …
- ihn richtig zu strukturieren.
- nur relevante Informationen zu nennen.

S ▶ **S20 Eine Bewerbung schreiben**

Denken Sie daran, …
- sie richtig zu strukturieren.
- den Job zu nennen.
- Ihre Fähigkeiten, Kenntnisse und Berufserfahrungen zu beschreiben.
- die Gründe zu nennen, warum Sie perfekt für den Job sind.
- sich höflich und formal auszudrücken.
- die Inhalte mit Ihrem Lebenslauf abzugleichen.

V ▶ **V14 Writing a letter of application**

Dear Mr / Ms, … | To whom it may concern, …
I would like to apply for the job as … | I am interested in your position as …
I read your advertisement for … in / on … | I refer to your advertisement in / on …
I am well-qualified for the position because … | My skills are …
I have a part-time job as … | I have work experience as … | Although I have no experience, …
I am very interested in this job because … | I would like to work for you because … |
I would welcome the opportunity to train / work in your company (because …)

Please find my CV attached.
I look forward to hearing from you.
Yours sincerely, …

---

e) Exchange your application and your CV in small groups. Give feedback.
   ▶ **M8** Writers' conference   ▶ **M10** Tip-top
   Would you invite him/her to a job interview if you were the manager of this company? Give reasons.
   Example: I would invite you because you have the perfect skills which match the job requirements. / I wouldn't invite you because you made a lot of spelling mistakes.

Now I can write a job application.

thirty-five 35

2 Reading workshop

Writing a dialogue between two fictional characters

Returning to Dublin

Ireland has changed a lot in the last 30 to 40 years. Today it is a young and modern country. Irish people who come back after several years are often surprised.

1 Then and now ▶ G5 Simple past / Present perfect

a) Have you ever returned to a place you went to when you were younger? Did the place change? Did you like the changes? How did you feel when you went back? Talk about it in class. ▶ M2 Think-pair-share
Example: When I visited the school I went to when I was 10, it felt really strange.
The school hadn't changed at all.

b) Look at the two pictures of College Street in Dublin. One was taken in 1919 (A) and the other photo was taken in 2020 (B). Describe the two pictures. Then compare them. What has changed? Work with a partner. You can use the words from the word bank. ▶ H2 ▶ S15 Bildbeschreibung ▶ G11 Past progressive
▶ V11 Pictures

| horse and carriage | elegant clothes | asphalt | advertising | cobblestone | sit on the roof | tram |

| police officer | double-decker bus | traffic light |

A

B

2 A conversation at the café ▶ S3 Textsorten ▶ S9 Leseverstehen

a) Read the novel extract from *Evening Class* by Maeve Binchy. The novel is about different students of an Italian course in Dublin and their teachers Signora and Aidan. Match the titles (1–6) with the text passages (A–F).

1 I just came back from Sicily
2 Meeting Jerry
3 A recommendation where Signora could stay
4 Looking for a place to stay
5 The young and modern population
6 The reason why Suzi moved out

After many years in Italy, Signora has just arrived in Dublin to start a new life.

A Signora got out of her bus and walked up beside the Liffey to O'Connell Bridge. All around her there were young people, tall, confident, laughing, in groups. She remembered reading somewhere about this youthful population, half the country under the age of twenty-four, was it? She hadn't expected to see such proof of it. And they were dressed brightly, too. Before she had gone away, Dublin had been a grey and drab place.
A lot of the buildings had been cleaned, there were smart, expensive cars in the busy traffic lanes. She remembered more bicycles and second-hand cars. The shops were bright. […] For some reason she kept walking down the Liffey after O'Connell Bridge […] and there she found Temple Bar.

It was like the Left Bank in Paris when once she had gone there so many years ago with Mario for a long weekend. Cobbled streets, outdoor cafés, each place full of young people calling each other and waving at those they knew. [...]

Signora thought it was wonderful. It was a whole new world, she couldn't get enough of it. Eventually, she sat down to have a coffee.

B A girl about eighteen with long red hair, like her own many years ago, served her coffee. She thought Signora was a foreigner.

'What country are you from?' she asked in slow English. [...]

'Sicilia, in Italia,' Signora said.

'Beautiful country, but I tell you I'm not going there until I can speak the language though.'

'And why is that?'

'Well, I'd want to know what the fellows are saying, I mean you wouldn't know what you were letting yourself in for if you didn't know what they were saying.'

'I didn't speak Italian when I went there, and I sure didn't know what I was letting myself in for,' Signora said. 'But you know, it worked out all right ... no, more than all right. It was wonderful.'

'How long did you stay for?'

'A long time. Twenty-six years.' [...]

The girl [...] looked at her in amazement. 'You stayed all that time, you must have loved it.'

'Oh I did, I did.'

'And when did you come back?'

'Today,' Signora said. [...]

C The girl was about to move away.

'Excuse me, this seems a very nice part of Dublin. Is this the kind of place I could rent a room, do you think? [...] Just somewhere simple,' Signora said. She listened glumly as she learned that this was one of the most fashionable parts of town; everyone wanted to live here. There were penthouse apartments, pop stars had bought hotels, business people had invested in townhouses. The place was full of restaurants. It was the last word. [...]

'And please could you tell me where would be a place that would be good value to stay, somewhere that hasn't become the last word?'

The girl shook her head of long, dark red hair. It was hard to know. She seemed to be trying to work out if Signora had any money at all, if she would have to work to pay her rent, how long she would stay wherever she landed. Signora decided to help her. 'I have enough money for bed and breakfast for a week, but then I'll have to find a cheap place and maybe somewhere I could do some jobs ... maybe look after children.'

The girl was doubtful. 'They usually want young ones to look after kids.'

'Or maybe over a restaurant and work in it?' Signora asked.

'No, I wouldn't be too hopeful about that, honestly [...].

They're very hard to get.'

She was nice the girl. 'Is that your name on the apron? Suzi?'

'Yes, I'm afraid my mother was a Suzi Quatro fan. [...] The singer, you know? She was big years ago, maybe not in Italy.'

'I'm sure she was, it's just that I wasn't listening then. Now Suzi, [...] I'd love you to tell me what area would be a nice cheap one where I should start looking.'

Suzi listed off the names of places that used to be small areas, suburbs if not exactly villages, well outside the city when Signora was young, but now [...] they were big [...] working-class estates. Half the people there would take someone in to rent a room if their kids had left home maybe. As long as it was cash. [...]

D 'You're very good to me, Suzi. How do you know all about things like that at your age?'

'Well, that's where I grew up, I know the scene.' [...] She saw Suzi pause and bite her lip. [...]

'Are you serious about not minding what kind of place it is?'

'Absolutely serious. [...]'

'Listen. I don't get on with my family myself, so I don't live at home any more. And only a week ago they were talking about trying to get somebody to take my room. They could use a few pounds a week – it would have to be cash, you know, and you'd have to say you were a friend if anyone asked ... because of income tax.'

'Do you think I could?' Signora's eyes were shining.

'Listen, now.' Suzi did not want any misunderstandings. 'We're talking about a very ordinary house in an estate of houses that look the same, some a bit better, some a bit worse. [...] They have the TV on all the time, they shout at each other over it and of course my brother's there, Jerry. He's fourteen and awful.'

2 Reading workshop

'I just need a place to stay. I'm sure it would be lovely.'

E Suzi wrote down the address and told her which bus to take. 'Why don't you go down the road and ask a few people who I know definitely won't be able to have you and then go by chance, as it were, to my house and ask. Mention the money first and say it won't be long. They'll like you because you're a bit older, respectable is what they'll say. They'll take you, but don't say you came from me.' Signora gave her a long look. 'Did they not like your boyfriend?'

'Boyfriends.' Suzi corrected her. 'My father says I'm a slut, but please don't try to deny it when he tells you because it will show you've met me.' Suzi's face looked hard.

Signora wondered if her face had been hard like that when she left for Sicily all those years ago.

F She took the bus and wondered at how the city [...] had grown so big. In the evening light children played in the streets among the traffic, and then [...] there were small gardens and children cycled round in circles [...].

Signora called at the houses that Suzi had suggested. Dublin men and women told her that their houses were full and they needed all the space they had.

'Can you suggest anyone?' she asked.

'Try the Sullivans,' someone suggested.

Now she had her reason. She knocked on the door. Would this be her new home? Was this the roof she would lie under and hope to ease the pain of losing her life in Annunziata? [...]

Jerry opened the door, his mouth full. He had red hair and freckles and he had a sandwich in his hand.

'Yeah?' he said.

b) Read the novel extract again. Choose the correct answer.

1. She remembered that half the country was under the age of …
   a) thirty-one.
   b) twenty-five.
   c) twenty-four.

2. She remembered more …
   a) motorbikes in the busy traffic lanes.
   b) bicycles and second-hand cars.
   c) expensive cars.

3. Suzi wouldn't go to Italy until …
   a) she can speak the language.
   b) she can travel by herself.
   c) she can cook spaghetti.

4. What did Signora think of her time in Sicily?
   a) She thought she stayed there for too long.
   b) She thought it was wonderful.
   c) She missed Ireland too much.

5. What does Signora look for in Dublin?
   a) for a bed and breakfast to stay for a week
   b) for her boyfriend Mario
   c) for a place to stay and a job

6. Where does Suzi suggest Signora could stay?
   a) at her uncle's apartment
   b) at her home where she lives with her brother
   c) at the house where she grew up

Reading workshop 2

c) Fassen Sie den Romanauszug auf Deutsch zusammen. Schreiben Sie pro Abschnitt (A–F) ein bis zwei Sätze. ▶ **S17** Mediation

d) Write two questions to ask Signora or Suzi about their lives. Use different question forms or tenses. Let your partner answer the questions. ▶ **G1, G5, G6, G7** Tenses

3 Many contrasts ▶ S7 Sammeln und ordnen ▶ G8 Comparison of adjectives

The story is full of contrasts – about people, times and places. Get into groups. Compare one of the following topics. Take notes. Then present your results in class. ▶ **S4** Präsentation ▶ **V1** Presentation

- **A** Signora's past and present
- **B** The similarities and the differences between Signora and Suzi
- **C** Dublin 30 years ago and Dublin today
- **D** The area around the café and the area where Suzi's family lives

4 Focus on words

a) Match the phrases (1–5) from the novel extract on pages 36–38 with the correct meanings (A–E).

1 to think sb is a foreigner (line 30) | 2 to let oneself in for sth (lines 37–40) | 3 to be the last word (lines 60–61) | 4 to know the scene (line 99) | 5 to have a hard face (lines 132–133)	**A** to accept a challenge | **B** to understand how this part of the city works | **C** to guess sb. comes from another country | **D** to be very trendy | **E** to look very serious

b) Find a word or phrase in the extract which means more or less the same (=), or the opposite (↔).

1. sad = ■ (lines 3–25)
2. dark ↔ ■ (lines 3–25)
3. finally = ■ (lines 3–25)
4. happily ↔ ■ (lines 53–97)
5. unsure = ■ (lines 53–97)
6. money = ■ (lines 53–97)
7. normal = ■ (lines 98–120)
8. to recommend = ■ (lines 137–155)
9. to make sth worse ↔ ■ (lines 137–155)

c) Explain these words from the extract. Write complete sentences.

1. fashionable (line 57)
2. misunderstanding (line 113)
3. freckles (line 152)

d) Copy the table and complete it with words from the same word family. Then choose a word from each line and write a sentence with it. ▶ **S19** Wortarten
Example: I wanted to buy a house, so I had to invest a lot of money.

	noun	verb	adjective
1.	amazement	■	■
2.	■	to invest	■
3.	■	■	respectable

5 Your turn   A conversation with Jerry ▶ S15 Geschichte (Fortsetzung) ▶ V5 Story

a) Read the two last sentences of the novel extract again. Write the dialogue Signora and Jerry with a partner. Write about 100 words. ▶ **S16** Schreibstil

b) Practise the dialogue. Then present it to the class. In class, vote for the best dialogue. ▶ **M9** Read and look up

Now I can write a dialogue between two fictional characters.

2 Video lounge

Meet the experts: Doing a good job interview

To do a good job interview, you need to follow some rules.

1 Dos and don'ts at a job interview ▶ S5 Hörsehverstehen

a) Before you watch the tutorial: decide which of these things you should do before a job interview.

1. Think about your outfit and wear suitable clothes.
2. Eat a big, spicy meal.
3. Come to the interview a little late to show that you're a very busy person.
4. Check out the website of the company.
5. Ask your mum to come with you.
6. Turn off your phone.
7. Write down what you want to say and ask during the interview.
8. Take some coffee to go to the interview so you'll stay awake.

b) Watch the tutorial and check if you were right.

c) Think of more interview tips and collect them in class. ▶ M2 Think-pair-share

2 Doing a good job interview ▶ S5 Hörverstehen

a) Read the questions and answers. Watch the tutorial again and decide: which answers are from Andrew, which answers are from Rebecca?

1. Please tell me something about yourself.
   a) I'm doing a course at a vocational college.
   b) I like partying and getting up late.

2. Why do you want to work for us?
   a) I would learn a lot working with you.
   b) I don't mind which company I work for.

3. Why should we choose you for the traineeship?
   a) Uhm …
   b) I've helped organise a summer camp for the last two years and I really enjoyed working in a team.

4. Do you have any questions?
   a) Trainees will work in different parts of the company. Can you tell me more about that?
   b) Are we finished?

 b) What did Andrew and Rebecca do well? What didn't they do well? Talk to a partner. You can use the words from the word bank. ▶ G8 Comparison of adjectives ▶ G13 Adjectives und adverbs ▶ V15 Opinion

| interested | open | bored | not prepared | friendly | excited | rude |

c) What do you think: who will get the job? Why?
Example: I think … will get the job because … made a better impression than … because …

40 forty

Speaking workshop 2

Acting out a job interview

Job interviews

1 Questions in a job interview ▶ S10 Hörverstehen

a) Ms White, the manager of Wanderlust Outdoor Shop, does phone interviews with candidates for a sales assistant position. What do you think: which questions can she ask? Talk about it in class.

1. Are you Muslim?
2. Do you drink alcohol or smoke?
3. Which school subjects do you like?
4. Which country do you come from?
5. Do you want to have children?
6. Can you tell me something about yourself?
7. Do you have a boyfriend/girlfriend?
8. Do you have any questions?
9. What are your skills?
10. When can you start work?
11. Are you over 18 years old?
12. Why should we choose you for the job?

b) Listen to the phone interviews. Check your guess from a). Why didn't Ms White ask all the questions?

c) Listen to the phone interviews again. What do the candidates answer? Take notes. Who will get the job? Discuss in class. ▶ H2

Questions	Michael	Liam	Laura
1. Can you …?	Has part-time job in a shop, likes running	…	…

2 Preparing for and doing a job interview ▶ S18 Sprechen (Dialog/Rollenspiel) ▶ V16 Job interview

a) Choose one of the jobs on page 30 or 32. Prepare for the interview and practise it. Look at your application from page 35, ex. 8. ▶ M9 Read and look up

b) Do a job interview with a partner. Take turns. You can record the interview on your phone.

Bewerber/-in

1. Melden Sie sich am Telefon.

3. Begrüßen Sie den/die Interviewer/-in und bedanken Sie sich für den Anruf.

5. Erzählen Sie, welche Schule Sie besuchen und ob Sie einen Nebenjob haben.

7. Nennen Sie zwei Ihrer Eigenschaften/ Stärken, die für den Job wichtig sind.

9. Sagen Sie, warum Sie die Arbeit interessant finden.

11. Stellen Sie eigene Fragen, z. B. wann der Job anfängt.

13. Bedanken Sie sich. Sagen Sie, dass Sie sich freuen, bald wieder von ihm/ihr zu hören.

Interviewer/-in

2. Begrüßen Sie den/die Bewerber/-in. Sagen Sie, dass Sie gern ein kurzes Telefoninterview führen möchten.

4. Bitten Sie ihn/sie, etwas über sich zu erzählen.

6. Bitten Sie ihn/sie, zwei Eigenschaften/ Stärken von sich zu nennen.

8. Fragen Sie, warum er/sie diese Stelle haben möchte.

10. Fragen Sie, ob er/sie eigene Fragen hat.

12. Beantworten Sie die Fragen.

14. Bedanken Sie sich für das Interview und verabschieden Sie sich.

Now I can act out a job interview.

2 Check out

Check out: Ireland

1 Listening

A10

a) Listen to the job interview of Dana Harris, who is applying for a job as a sales assistant in a cosmetics shop via phone. Put the questions (A–I) into the correct order.

A What do you do in your free time?
B What salary do you expect?
C How has your past work experience prepared you for this job?
D What are your personal strengths?
E Why did you leave your last job?
F How would your friends describe your character?
G Do you have any questions?
H Could you tell me something about yourself?
I What was your biggest personal success last year?

b) Listen again. Are the statements true or false?

1. The candidate has worked in the cosmetics field before.
2. The candidate knows how to organise products like clothes in a store.
3. The candidate is interested in beauty, but not in health products.
4. The candidate doesn't like working shifts.
5. The candidate couldn't finish the Dublin Marathon.
6. The candidate likes making decorations for her home.
7. The interviewer is going to call the candidate next week.

2 Reading

a) Read the article on page 43. Match the tips for assessment centres (A–F) with the paragraphs from the article (1–4). There are two tips more than you need.

1 lines 5–16
2 lines 17–30
3 lines 31–38
4 lines 39–51

A Inform yourself about the company.
B Quality is more important than speed.
C Dress elegantly.
D Show off your skills, even if you're shy.
E Be a team player.
F Listen to the instructions carefully.

 An assessment centre is a way to test which candidate is the best choice for a job. Candidates usually have to do interviews, take tests and complete tasks. Often they have to work on a task together, which can include role plays, group discussions, etc.

Check out 2

Q & A

by N. Miller | 22 November 20…

DUBLIN – A lot can go wrong in assessment centres, says expert and job advisor Maureen Snyder.
In today's Q&A, Maureen offers tips to people who have made mistakes at an assessment centre.

Mi Wang was invited to an assessment centre last week and doesn't understand what went wrong.

Q: My group got a list of tasks and had to sort them from most to least important. My ideas were very good but I couldn't convince the others. They didn't listen to me and I got quite angry. Why did I fail?

A: You have to show that you can work in a team. Even if you think your idea is the best, you need to listen to others. Most companies want candidates to show their motivation and offer solutions but at the same time allow other ideas. Employers don't give a chance to candidates who can't control their feelings.

Mark Twining arrived on time and well-dressed at the assessment centre but never got the job.

Q: In the role play they asked me about my vision for the company's future. I said, "If you asked me, I would invest in green energy." I thought they look for people with fresh ideas, don't they? What I didn't know is that the company already runs on solar power.

A: You will only make a good impression if you know what you are talking about. It's great if you have exciting ideas. But you have to do some research about the company you want to work for. Find out about past projects and special market interests. That's the first step to doing well at an assessment centre.

Sarah McMaster is invited to an assessment centre in two weeks' time. She wants to know:

Q: What if they can see how nervous and shy I am? Will they dislike me? If I prepare well, will I get the job?

A: Speak loud and clear and make eye contact. Control your body language. It's not a problem if you are introverted. However, you should show that you are competent and patient, even when under pressure.

Marie DeWitt remembers her experience at an assessment centre for a job at a hospital.

Q: I had to work out the right medicine for a patient, but at the same time, the employer tried to interrupt me. He thought I would make a mistake if he made noisy telephone calls. He also asked me many questions and almost left because I was too slow. He was impolite and I got nervous. What could I have done better?

A: You must stay calm and finish your task under stressful conditions. Even if you are slow, convince the employer with the quality of your work – then you will pass the test and show that you're a good fit. Quality is more important than being fast!

(475 words)

b) Answer the questions in complete sentences. Use your own words.

1. What did Mi Wang have to do in the assessment centre?
2. What is Maureen's advice for Mi Wang?
3. What was the idea Mark Twining mentioned and why wasn't it a good one?
4. Which solution does Maureen give Mark for his problem?
5. What is Maureen's tip for Sarah McMaster's worries?
6. What advice does Maureen give to Marie DeWitt if people test your stress levels?

c) Fassen Sie auf Deutsch in Stichpunkten zusammen, wie der Arbeitgeber getestet hat, ob Marie DeWitt mit Stress umgehen kann.

2 Check out

3 Writing

a) You do an internship at the tourist office in Kilkenny, Ireland. Write a recommendation for people to visit this town. Use the information from the notes. Write about 100 words.

Notes:
- town in the east of Ireland
- historic medieval streets, but also modern
- old pubs and restaurants (traditional Irish food)
- small shops with hand-made products
- music festivals (traditional Irish music, jazz, pop)
- important sights: Kilkenny Castle (Norman castle), St Canice's Cathedral (second-largest cathedral in Ireland), Smithwick's Experience (tour where you learn how beer is produced and taste some of their beer)

b) You are looking for your first job. You find two job adverts. Choose one of them and write a letter of application. Write about 160 words.

FITNESS COACH ON CRUISE SHIP

You …
- are a fitness coach with certificate
- have experience with personal and group training
- are highly motivated and able to motivate others
- are willing to work six days a week
- don't mind being away from home for a long time
- are OK with being on a ship
- want to see the world

Become part of the SunFitFun Cruises family and join our team with a one-year contract.

Apply online: www.sunfitfun-cruiseship.com/jobs

OFFICE ASSISTANT

QQ Equipment is hiring an office assistant (permanent contract)

Tasks:
- general business communication in English, German
- translating documents
- helping out at (video) conferences

Requirements:
- fluent in English, German and another language
- great communication and computer skills (MS Office)
- friendly and well-organised

Apply via email: mr_davids@qq-office...com

Check out 2

4 Use of language

a) Find words or phrases in the article on page 43 which mean more or less the same (=), or the opposite (↔).

1. to pass ↔ ■ (lines 10–14)
2. emotions = ■ (lines 15–20)
3. late ↔ ■ (lines 21–22)
4. stress = ■ (lines 39–42)
5. loud = ■ (lines 45–50)
6. nervous ↔ ■ (lines 51–55)

b) Explain one of these words from the article on page 43. Write complete sentences.

1. to convince sb (line 9)
2. green energy (line 21)
3. patient (line 38)

c) Write two questions you would like to ask Maureen about assessment centres. Use different question forms or tenses.

d) Change the category of these words. The categories are given in brackets. You can find the missing words in the article on page 43.

1. importance (noun) – ■ (adjective)
2. thoughtful (adjective) – ■ (noun)
3. investment (noun) – ■ (verb)
4. preparation (noun) – ■ (verb)
5. patience (noun) – ■ (adjective)
6. stress (noun) – ■ (adjective)

e) Complete the sentences with the correct prepositions and words from the word bank. Sometimes you need to change the category of the word.

| of | to advertise | internship | at | temporary | requirement | colleague | for (2 x) |

1. Candidates have to be good ■ solving problems. This is one of our most important ■.
2. Have you ever thought ■ doing an ■ in Ireland?
3. I would like to apply ■ the job you have ■ on your website.
4. Your contract is ■, but after the first year we consider you as a candidate for a permanent position.
5. My ■ and I were well-prepared ■ the meeting, so our boss was very happy with the result!

f) Complete the text with the correct words. You need to change the words on the right, or choose the correct word if two options are given.

Working as a tourist guide in Dublin

I've been working as a tourist guide in Dublin for five years now. Usually I work on a hop-on-hop-off bus in the afternoon and do ■ (1) tours in the evenings. That's great because on the one hand you get some fresh air, and on the other hand your ■ (2) don't get tired. Dublin is an interesting city with a lot of things to see and do. Most tourists enjoy the Temple Bar area with its ■ (3) streets and pubs, where you can listen ■ (4) talented Irish ■ (5) and have drinks with your friends. I like my job because I get ■ (6) a lot of people from all over the world – from Germany, for example. I don't speak ■ (7) German, but my German guests always find it funny when I say "Auf Wiedersehen" with my Irish accent. When the tourists clap their hands ■ (8) at the end of the tour, I know they enjoyed it, and that makes me feel ■ (9). The reviews on the internet also show that the tour is the ■ (10) in town. It really makes me proud!

1 to walk
2 foot
3 tradition
4 with/to   5 music
6 knowing/to know
7 much/many
8 loud
9 happiness
10 good

v877f8

3 Multicultural South Africa

Rainbow nation

In this unit you will:
- prepare and do an interview.
- write the story behind a picture.
- plan and promote an event against racism.
- talk about and suggest free-time activities.

Most people think of safaris, elephants and lions when they imagine South Africa. In fact, South Africa is a country with many different interesting aspects: its multicultural population, its amazing nature, and its rich history and culture. South Africa's motto is "!ke e: /xarra //ke", or in English "diverse people unite".

A

D

B

C

E

1 This is South Africa ▶ V17 Multiculturalism

a) With a partner, give each picture a title.

b) Why do you think South Africa is called "rainbow nation"? Talk about it in class.
   ▶ M5 Round robin

c) How is the title "rainbow nation" reflected in the pictures? ▶ H3 ▶ M2 Think-pair-share

d) Is Germany also a "rainbow nation"? Discuss in class.

V township | safari | plant | clothes | medal | fruit and vegetables | to celebrate | wildlife | colourful | diverse | different peoples

🏳 South Africa's population is made up of 80.8% black South Africans, 7.9% white South Africans, 8.7% coloured South Africans (mixed race) and 2.6% Asian / Indian South Africans. The country has 11 official languages. These include Afrikaans, English, Xhosa and Zulu. Xhosa and Zulu are the two most common languages spoken in the black townships like Soweto. Who speaks more than one language in your class?

46 forty-six

Starter 3

2 People of South Africa ▶ S10 Hörverstehen

a) Before you listen: which three of the things in the word bank are important for getting on with other people? What do you think? Read the culture box on page 46.

| education | same interests | respect | similar background | language | hobbies | common goals |

b) Listen to the interview with Lionel. Choose the sentence which best summarises it.

1. Nelson Mandela liked the almost all-white rugby team.
2. Sports are a good place to start changing societies and learning to be more open.
3. It's important for groups of people to have their own sports.

> Apartheid was a system of racial segregation that existed in South Africa from 1948 until 1994. According to this system, the country was dominated politically, socially, and economically by the nation's white population. White citizens had the highest status, followed by Asians and Coloureds, then black Africans. The social effects of apartheid continue to the present day.

c) Listen again and answer the questions. ▶ H3

1. Which sport does Lionel play?
2. What did Mandela do after the World Cup in 1995?
3. What happened after the 2019 World Cup?
4. What is the benefit of rugby and sports?

3 Your turn An interview with a famous person ▶ S22 Interview ▶ V17 Multiculturalism ▶ V18 Interview

a) With a partner, write a list of famous people with multicultural backgrounds. Agree on one person.

b) Research the person and take notes on these aspects: ▶ S1 Informationen
- age
- family background/origin
- language(s)
- challenges
- career
- biggest success
- lifestyle
- influences

c) Write a list of questions that you would like to ask this famous person. ▶ G1, G5, G7, G11 Tenses
Example: Which Iranian traditions do you still practise in Germany?

d) Practise and record the interview with the notes from b) and c). One of you is the famous person and the other one the interviewer. ▶ S18 Sprechen (Dialog: Rollenspiel) ▶ M9 Read and look up

e) Present the interview to the class. Are you happy with the result (acting, speaking, body language)?
▶ M10 Tip-top

S ▶ S22 Ein Interview führen
- Stellen Sie möglichst keine Entscheidungsfragen (Ja/Nein-Fragen).
- Gestalten Sie das Interview so, dass ein Gespräch entstehen kann.

V ▶ V18 Doing an interview
Questions
When/What/Who/Where/Why/How ...?

Answers
My family comes from ...
I speak ... fluently/a little.
A big challenge in my life was/is ...
I wish I had learned ... before ...
A big step in my career was ...
My biggest success in life is ...
I really enjoy ...
... is/isn't the most important thing in my life.
... taught me ... | ... inspired me.
I'm most thankful for ...

Now I can prepare and do an interview.

3 Workshop

Writing the story behind a picture

Step A: South Africa in pictures

The area that today is the Republic of South Africa was the home of the Zulu and Xhosa people before Dutch traders arrived. From that time on, the history of South Africa was troubled with wars, slavery, discrimination, segregation and apartheid. Although apartheid has ended, it can still be felt in the country today.

1 A timeline of South African history

a) Read the timeline and match the pictures (A–D) with a year or event. Give reasons.

1652	The *Dutch East India Company* builds a military base in Table Bay, near today's Cape Town, as a stop for its trading ships on their way to India.
1684–1838	Thousands of Indians are brought to the Dutch colony as slaves.
1806	The British Empire takes control of the Cape Colony.
1860s–90s	Large gold and diamond fields are discovered; the British defeat the native Xhosa; Indians are brought to the colony to work on farms, in mines and to build the railway.
1948	The National Party comes to power and introduces apartheid. The non-white people weren't treated equally and had to live in segregated neighbourhoods.
1962	Nelson Mandela, a leader of the African National Congress (ANC) - the party that represents blacks and coloureds - is put into prison.
1964–1991	South Africa is not invited to take part in the Olympics.
1976	The Soweto Uprising takes place.
1990	Mandela is released from prison and the ANC becomes a legal party.
1994	The ANC wins South Africa's first universal elections; Mandela becomes the country's first black president and apartheid officially ends. The country gets a new flag.
2010	South Africa hosts the FIFA World Cup.
2017	The government under Jacob Zuma and the ANC is criticised for corruption.

 A
 B
 C
 D

b) Read the timeline again. Answer the questions in your own words.
1. Who had a trading relationship with India?
2. What happened to the Xhosa people in the 19th century?
3. When did apartheid start and end?
4. Why is Nelson Mandela so important for South Africa's history?

c) Choose 2–3 dates which you think are important in German history. Write a sentence about each event. ▶ H3

Workshop 3

2 Describing and analysing pictures ▶ S13 Bildbeschreibung ▶ V11 Pictures

Every photo has its own story which it tells the viewer when he or she looks at it closely.

a) Read the description of this iconic picture. Note the phrases that you can use for a picture description in general.

> An **iconic picture** shows a dramatic moment in history. The picture becomes the symbol of an event or a person that will be remembered like this forever. Which iconic pictures do you know?

In the foreground, you can see three children: a girl and two boys. One of the boys is carrying the other one and they are running away fast from something we can't see but which must be horrible. Antoinette, the girl on the left, is wearing her school uniform.

You can tell by Antoinette's face that she is scared, even terrified and in great pain over something. She is running with her eyes closed like she doesn't want to see what is happening. You can almost hear the loud cries coming from her open mouth. Her raised right hand seems to be saying, "Stop this horror! Save my brother!" Mbuyisa, the boy next to her, seems to be strong, but he is still struggling to quickly hurry away from the horrible scene. While carrying the lifeless body of Hector, Antoinette's brother, the young man has a strong hold on Hector's legs; however, his arms are slowly slipping away with every step and Hector's head is falling back over Mbuyisa's arm. Mbuyisa has a determined but pained expression on his face. The picture seems sadder and more serious as it is in black and white.

b) Read the text again. Which tense is used to describe actions and which to describe the situation, location or feelings? ▶ H3 ▶ G1, G5, G7, G11 Tenses

 c) Was ist an dieser Bildbeschreibung besonders? Legen Sie sich auf drei Aspekte fest. ▶ M4 Placemat

G ▶ **G19 ADVERBS AND SEQUENCE OF ADVERBS**

GV13
GV15

a) Complete the sentences from the text above.
1. … he is still struggling to ■ hurry away from the horrible scene.
2. … his arms are ■ slipping away with every step …

b) Most **adverbs of manner** (how something is done) are built like this: adjective + ly.
Exceptions: hard, fast, early, high, near, well

There are other kinds of adverbs too:
adverbs of time (when something is done): tomorrow, at ten o'clock, at night, …
adverbs of place (where something is done): in South Africa, to Cape Town, …

Look at the sentence below. What is the correct order of the adverbs in the sentence?

He <u>regularly</u> is <u>at home</u> <u>at six p.m.</u>   1. ■ → 2. ■ → 3. ■

3 Workshop

3 Focus on grammar ▶ G13 Adjectives and advrbs ▶ G18 Word order ▶ G19

Put the parts of the sentences in the correct order.

1. every morning • the guide at the Hector Pieterson Museum • for visitors • patiently • waits • at the door
2. at 9:00 today • to take a tour • a school group arrives • at the museum
3. the students • through the museum • walk silently • because there is so much to learn • from 9:00 to 11:00
4. eagerly • ask questions • because they want to learn more • most of the visitors • in front of the old photos
5. happily • answer all of the questions • every day • the museum guides • on the tours
6. before they go in • new groups • outside the museum • quietly • read the sign

4 More pictures ▶ S13 Bildbeschreibung ▶ G1 Present progressive ▶ V11 Pictures

Choose a picture and describe it to your partner. Use the words from the word bank. ▶ H3

Photo A: to celebrate   goal   goalkeeper   exciting   angry   victory   to defeat

South African / German team   match

Photo B: tourist   elephant   dangerous   to take a close-up picture   to come towards   bush

Photo C: to perform   ballet dancer   to dance   in front of   costume   classroom   school uniform

from South Africa

Photo D: view   Cape Town   sea   sports clothes   to pose   on top of   Table Mountain   to enjoy

Workshop 3

Step B: The story behind the picture

On 16 June 1976, students began protesting in Soweto because the government announced that important subjects must be taught in Afrikaans in the township schools. Today the Hector Pieterson Museum is dedicated to this event.

5 The Soweto Uprising ▶ S9 Leseverstehen

a) Before you read: why would you go out into the streets and take part in a demonstration or protest march? Think of reasons and make a list in class.

b) Look at the picture. What would you like to ask the children? Write down 2–3 questions. ▶ G1, G5, G6, G7 Tenses

c) Read the story behind the picture. Did you find the answers to your questions?

On the morning of 16 June 1976, students arrived at school and saw that a protest march was forming. Students from one of the high schools in the township had formed an action committee earlier that month in order to plan a march for that day. Even students who hadn't been told about the protest spontaneously joined the crowd on the playground when they got to school that morning. Soon there were thousands of students marching through the streets towards Orlando Stadium, a football stadium in Soweto.
Hector Pieterson, a 12-year-old student, also joined the protest with his 17-year-old sister Antoinette. They began peacefully marching with the crowd near Orlando West High School. The students were singing loudly and holding signs with slogans like "No to Afrikaans!" to show their dissatisfaction. Although it was a peaceful demonstration, the police soon arrived and intimidated the students, who began throwing stones at the police. Another report said that students killed a police dog after the dog tried to attack the protesters. Others said that the police first used tear gas to force the crowd to leave. Nobody knows who gave the command, but suddenly the police started firing their guns at the students. The children panicked and began running in all directions, because they wanted to get away. Nevertheless, the police continued shooting. When Mbuyisa Makhubo saw young Hector fall down and heard Antoinette screaming, he immediately picked up the lifeless, bleeding boy from the street. Hector was one of the first children who was shot and killed on that day. A newspaper photographer, Sam Nzima, took the picture that soon became the symbol of the "Soweto Uprising". However, for a long time the picture was banned in South Africa.

d) Read the story again. Put the events (1–9) in the correct order. Start with no. 5.

1. The students were singing and carrying signs.
2. Mbuyisa and Antoinette hurried away from the protest.
3. Mbuyisa Makhubo picked up Hector.
4. They started the march at their school.
5. Students from the townships planned a protest march for 16 June.
6. Soon the police arrived.
7. Hector Pieterson was shot.
8. The police started shooting at the protesters.
9. Feeling scared, the students threw stones at the police.

3 Workshop

6 Focus on words

a) Find a word or phrase in the text on page 51 which has more or less the same meaning.

1. without a plan = ■ (lines 6–11)
2. without violence = ■ (lines 12–18)
3. to frighten = ■ (lines 14–21)
4. to go away = ■ (lines 22–27)
5. right away = ■ (lines 30–35)
6. not moving, dead = ■ (lines 30–35)

b) Explain these words and phrases. Write complete sentences. ▶ H3

1. dissatisfaction (line 18)
2. to bleed (line 32)
3. uprising (line 37)

c) Complete the text with words from the same word family. You can find them all in the texts in ex. 2. Look at the example. ▶ S19 Wortarten

Last week the government decided that they would spend less money on school equipment. A group of about 75 **students** (1 to study) ■ (2 spontaneous) met at school. They were carrying signs. An older student gave the ■ (3 to command) "Go!", and they all started marching in the same ■ (4 direct). More and more students joined the ■ (5 crowded). Soon there were at least 200 ■ (6 to protest). Although they were marching ■ (7 peaceful), police showed up quickly. They told them that they needed permission for their protest. They had to end their ■ (8 to demonstrate) for that day.

> **G** ▶ **G20 CONJUNCTIONS AND ADVERBIAL CLAUSES**
>
> a) Complete the sentences from the text on page 51.
>
> 1. Even students who hadn't been told about the protest spontaneously joined the crowd on the playground ■ they got to school that morning.
> 2. ■ it was a peaceful demonstration, the police soon arrived and intimidated the students …
> 3. The children panicked and began running in all directions ■ they wanted to get away.
>
> b) Conjunctions introduce adverbial clauses of time, reason, result, purpose and concession. Match the sentences (1–4) with the words (A–D).
>
> 1 Give me your phone number **so that** I can call you.
> 2 **After** I spoke to my friend, I felt much better.
> 3 **Though** they were best friends, they had a fight.
> 4 The student talked to a teacher **because** he had a problem.
>
> A time
> B reason/result
> C purpose
> D concession

7 Focus on grammar ▶ G20

a) Match the conjunctions (1–11) with their German translations (A–K).

1 after | 2 although | 3 because | 4 before | 5 despite | 6 however | 7 in contrast to | 8 since | 9 so that | 10 until | 11 while	A bevor | B bis | C damit | D im Gegensatz zu | E jedoch | F nach/nachdem | G obwohl | H seit | I trotz | J während | K weil

b) Complete the text about a school in Soweto with conjunctions from a).

■ the school doesn't have good equipment, it has a group of very motivated teachers. ■ other schools, parents don't have to pay for their children's education here. There is a library at the school; ■, there is no teacher to take care of it. The school offers a high-quality education ■ the difficult living conditions in Soweto. The school also offers rooms and meals ■ some students live hours away. ■ native languages are used in grades 1–3, in grade 4 only English is used.

Workshop 3

8 On top of the world ▶ S10 Hörverstehen

a) Listen to the story behind the picture. What was the woman's trip to Cape Town like? Write down keywords.

b) Listen again. Choose the correct answer.

1. What information did the woman collect before her trip?
   a) about the weather, people, doctors
   b) about what to wear, money, papers
   c) about trips, towns, planes

2. How much time did she have to wait for her plane?
   a) three hours
   b) two hours
   c) five hours

3. What happened during the first part of the flight?
   a) Nobody cared about her.
   b) All the passengers felt sick.
   c) She wasn't able to sleep and eat.

4. What happened at Cape Town airport?
   a) She was arrested by the police.
   b) She didn't have her passport.
   c) She didn't have all her bags.

5. What did the woman do after she left the airport?
   a) She went directly to Table Mountain.
   b) She went directly to the hotel.
   c) She went directly to her friend George.

6. What did she do during the rest of her trip?
   a) She explored Cape Town.
   b) She climbed Table Mountain every day.
   c) She travelled around South Africa.

9 Your turn The story behind the picture ▶ S15 Geschichte (zum Bild) ▶ G5 Simple past / Present perfect ▶ G20 Conjunctions ▶ V5 Story

a) Look back at the story about the Soweto Uprising on page 51. Find the different parts of a story. Give the lines.
   1. where and when it takes place
   2. who is telling the story
   3. main characters
   4. what happened before the picture was taken
   5. the most exciting or suspenseful part
   6. ending (solution or open ending)

b) Choose picture A, B or C from ex. 4. Take notes on what you think happened before, during and after the photo.
   – Who took the photo?
   – Where was it?
   – What were the people feeling and thinking?

c) Write the story behind the picture. Think about the different parts (1–6) in a). ▶ S16 Schreibstil

d) Get into groups and read your stories to each other.
   ▶ M8 Writers' conference

S ▶ S15 Eine Geschichte zu einem Bild schreiben
- Eine Geschichte wird meist im *Simple past* geschrieben.
- Machen Sie die Geschichte durch die Beschreibung von Sinneseindrücken lebendig (Sehen, Hören, Riechen, Schmecken, Fühlen).
- Verwenden Sie unterschiedliche Konjunktionen.
- Die Geschichte sollte nur einen Höhepunkt haben.

Now I can write the story behind a picture.

fifty-three 53

3 Reading workshop

Planning and promoting an event against racism

The Big Five Marathon

The Big Five Marathon in South Africa takes place every year in a reserve in Entabeni. Runners from all over the world run through some of Africa's most beautiful landscape.

> South Africa is home to the so-called *Big Five* of Africa. These animals are the lion, leopard, rhinoceros, elephant and Cape buffalo. Which animal is Germany famous for?

1 Ready for a marathon in South Africa?

a) Before you read: how important is fitness to you? Take this quiz. Look at the results on page 192.

1. **How often do you do sport?**
   A Exercise? I don't know the word.
   B Does walking to the kitchen count?
   C About 1–2 times per week.
   D Every day. Sometimes more than once.

2. **How much do you walk every day?**
   A less than 1 km
   B 1.5 km
   C 2 km
   D more than 3 km

3. **How do you usually get to places?**
   A I stay home.
   B I go by car.
   C I take the bus or the train.
   D I walk or take the bike.

4. **It's Saturday! What are you going to do?**
   A watch my favourite series
   B read and cook
   C go shopping
   D do sports

b) Imagine you travel to South Africa: what kind of animal would you like to see? Give reasons.
   ▶ M1 Milling around   ▶ V19 Animals

2 A unique marathon   ▶ S9 Leseverstehen

a) Skim the text and choose the sentence that best summarises it.

1. It is an objective report about an event that took place.
2. It is an autobiographical story about someone's personal experience.
3. It is a story being told about a person who ran a marathon.

🗨 A15

When my alarm clock rang at 5 a.m., it was dark and there were still another two hours until sunrise.
I heard the night sounds slowly changing to morning sounds. The first birds were happily chirping and I could hear the wind blowing over the bushes around the lodge. In my imagination it was a lion silently looking for its breakfast. I, too, wanted to eat soon because I had a big day before me.

Ten months ago I had decided to make my dream a reality and now the day had come. I had read a lot about this country so the landscape and the atmosphere felt familiar. Although the sounds of the native languages were still foreign to my ears, the people wore their friendliness on their faces, making communication easy and natural.
Just like my role model had done almost every day of his life, even when he was in a 5-m^2 prison cell, I started my morning with exercise. Feeling full of energy, I then went to find breakfast. I still had almost three hours before the marathon.
Having read many reports about the run, I knew it would be difficult, so I had trained hard. I also knew the race was unique since the course was through a private game reserve, where Africa's 'big five' live.

54 fifty-four

But my knowledge and my training didn't completely prepare me for the experience. Probably nothing could have.
When the gunshot to start the race was fired at 9 a.m., I took a deep breath and my feet started running all by themselves, just like they had been taught to do. 600 other feet did the same thing. People from all over the world had come to this magical place.
During the first part of the race, I had time to think. I thought about my hero, about the reason I was there. Nelson Mandela had never run a marathon. He had been a boxer in his younger days, but by the time he got out of prison at the age of 71, he was too old and sick to start this tough sport. But still I was running in Mandela's home country to thank him for inspiring me with his determination. He had overcome near impossible obstacles and achieved so much. If he survived many years of apartheid and prison to achieve racial equality in his country, then I could get through 6 hours of running.
However, now it was time to concentrate on the race. In front of me was the path down the hill called Yellow Wood Valley, which everyone was afraid of. With every step, I heard the sound of my shoes when they touched the road. I concentrated on this noise to keep myself from falling. This wasn't the time to daydream or enjoy the landscape. Once I reached the bottom, I was in lion country. The next nine kilometres were flat, but difficult because of the deep sand. I looked around and used the landscape to distract myself from the pain in my legs. Could that be a lion over there, under the large tree? Was that quick movement a lion walking behind the bushes? While my eyes and mind played tricks on me, my legs kept moving. It wasn't my job to worry about the lions. There were rangers along the whole course to guarantee the safety of the runners. Suddenly a zebra showed up on my right and I knew that one zebra usually meant a herd of zebras.

I turned to look and there was the herd. I had two choices: I could quickly run past and continue the marathon, or I could stop and let the herd pass. I stopped because seeing the zebras was more important to me than any race. But a loud noise interrupted me from watching.

***

One hour later, I was ready to continue the marathon. The scene I had watched kept playing like a film in my head. That hour in the safety of the ranger's jeep was one of the most impressive things I had ever seen. The herd of zebras was followed by a family of majestic elephants. Slowly they walked through the sand with giant steps, the young elephants staying close to their mothers' legs. The ranger pointed to a tree far away and showed me the lions relaxing there. They had already had their breakfast and were, therefore, not interested in the animals on their way to the waterhole.
The rest of the run was like a dream. I looked at the land around me in admiration and couldn't imagine that there could be a place as picturesque as this anywhere else in the world. Mandela had also loved this. He saw his people's health and the health of the land, air and water as one and the same. What a wonderful vision.

b) Scan the story. Are the statements true, false or not in the text?

1. A lion was walking around outside the lodge.
2. The narrator isn't from South Africa, but he feels at home in this country.
3. The Big Five Marathon was the narrator's first marathon.
4. The runner felt well prepared for the marathon.
5. There were 300 other runners in the marathon.
6. The narrator looks up to Nelson Mandela as a role model.

3 Reading workshop

c) Match the sentence beginnings (1–5) with the endings (A–G). There are two endings more than you need.

1. When Mandela got out of prison,
2. Running down the hill
3. Lions lived
4. The runners didn't worry about the animals
5. The narrator was more interested in zebras

A because there were rangers along the path.
B took a lot of concentration.
C he was already president.
D than in running a fast race.
E he was too old and sick to run marathons.
F because they weren't real.
G in the sandy area at the bottom of the hill.

d) Write two questions to the narrator about the event. Use different question forms and tenses. Let your partner answer the questions. ▶ **G1, G5, G7, G11** Tenses

3 Decorating a text ▶ **V20** Sensations

a) Do these words describe sounds, feelings or sights? Copy the table and complete it. Add more words.

admiration chirping loud motivated familiar foreign impressive wonderful natural noise

sounds	feelings	sights
chirping	admiration	…
…	…	

b) Complete the sentences with words from the table in a).

1. In the evenings you can often hear ■ insects.
2. The ■ landscape was perfect for a postcard.
3. The runners felt ■ when the crowd cheered for them.
4. When the race started, 600 feet made a ■ noise across the running track.
5. The ■ mountain was much higher than the rest of the land.
6. I was in ■ of the landscape around me. I never knew anything could be that beautiful.

4 What happened after the loud noise

a) One part (***) in the story on pages 54–55 is missing. What happened in the one hour between the loud noise and the rest of the run? Write about the runner's experience. ▶ H3
▶ **S15** Geschichte (Fortsetzung) ▶ **S16** Schreibstil
▶ **G20** Conjunctions ▶ **V5** Story
Example: The loud noise I heard was …

V
At first there was …
Soon there was a smell of …
The next thing I heard was …
Afterwards I realised that …
Finally I noticed that …
Next time I'll pay attention to …

b) Work with a partner and read your texts to each other. Give feedback. Was it creative? ▶ **M7** Peer correction

5 Focus on words ▶ **S19** Wortarten

a) Match the word parts (1–8 and A–H) to form correct words.

1 imagin- | 2 equal- | 3 run- | 4 impress- | 5 box- |
6 pictures- | 7 friendli- | 8 majest-

A -ity | B -er | C -ness | D -ic | E -ation | F -ive | G -ner |
H -que

Reading workshop 3

b) Look at the words from a). Are they nouns or adjectives? The skills box can help you.

> **S ▶ S19 Wortarten**
> Es gibt Übungen, in denen Sie Wortarten ändern müssen. Im Satz „The ■ was very talented. (*sing*)" müssen Sie das Verb (*sing*) in ein Nomen (*singer*) wandeln. Typische Endungen für die jeweiligen Wortarten sind:
>
> *nouns*: -ment, -ion, -ness, -ity
> *adjectives*: -able, -ible, -ive, -al, -ic, -ed, -ing
> *adverbs*: -ly
>
> *person nouns*: -er, -or, -ist, -ian
> *verbs*: -ise, -ate, -en
> *Negative adjectives often begin with*: un-, im-, dis-

c) Copy and complete the table with the missing words from the same word family. Work with a dictionary.

	noun	verb	adjective	negative adjective	adverb
1.	admiration	■	■	–	–
2.	■ ■	–	friendly	■	■
3.	■	know	■	■	–
4.	■	–	possible	■	■

d) Complete the sentences with words from the table in c). ▶ H3

1. I ■ Nelson Mandela for his determination.
2. The runner ■ a lot about the surrounding nature. He could explain everything in this area.
3. It is ■ to run this marathon without preparing for it.
4. One of the rangers seemed ■ when I asked him for help. He didn't help me at all!

6 Your turn No racism ▶ S4 Präsentation ▶ S11 Visualisierung

Your school wants to take part in a project called "Schule ohne Rassismus". Therefore, you want to organise an event to bring people from different backgrounds together.

a) Make a list of events you could organise to help fight racism.

b) In your group, prepare one of the events from the list. Answer these questions:
▶ G7 Will-future / Going to-future ▶ G21 Quantifiers ▶ V17 Multiculturalism

1. Who can organise it?
2. Who and how many will be invited?
3. Where and when will it take place?
4. What equipment do you need?
5. How much money do you need?
6. What makes the event special?
7. How can people interact / get to know each other during the event?

c) To promote your event, film an advert or make a poster about it.

d) Each group presents their event to the class. Give feedback to each other. Then vote for the best event in class. ▶ M3 1-minute presentation ▶ M10 Tip-top ▶ V1 Presentation

Now I can plan and promote an event against racism.

3 Speaking workshop

Talking about and suggesting free-time activities

Happy times

1 Free-time activities ▶ **S18** Sprechen (Monolog) ▶ **G22** Quantifiers ▶ **G24** Gerund ▶ **V21** Free time

At a party a new friend is asking you about your free time. Tell him/her:

1. what you do in your free time.
2. how much time you spend with your family and your friends.

> **V** ▶ **V21 Free time**
>
> I like meeting my friends / playing video games / relaxing / staying over at friends' / going to the gym / …
> I love football / talking to my friends / shopping / …
> I'm crazy about films / series / riding my bicycle / …
> I enjoy playing the piano / reading comics / going out / …
> I have to help with the household / …
> I spend every day / every hour / some time with …

2 What can we do with them?
▶ **S18** Sprechen (Dialog) ▶ **G2** Modals
▶ **V22** Sightseeing

a) A group of exchange students from South Africa is coming to your school. Make a list of activities you want to do and places you want to see with them in your town. ▶ **S7** Sammeln und ordnen

A places to eat out

B parks/nature

C sights/attractions

D shops/markets

E sports

F entertainment

b) Discuss the options with a partner.
▶ **V8** Discussion

c) Then decide on five activities.
▶ **V23** Suggestions

> **V** ▶ **V23 Making suggestions and finding a compromise**
>
> Let's … / I suggest … | We could / should …
> What about …? / Would you be OK with …?
> How about …? | Why don't you …?
> If I were you, I would …
> Don't you think it's a good idea to …?
> Do you mind (if) …?
> Yes, I'd like / love to. / That's a great idea.
> Well, I'd rather … / I like your idea, but could we …?
> I don't think … will work. / I don't feel like …
>
> Sounds great. | Good point. | Brilliant!

Now I can talk about and suggest free-time activities.

Video lounge 3

 Discovering South Africa

1 Destinations in South Africa ▶ V24 Locations

a) Look at the map and find these places: Cape Town, Durban, Kruger National Park, Robben Island and Soweto. Describe the position of the places.

Example: Soweto is located in the north of the country. It is situated close to …

> **V** ▶ V24 Talking about locations
> … is located in the north / south / west / east / middle / north-east of the country.
> … is situated close to / between / next to the sea / mountains / a river / the city of …

b) Have you heard of any of the places from a)? What do you know about them? Talk to a partner.

c) Divide the class into six groups. Each group researches videos about one of the places from a). Make a table for this place and complete it with information from the videos you have found. ▶ S1 Informationen
▶ S5 Hörsehverstehen

- Where is it?
- What is it known for?
- What can tourists do / see there?
- Interesting facts?
- Events, festivals, celebrations?

d) Write a short text and recommend the place you have researched. Then present it to the class.
▶ G2 Modals ▶ M3 1-minute presentation
▶ V7 Recommendation
Example: I can highly recommend … It is the most popular destination for …

> **V** It is known around the world for its / as …
> The main tourist attractions / destinations are …
> It has the biggest / most important / fastest …
> It was built / founded / started in …
> There is … every year / month / week.

fifty-nine

3 Check out

Check out: South Africa

1 Listening

a) Listen to the radio programme. Which group of listeners (1–3) is the programme made for?

1. It's for Germans who live abroad.
2. It's for people from different countries who live in Germany.
3. It's for people who want to leave Germany.

b) Listen again. Copy the table and complete it with the correct information. Take notes.

	Dan	Iminathi	Perry
Age	…	…	30
Home country	…	South Africa	…
Time lived in Germany	…	…	nine years
Reasons for moving to Germany	His father's job	…	…
Differences: Germany and home country	…	South Africa more colourful; …	…

c) Match the sentence beginnings (1–6) with the endings (A–H). There are two more endings than you need.

1. Before moving to Germany Dan lived
2. Dan often visits
3. Iminathi takes care of
4. In her free time Iminathi takes
5. Perry met his future wife while she was
6. Perry and his wife had

A a boy and a girl.
B a long-distance relationship for two years.
C in France, Italy and Belgium.
D his friends in other countries.
E German lessons.
F working at a hotel.
G his family back in Ireland.
H backpacking.

2 Reading

a) Read the wiki entry. What is it about? Choose the four correct topics.

A tourism
B apartheid
C dangerous animals
D protecting nature
E locals getting active
F shelter for elephants
G poaching
H accidents

South Africa's national parks

Every year millions of tourists travel to South Africa to see the so-called Big Five – lions, leopards, rhinos, elephants and Cape buffalos – and of course lots of other animals, such as giraffes, zebras and many more. South Africa has many different species of plants and animals. Thus, safaris through South Africa's national parks are popular tourist attractions. In Kruger National Park, for example, you can choose from

Check out 3

many different types of safari. These can be adventure walking tours with a guide, family safaris in jeeps, and also 5-star packages with excellent meals. If you want more freedom and flexibility, you can also do a self-drive safari with a rented car. You can sleep in tents, lodges or even in luxury accommodation.

While this sounds like a lot of fun, South Africa's national parks are much more than just tourist attractions. They're protected areas where South Africa's unique wildlife and nature are conserved. However, tourism is an important source of income for the national parks, which need a lot of money in order to conserve their plants and animals. Special attention is being paid to the sustainability of tourism in the national parks. In Kruger National Park, for example, visitors can only see 3% of the park from the roads so that the animals have enough space to feel free.

South Africa's national parks also have educational programmes to teach locals how important South Africa's animals and plants are to the country. They work together with communities in the neighbourhood to form a connection from which both sides can benefit. For example, school groups can enter Kruger National Park for free if they take part in an educational programme.

One big problem the national parks have is the illegal hunting of big game, which is called poaching. South Africa's national parks are home to species which are in great danger, such as elephants and rhinos. Poachers kill rhinos for their horns, which are used, for example, in traditional Asian medicine. Elephants are killed for their ivory. The ivory is used to make jewellery or other decorations. Some people hunt just for fun and to show off their hunting talent. These animal parts are sometimes cut off while the animals are still alive, which is extremely brutal.

South Africa's national parks are fighting a battle against poaching. Rangers are always searching the area on foot, by car or even by plane using technology to find illegal hunters. The fight against poaching is dangerous as rangers come into direct contact with the poachers who are often violent. Sadly, it also happens that rangers are killed by poachers. That's why the fight against poaching is sometimes compared to a war.

(450 words)

b) Complete the sentences.

1. Safaris through South Africa's national parks are popular tourist attractions because …
2. The national parks have the goal of conserving …
3. The national parks rely on tourism because …
4. Tourism in the national parks should focus on …
5. If school groups take part in an educational programme, they …

c) Answer the questions in complete sentences. Use your own words.

1. Why are rhinos hunted by poachers?
2. How do park rangers fight against poaching?
3. Why is the fight against poaching dangerous for the rangers?

d) Welche Safaris gibt es im Kruger National Park? Fassen Sie die Information auf Deutsch zusammen.

3 Check out

3 Writing

a) Write a statement on safaris: would you like to take part in one? Write about 100 words.

b) Choose one of the photos (A–B) and write the story behind the picture. Write about 160 words.

You can include these aspects:
- Where and when was the picture taken?
- Who took it? Why?
- What happened before and after the picture was taken?
- What did the people feel? What did they think?
- What is the most suspenseful/exciting part in the story?
- Does the story have a happy ending?

A

B

4 Use of language

a) Find words or phrases in the article on pages 60–61 which mean more or less the same (=), or the opposite (↔).

1. low ↔ ■ (lines 9–14)
2. to protect = ■ (lines 9–14)
3. room = ■ (lines 9–14)
4. relationship = ■ (lines 15–18)
5. trouble ↔ ■ (lines 19–28)
6. legal ↔ ■ (lines 19–28)
7. to poach = ■ (lines 19–28)
8. dead ↔ ■ (lines 23–28)
9. brutal = ■ (lines 29–33)
10. to be murdered = ■ (lines 29–33)

b) Explain one of these words from the article. Write complete sentences.

1. tourist attraction (line 9)   2. for free (line 18)   3. to hunt (line 26)

c) Write two questions for a ranger in a national park about safaris in South Africa.
Use different questions forms and tenses.

d) Complete the text with adjectives and adverbs.

Last year we went on a ■ (1 fantastic) safari in Kruger National Park. We had a guide who drove us around in a jeep. We saw leopards that walked almost ■ (2 silent) through the ■ (3 wide) landscape and a herd of antelope that ■ (4 quick) jumped away at the sight of the leopard. Suddenly, we saw a ■ (5 majestic) elephant coming towards us from behind the bushes. It was looking at us and shaking its ears. We thought it was ■ (6 angry) and got a little ■ (7 scared). However, our guide told us ■ (8 calm) that it was just shaking its ears to cool its body down. We watched it ■ (9 quiet) for a while until it ■ (10 slow) went back behind the bushes.

Check out 3

e) Rewrite the sentences with the adverbs in brackets. Put them in the correct position.

1. Mason and Janet play basketball. (often / in the park / in the evenings)
2. I'm meeting Peter. (at nine o'clock / at the restaurant)
3. Tom goes swimming. (here / often / in the mornings)
4. I'm at the bowling alley. (on Sundays / always)
5. We go hiking. (at the weekend / in the mountains / sometimes)

f) Complete the sentences with the correct conjunction.

| so | because | until | while | although |

1. Nelson Mandela spent more than 35 years in prison ■ he was released in 1990.
2. ■ Mandela was in prison, apartheid set the rules in South African society.
3. South Africa was punished for apartheid ■ they couldn't take part in the Olympic Games in 1964.
4. ■ Mandela had spent such a long time in prison, he didn't give up.
5. Mandela became South Africa's first black president ■ the ANC had won the elections.

g) Complete the text with the correct words. You need to change the words on the right, fill in the word if there is a question mark, or choose the correct word if two options are given.

Rich against poor

In South Africa the gap between the rich and the ■ (1) is wide. That means some people are very rich while others are very poor.
Rich people often live in so-called 'gated communities'. These are areas which have walls around them and security guards ■ (2) them too. Residents and people who work in these communities can enter them ■ (3) with their fingerprints, while guests can get an entry card or a code. Thanks to these regulations, residents of the gated communities feel ■ (4) in view of the high crime rate in South Africa. Gated communities are usually very clean areas with beautiful houses. As the ■ (5) of the people who live in these communities are white, these areas are said to be places where a white elite feels better than the rest.
The ■ (6) of life in South Africa's townships is very ■ (7). Townships are poor areas of the city. During apartheid they were for black people and even today ■ (8) black people live there. The conditions of ■ (9) are very different from those in the gated communities. The poorest people in the townships live ■ (10) cabins or in places where more than one family shares one room.

1 poverty

2 controlled

3 easy
4 to save

5 major

6 real
7 difference

8 most
9 to live

10 ?

sixty-three 63

⊕ h87gg2

4 Digital Hong Kong

Discovering the city

In this unit you will:
- recommend a selfie spot.
- create a poster about media addiction.
- write a profile of your favourite influencer.
- talk about and discuss mobile phone habits.

Hong Kong is a region on the south-eastern coast of China. With over 7.5 million people living in quite a small area, Hong Kong is a megacity. It is famous for its important financial district, a huge skyline, a big container terminal and a lot of shopping streets.

A

B

C

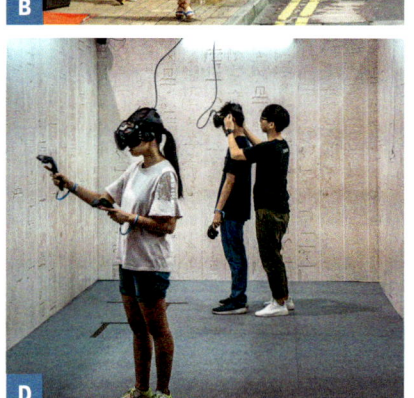
D

E

1 Things to do in Hong Kong ▶ V22 Sightseeing

a) Look at the pictures (A–E). Match the pictures with the words from the word bank.

| billboard | Chinese letters | crowded | dragon | e-sport | impressive | joystick | Monster Building |

| selfie spot | shopping | skyscraper | skyline | to go sightseeing | sailing boat | to pose |

| tourist attraction | traffic | urban | Victoria Harbour | Victoria Peak | view | virtual reality | VR goggles |

b) Write a question for each picture (A–E). With a partner, take turns in answering your questions. Use the words from a).
▶ H4 ▶ G1, G5, G6, G7, G11 Tenses
Example: Where is a good spot to take a selfie?
– Victoria Peak is a great selfie spot.

> Hong Kong became a colony of the British Empire in 1841. It was given back to China in 1997. It has three main parts: Hong Kong Island, Kowloon and the New Territories. Hong Kong's official languages are Chinese and English.

Starter 4

2 Top selfie spots in Hong Kong ▶ S10 Hörverstehen

A17

a) Listen to the radio programme. Which of these places does influencer Vera recommend as top spots to take selfies? Choose the correct attractions.

A Victoria Harbour   C Temple Street   E International Commerce Centre
B The Monster Building D Victoria Peak   F AME Stadium

b) Listen again. Choose the correct answer.

1. When did Vera begin writing her blog?
   a) five months ago
   b) two years ago
   c) five years ago

2. On which floor is the observation deck?
   a) 100th floor
   b) 36th floor
   c) 60th floor

3. Which sight is one of Hong Kong's most Instagrammable places?
   a) the International Commerce Centre
   b) the Monster Building
   c) Victoria Harbour

4. When was the Monster Building built?
   a) in the 1950s
   b) in the 1960s
   c) in the 2000s

5. How high is Victoria Peak?
   a) 252 metres
   b) 525 metres
   c) 552 metres

6. What kind of transportation goes up to Victoria Peak?
   a) a tram
   b) a train
   c) a bus

c) Research more information about two sights and attractions from a). Describe each of them in one sentence. ▶ H4 ▶ S1 Informationen

d) Which sights would you like to see? Where would you take a selfie? Tell your classmates. ▶ H4
▶ M5 Round robin

3 Your turn   A recommendation ▶ S3 Textsorten ▶ V7 Recommendation ▶ V22 Sightseeing

a) Imagine an exchange student from Hong Kong is coming to stay with you. Which places and attractions in Germany would you recommend to him/her for a visit? Make a list in class.

b) With a partner, choose 1–3 attractions that are good selfie spots and write a recommendation for them. Write 80–100 words. ▶ S16 Schreibstil ▶ G2 Modals

> **S** ▶ S3 Textsorten
>
> In einer Empfehlung geben Sie anderen Personen Rat zu einem Thema oder einer Situation.
> • Fragen Sie sich vorab, welche Information hilfreich ist.
> • Drängen Sie Ihre Meinung der anderen Person nicht auf.
> • Sprechen Sie über Ihre eigenen Erfahrungen.

c) Exchange your recommendations with another pair. Give feedback to each other. Would you like to visit the attractions? Give reasons. ▶ M7 Peer correction

Now I can recommend a selfie spot. ✓

sixty-five 65

4 Workshop

Creating a poster about media addiction

Step A: Media habits

The World Wide Web (www) was developed at the end of the 1980s. With all its functions and all the devices we use it on today, we can't imagine a world without it any more.

1 Me and my smart device

a) Make a mind map for "media". ► **S7** Sammeln und ordnen

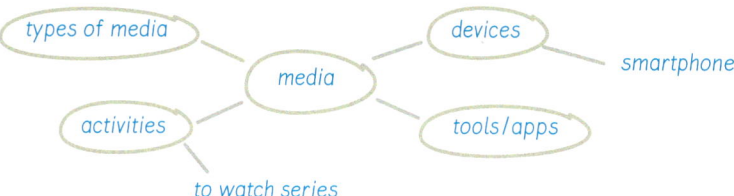

b) Compare your mind map with a partner's. What do you have in common? Then talk about your results in class.

c) What do you think: how much time do you spend online every day? Write down an amount of time.

d) Write a media diary for seven days.
Take notes about: ► **G19** Adverbs and sequence of adverbs ► **V25** Media ► **V26** Media habits

- how often you use media,
- when you use it,
- for how long you use it,
- what you use it for.

 ► **V26 Talking about media habits**

I spend … hours on media every day.
I spend most time …
I use my phone/device for …
I didn't realise I spent so much time doing …
I could/couldn't live without it.
I think I spend too much / a normal amount of time on my phone.

e) Check your guess from c) and discuss your results in class.

2 Screen time ► **S10** Hörverstehen

a) Listen to Matthew. Answer the questions:
- Who is he talking to?
- Where are they from?

b) Listen again. Copy the table and complete it with the correct information. Then compare your results with a partner. ► **H4**

	Davis	…	…	…	…
Phone usage per week	20 h 47m	…	…	…	…
Most used feature	Music streaming app	…	…	…	…
Pickups	21	…	…	…	…

c) Which person in the interview can you identify with the most? Give reasons.
Example: I can identify with Davis the most because …

Workshop 4

Step B: Media usage in Hong Kong

More and more of our interaction takes place online. That's why the time people use digital media is rising constantly.

3 Time spent on media by Hong Kong's population ▶ **S9** Leseverstehen

a) Before you read: look at the infographic which was published in an online magazine. In class, talk about the information it shows. ▶ **S2** Diagramm ▶ **V27** Analysing charts
Example: The infographic shows that Hong Kong's youth uses the internet for … hours and … minutes on average every day.

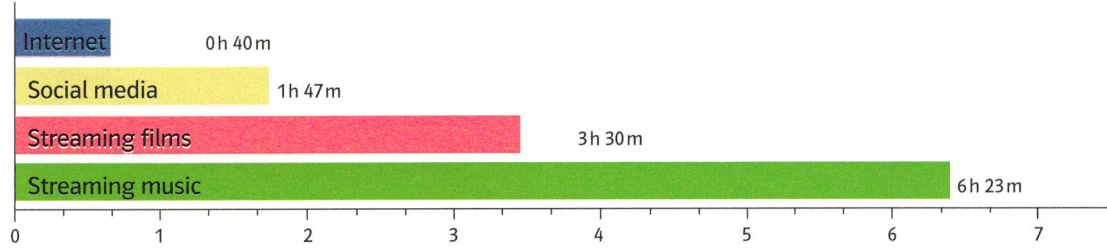

Base: Internet users from Hong Kong, aged 16–64   Source: we are social, 2019; Hootsuite, 2019; Global Web Index, 2018

b) A lot of people saw the infographic online and posted comments on the magazine's website. Read the comments and write down one keyword for each of them.

A19

LOONY_LUKE
I was shocked when I read your infographic on media use among students in Hong Kong. According to the infographic, some students who took part in the survey said that they used social media for nine hours a day. That's crazy! These students can't be making time for any other free-time activity. This is not a healthy lifestyle.
It's clear that these young people – who should be having the time of their lives – are addicted not only to certain social media platforms, but to their phones in general. It is extremely worrying that they are taking up habits that they may never be able to break.
As everybody knows phone addiction comes with anxiety, depression and problems with sleeping. It can lead to feelings of low self-esteem, relationship conflicts, and bad school or work performance. We know all this, and it still seems impossible to do anything about it. I find it really alarming that nothing is being done to help young people manage the time they spend with new technology. Isn't it time that smartphones came with health warnings and age restrictions like tobacco and alcohol?
5 h ago

4 Workshop

SOPHLEE

This addiction isn't limited to the young. People of all ages are addicted. And it's not surprising when you consider that smartphones are available to almost everyone and almost everyone has one. In my opinion, problematic smartphone usage presents a much bigger public health problem than alcohol or drug addiction. But this is new technology. When cars were invented, there weren't any regulations at first either. It wasn't until later that laws were passed to protect people. I hope the same happens with smartphones.

4 h ago

MEDIAGEEK123

I don't understand your frustration about smartphones. I use mine all the time and I couldn't imagine living without it. And I don't want to! It's very helpful because I can send messages to my friends if I'm too late or I can check for the correct way if I'm lost. Maybe you are too old to understand my way of thinking.

3h ago

MRSCHEUNG

As a parent, I think rules are important. My 16-year-old daughter uses social media to talk to her friends online, which I think is good. However, she isn't allowed to use her phone during meal times or after bedtime. It's a simple rule but it's fair and my daughter says it helps her to develop good habits.

2 h ago

BRIGHTSMILE

I think the impact of social media on a person is largely dependent on the user. However, most children and teenagers do need help when it comes to controlling their phone usage. It's up to parents to set the rules and limits, but parents who didn't grow up with smartphones need support too.

1h ago

VICTORIAPEAK3

I don't use social media very often, but on my smartphone there are apps for checking the weather, looking at maps, looking at photos, listening to music, watching TV, learning languages, reading books and newspapers, booking flights and much more. It's not all bad!

1h ago

c) Read the comments again and match the sentences with them. Who says what?
   Sometimes there is more than one possible solution.

1. It's bad for your health when you spend too much time online.
2. It's very difficult to change one's habits.
3. There should be rules and laws which are for everyone.
4. Families can make their own rules too.
5. There are very useful things that you can do with your smartphone.
6. Older people didn't have smartphones or social media when they were young.
7. I'm not frustrated by my mobile phone.

d) Fassen Sie jeden Kommentar in einem Satz zusammen. ▶ **S17** Mediation

e) Which comment do you disagree with the most? Give reasons. ▶ **V15** Opinion

Workshop 4

4 People's feelings ▶ H4 ▶ S7 Sammeln und ordnen ▶ G13 Adjectives and adverbs ▶ V28 Feelings

a) Read Loony_Luke's comment on page 67 again. Find three adjectives which show his feelings about students' phone usage.

b) Copy the table and add more adjectives that describe feelings. You can use a dictionary.

positive	negative	neutral
helpful, …	shocked, …	…

5 Focus on words

a) Find media words in the comments and add them to the "media" mind map in ex. 1a).

b) Match the underlined words from the posts with the German words in the word bank.

   Altersbegrenzung   Ängstlichkeit   Auswirkung   Gesundheitswarnhinweis   Gewohnheit   Grenze

   problematisch   Selbstwertgefühl   Sucht   Vorschrift

c) Complete the sentences with words from b).
   1. The government announced the new safety ■ on Friday.
   2. It's normal to feel a lot of ■ before and during exams.
   3. I have the ■ of leaving my phone in the living room when I go to bed.
   4. Getting so many likes on the picture she posted was good for her ■.
   5. Alcoholic drinks have ■ on their labels.

d) Explain these words. Write complete sentences.
   1. lifestyle (line 5)   2. limited (line 16)   3. habit (line 32)

G ▶ G4, G12 THE PASSIVE VOICE I & II

GV20

a) Complete the sentences from the comments on pages 67–68. Use the correct form of the verbs in brackets.

   1. When cars ■ (invent), there weren't any regulations at first either.
   2. It wasn't until later that laws ■ (pass) to protect people.
   3. She ■ (not allow) to use her phone during meal times or after bedtime.

b) Complete the rule. Use the words from the word bank.

   action   am/is/are   by   past participle   to be   unimportant   was/were   who or what

   FORM
   The correct form of ■
   → simple present: ■   } + the ■ (3rd verb form)
   → simple past: ■

   USE
   The passive voice is used to show that ■ caused the action is ■ or unknown.
   To say who or what caused the ■ you can use ■.

4 Workshop

6 Focus on grammar ▶ G4, G12 Passive voice I & II

a) Complete the sentences with the correct form of the verbs in brackets. Use the passive voice.

1. Not everybody knows that the World Wide Web ■ (invent) by Tim Berners-Lee.
2. Last night some laptops ■ (steal) from the computer shop.
3. One of the richest influencers I know ■ (follow) by over 118 million people.
4. I wanted to look something up in class but I ■ (not allow).
5. Today we ■ (show) around the city by a funny young tour guide.
6. The posts ■ (not remove) from the web page although they are rude.

b) Rewrite the sentences. Use the passive voice.

1. They don't update the school computers regularly.
2. More than 100 people liked her picture.
3. They tell us not to share pictures on the internet.
4. Trolls posted very rude comments on her page.
5. They removed one of the comments later.
6. People from all over the world use the internet every day.

c) Work with a partner. Ask and answer questions about the pictures (A–F). Use the phrases in the passive voice. ▶ G1, G5, G6, G7 Tenses ▶ G16 Prepositions
Example: Picture A: Where was the selfie taken? – It was taken at Victoria Harbour in Hong Kong.

A — take a selfie (Victoria Harbour, Hong Kong)

B — finish construction of the Buddha statue (1993)

C — celebrate Chinese New Year (21 Jan–20 Feb)

D — open the garden to the public (2006)

E — make noodles (water, salt, eggs and flour)

F — organise demonstration (fight for democracy)

Hong Kong has different governing and economic systems to mainland China. In the summer of 2019, mass protests against the Chinese government took place in Hong Kong because China wants to integrate Hong Kong into its legal system. The conflict isn't over yet. Do you know any other regions with such conflicts?

Step C: Am I addicted to my phone?

A lot of people can't control their smartphone usage any more. They spend more time with it than with any other activity or person. Smartphone addiction is an illness and can cause serious physical and mental problems.

7 Signs of smartphone addiction

a) Take the test and find out if you are addicted to your phone.

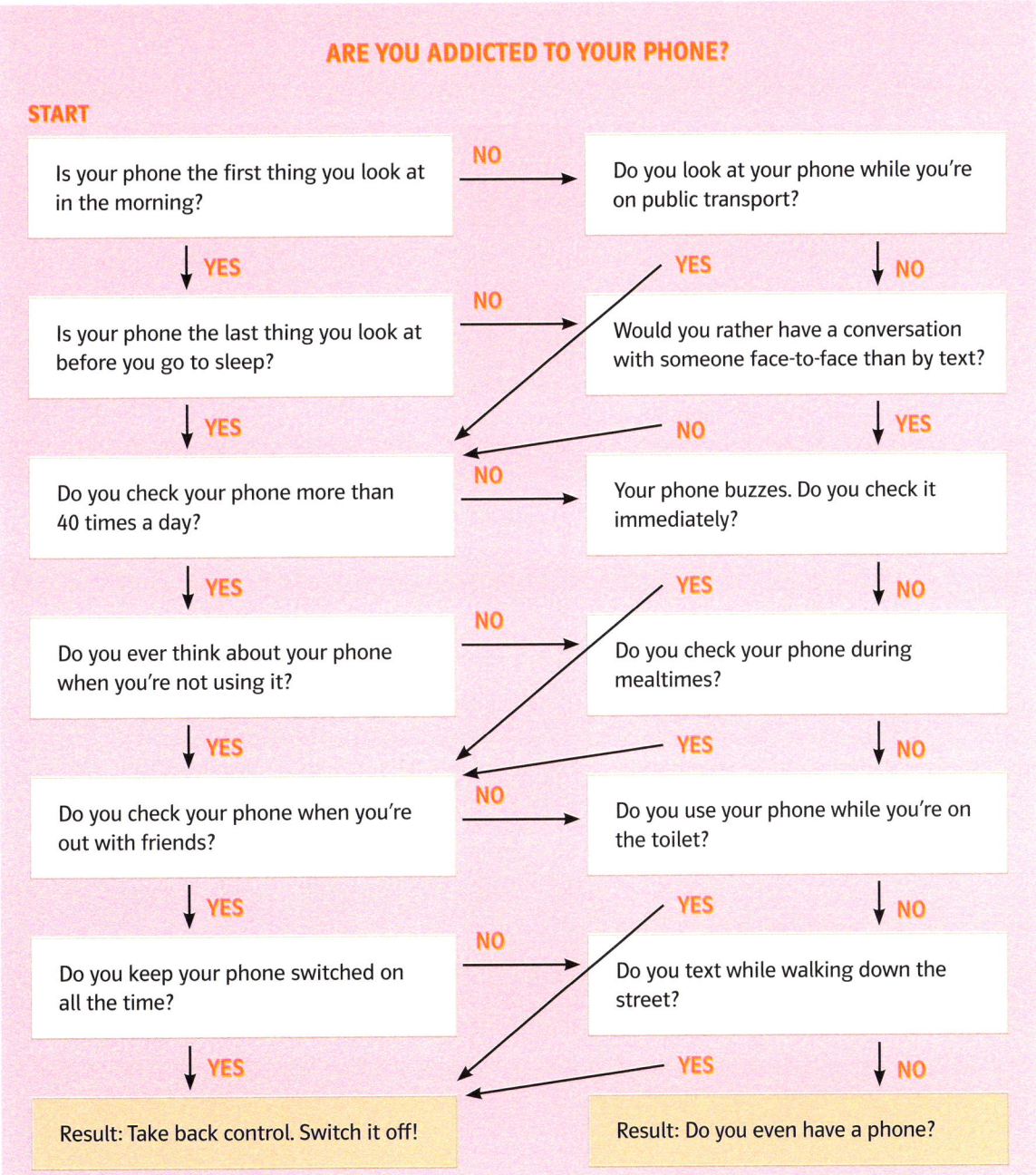

4 Workshop

b) Do you agree or disagree with the result? Is there anything about your smartphone usage that you would like to change? Talk about it with a partner.

c) In which situations is it OK to look at one's smartphone? In which situations isn't it? Discuss with a partner.

d) Why do you think it is difficult for people to stop using their smartphones? Discuss in class.
▶ **H4** ▶ **V8** Discussion

8 Symptoms and measures ▶ S17 Mediation

Lesen Sie den Informationstext über Mediensucht und beantworten Sie folgende Fragen auf Deutsch in Stichworten.

1. Wie kann man feststellen, dass eine Person süchtig ist?
2. Wie kann man einer süchtigen Person helfen?

Signs
Many users use the internet to escape reality; they stop communication with people in real life and prefer online communication. They act differently on social media than they do in person.

Symptoms
- Depression: life satisfaction and the general feeling of well-being decrease; people get unhappy and lose their self-confidence.
- Anxiety: people are afraid of being judged in a negative way, or rejected in a social situation.

Diagnosis
1. a person uses social media to regulate his or her mood, or to escape real-world conflicts
2. social media starts to take control of what a person is thinking, which has an impact on other activities
3. a person spends more and more time on social media to experience good feelings they had while using social media
4. a person doesn't sleep or eat any more, even when they can't use social media
5. a person has conflicts with family and friends in real life

Measures
Medications have been tried but don't seem to be effective. Helpful methods can be:
- self-help by following rules and time limits
- professional therapy to learn to change one's own behaviour and habits
- professional support to organise one's tasks and activities

9 Your turn A poster about media addiction ▶ S1 Informationen ▶ S4 Präsentation ▶ S11 Visualisierung
▶ **V1** Presentation

a) Work in small groups. Create a poster to give students information about smartphone and media addiction. Research and collect information. You can use the information from this step and add your own aspects. Choose pictures and/or charts to visualise your message. ▶ **V25** Media ▶ **V26** Media habits

b) Present your poster in class. Give each other feedback. ▶ **M11** Gallery walk ▶ **M10** Tip-top

Now I can create a poster about media addiction.

Writing a profile of your favourite influencer

Reading workshop 4

Living for the likes

In every country, influencers on different platforms have millions of followers who want to find inspiration or look for information. In Hong Kong and China, influencers have to pay attention to what they post. The Chinese government doesn't like criticism.

1 Are you a follower?

Before you read: do you follow any influencers on social media? If yes: whom? Why? If no: why not? Tell the class. ▶ M5 Round robin

2 A traditional way of life ▶ S9 Leseverstehen

a) Before you read: match the words (1–12) from the article with their German translations (A–L).

1 ancient | **2** delicious | **3** empowerment | **4** ginger | **5** prospect | **6** plum | **7** rural | **8** seasonal | **9** to publicise | **10** to promote | **11** to praise | **12** urban

A alt | **B** Ermächtigung | **C** für etw. werben | **D** Perspektive | **E** Ingwer | **F** ländlich | **G** loben | **H** Pflaume | **I** saisonal | **J** etw. veröffentlichen | **K** städtisch | **L** köstlich

b) Read the article. Sum up the influencer's message in one sentence. ▶ H4 ▶ G23 Genitive

A20

Making farm life fashionable

3 June 2021
by Han Fong

Millions of people follow 29-year-old Bao Wang on social media.
So why are the videos of her quiet life in the Chinese countryside so popular?

5 HONG KONG – Bao has become one of China's biggest social media stars since she started sharing videos of her life in Yunnan in 2017. She now has 26 million followers across different social media platforms.
She first started making her videos by herself, but now a team of people work with her to help her create them. The
10 videos have soft guitar music playing in the background and show beautiful countryside and ancient traditions. Bao makes furniture from bamboo and makes her clothes with natural materials. She creates a lot of delicious meals from seasonal, natural ingredients such as soya beans,
15 ginger and plums.
The Chinese government has started to realise Bao's power as an influencer. Chinese politicians recognise and praise her for showing China's traditional culture to the rest of the world and a Communist youth programme even named her an ambassador for promoting the economic empowerment of young people living away from the main cities.
20 But as she becomes more and more famous, people have started to ask whether Bao's channel is Communist propaganda. Using social platforms to publicise rural commercial opportunities and showing traditional Chinese cultural aspects to millions of people, she seems almost too perfect for the Communist Party of China.

4 Reading workshop

> Dr Zhang Wei Li, a professor of Chinese culture and history at Nanjing University, told us: "Bao is one of many fresh new faces in the influencing industry. She's creative, she's attractive and she knows exactly what her audience wants – in China and other countries. I don't believe that it has anything to do with a Communist movement. Bao built her story upon finding her success in the country instead of in a city – which doesn't match with China's push for urban development and prospects.
> I believe that that's what has made her so popular and successful – she shows young people that success doesn't have to mean living the big city dream. In fact, she's made the opposite trendy and creative. The Chinese government has been clever in adapting its own position to advertise Bao as a symbol of traditional culture."
> Some Chinese media channels say that Bao's work is even more effective than propaganda. Why? Because it has created more real global interest in Chinese traditions than any professionally designed campaign has been able to do for many years.
> What goes without saying is that Bao has shown real determination to succeed in a way that is less conventional than others in the social media and influencing industry.

c) Read the article again. Complete the sentences with words from the article.
1. Bao Wang now works with ■ to create her videos.
2. The government has begun to use Bao as an ■ of traditional Chinese culture.
3. Using social media, Bao Wang shows commercial ■ in the countryside.
4. According to Dr Zhang Wei Li Bao isn't part of the Communist ■.
5. Bao has made country living ■ and creative.
6. Compared to other social media influencers, Bao's path to success isn't ■.

d) Answer the questions in complete sentences. Use your own words.
1. How successful is Bao? In what ways?
2. What sort of videos does she make?
3. Why do some people think that Bao's videos might be Communist propaganda?
4. Why does Dr Zhang Wei Li think the content of Bao's videos isn't propaganda?
5. According to Dr Zhang Wei Li, why are Bao's videos so popular?
6. Why do some Chinese media channels think that Bao's videos are more successful than government propaganda?

3 About Bao

a) Write two questions for Bao Wang about being an influencer. Use different question forms or different tenses. ▶ **G1, G5, G6, G7, G11** Tenses

b) Would you like to follow Bao Wang? Give reasons. Discuss in class. ▶ **V15** Opinion

4 Focus on words

a) Find a word or a phrase in the article on pages 73–74 which means more or less the same (=), or the opposite (↔).

1. busy ↔ ■ (lines 1–7)
2. to produce = ■ (lines 8–15)
3. to ignore ↔ ■ (lines 16–19)
4. outdated ↔ ■ (lines 29–32)
5. successful = ■ (lines 33–37)
6. local ↔ ■ (lines 33–37)

Reading workshop 4

b) Find words in the article which belong to the same word family. Copy the table and complete it.
▶ **S19** Wortarten

	noun	adjective	verb
1.	■ ■	influential	to influence
2.	recognition	recognised	■
3.	success	successful	■
4.	effect	■	to affect
5.	value	■	to value

c) Complete the text. Use five words from the table in b).

Bao Wang's ■ (1) has grown over the last years, so that she is now one of China's most popular ■ (2). Even official organisations ■ (3) her power – she is used by a Communist youth programme to promote economic (4) among young people who live outside of the main cities. Bao was ■ (5) to be successful, although she is sometimes seen as an unconventional influencer because she comes from the country.

5 When do we trust influencers?

Many people trust Bao. What makes you trust an influencer? What makes you doubt him/her?
▶ **M2** Think-pair-share

> **V** to influence | to advertise | to know about a product/topic | many followers/ (dis-)likes/positive ↔ negative comments I to identify with sb | interesting ↔ boring presentation | to be paid for sth I to hide sth from sb I to make sb feel good/bad | to trick sb into doing sth

6 Your turn My favourite influencer

a) Think about the influencers you follow or know and choose your favourite one.

b) Research more information about him/her. You can research online. Include: ▶ **S1** Informationen

- place of birth
- real name and alias
- topics
- which products he/she promotes and why
- message(s)
- popularity

> **V** … was born in …
> His/Her real name is …, but his/her alias is …
> … talks about/shows …
> … has a channel on …
> … is known for pranks/comedy/ …
> … promotes … because …
> His/Her message is …
> … has … followers on …

c) Write a profile for the influencer you have researched. Write about 120 words. ▶ **S16** Schreibstil

d) Exchange your text in a small group. Give each other feedback. ▶ **M8** Writers' conference

Now I can write a profile of my favourite influencer.

4 Video lounge

Meet the experts: Talking about contracts

1 Bad consequences

a) Match the English words (1–5) with their German translations (A–E).

> 1 storage | 2 to cancel | 3 fine print | 4 to revoke | 5 to include
>
> A umfassen, enthalten | B das Kleingedruckte | C stornieren | D Speicher | E widerrufen

b) Have you ever signed a contract or bought something and regretted it later? Why? Were you able to return or revoke it? Talk to your classmates. ► M1 Milling around

2 A great deal? ► S5 Hörsehverstehen

a) Watch the video. What happened to Claire? What did she do wrong? Take notes.

b) Watch the video again. Choose the correct answer.
1. How much did Claire's phone cost?
   a) Nothing, it was free.
   b) £19.99 per month flat rate for using the phone.
   c) £19.99 per month for the first six months, then £49.99 per month.

2. How long is the contract period?
   a) 12 months
   b) 24 months
   c) 48 months

3. How much would Claire have to pay for her phone contract all together?
   a) £119.94
   b) £899.82
   c) £1,019.76

4. After signing a contract, how much time do you have to revoke it?
   a) 7 days
   b) 14 days
   c) 30 days

c) Many companies offer deals that sound great at first but aren't. What can you do to protect yourself from such offers? Collect ideas in class.

3 Revoking a contract ► S12 E-Mail ► V29 Email

Claire wants to revoke the contract via email. Write Claire's email to the phone company.

> ► V29 Writing an email
>
> Dear Sir or Madam … | I am writing to you because … / to inform you … | I would like to … | I herewith revoke the contract I signed on … | Please find attached … | Please confirm … | Thank you for your help. / I look forward to … | Yours sincerely / Kind regards …

Talking about and discussing mobile phone habits

Speaking workshop **4**

How important is your mobile phone?

1 Mobile phone habits ▶ **S18** Sprechen (Monolog) ▶ **S4** Präsentation ▶ **V25** Media ▶ **V26** Media habits

Your class is going to have a discussion about mobile phone habits.
Prepare a short presentation.
▶ **M3** 1-minute presentation

Answer the following questions:

- How important is your mobile phone in your life and why?
- For which activities do you use it?

 2 Mobile phones in school ▶ **S18** Sprechen (Dialog: Diskussion)
▶ **V8** Discussion ▶ **V25** Media ▶ **V26** Media habits ▶ **V30** Help

Your school wants to ban mobile phones in school. You discuss the topic with a partner.

a) Look at the cartoon on the right. Analyse it.
▶ **S13** Bildbeschreibung ▶ **V12** Cartoon

b) Prepare for the discussion. Decide who plays which role:

- Partner A: You want to ban mobile phones.
- Partner B: You are against banning them.

Write down arguments for your position.

"Let's turn off the cellphone cameras for a moment and take some notes old-school"

c) Practise the discussion with a partner. ▶ **M9** Read and look up

V	▶ **V30** Asking for help and clarifying your idea
	I'm sorry, I don't understand … Can you repeat that, please? What do you mean by …? Could you explain …? Can you give me an example? If I understand you correctly, you're saying that … Let me explain it another way … In other words … Now I understand. Thanks a lot.

S	▶ **S18 Sprechen**
	Fragen Sie immer nach, wenn Sie etwas nicht verstanden haben. Das zeigt, dass Sie aktiv am Gespräch teilnehmen. Falls Sie merken, dass Ihr Gegenüber etwas nicht verstanden hat, umschreiben Sie Ihren Punkt oder verdeutlichen Sie ihn mit einem Beispiel.

d) Present your discussion to the class.
The others give feedback. ▶ **M10** Tip-top

e) Give your own opinion: is it a good idea to ban mobile phones in school?
Or do you have an alternative solution? Discuss in class.
▶ **M6** Opinion line ▶ **V15** Opinion

Now I can talk about and discuss mobile phone habits.

4 Check out

Check out: Hong Kong

1 Listening

a) Listen to the voice messages. Match the pictures (A–E) with the voice messages (1–5). Write down one keyword for each voice message.

A

B

C

D

E

b) Listen again. Choose the correct answer.

1. Carol will be at the hostel at …
   a) 5:30 a.m.
   b) 8:30 a.m.
   c) 8:30 p.m.

2. An online ticket to Madame Tussauds costs …
   a) £13.50.
   b) £25.00.
   c) £30.50.

3. Marc's grandfather wants to have a smartphone to check timetables and …
   a) take photos.
   b) send photos.
   c) receive photos.

4. Marc's grandfather doesn't want to spend more than … on his new smartphone.
   a) £250
   b) £350
   c) £450

5. Maggie talks about an influencer who presents tips on shopping and …
   a) selfie spots.
   b) bars and clubs.
   c) virtual reality games.

6. The food the influencer tastes is … the Chinese food.
   a) different from
   b) the same as
   c) better than

7. Tian says that while he's in the training camp, …
   a) they won't reach him.
   b) he'll only answer emails.
   c) they can't call him after 8 a.m.

8. Tian can't use his phone at the training camp because …
   a) it's broken.
   b) he should focus on training.
   c) it's forbidden.

9. Kiu My says playing VR games is like …
   a) reality, just better.
   b) entering a different world.
   c) flying to the moon.

10. The girl wants to pick Dan up at …
    a) 7 a.m.
    b) 7 p.m.
    c) 6 p.m.

Check out 4

2 Reading

a) Read the story. Match the paragraphs from the story (1–5) with the headings (A–G). There are two more headings than you need.

1 lines 1–23
2 lines 24–35
3 lines 36–43
4 lines 44–48
5 lines 49–65

A Lunchtime at the office
B Too much risk for a selfie
C The perfect spot
D Same city, new job
E And the winner is …
F The selfie challenge
G Happy to have survived

The perfect selfie

"Who is going to pick up lunch for everyone today?" Michael's boss asked. Michael, Karen and Curtis were looking at each other. They all had important tasks to finish and nobody wanted to lose too much time at the snack bar. Competition was high in the office where the three of them were doing a 6-month internship because only one of them would get the chance of a permanent job at the end. 'Why does she always send one of us?' Michael thought while saying, "OK, I'll go." He noted his colleagues' wishes down and left the office. Michael had been working in the office for three months now. The internship had been his chance to leave his hometown and move to the big city. He liked working at the office and he wanted to stay – even if the job was difficult sometimes. They often needed to work long hours to finish a project in time and because of that Michael hadn't had the time to find new friends yet. He had hoped to make friends with the other interns, but they didn't seem to be interested. They had been born in the city and already had enough friends.

Back in the office, Michael ate at his desk to make up for the lost time. "Next time, one of you needs to go," he said to Karen and Curtis. "I go more often than you do," Curtis replied, even if that wasn't exactly true. "I've got an idea," Karen said. "What about a selfie challenge over the weekend? Everyone takes one selfie and the one who gets the least likes by Monday morning has to pick up lunch for the next four weeks." Michael didn't think twice before he said yes. The idea of one month without having to pick up lunch was too good.

Also it sounded fun and maybe he and the others would even become friends through the challenge. Curtis said, "I'm in too. And I already know who's going to lose. Remember, Michael, we know all the good selfie spots in the city, so you'd better take a spectacular picture." Michael started to feel unsure. Maybe it hadn't been such a good idea to accept the challenge after all.

In the evening, he was walking around the city looking for a good spot when he saw a high tower. There was a small ladder that led to the top. 'If I can climb up there and take a picture at sunrise, it will be the perfect selfie,' he thought.

The next morning, he was back at the tower before sunrise. He knew he wasn't allowed to climb up there, but it was dark and there weren't any people around, so he went up. It was higher than he had thought. He began to feel very nervous. He reached the top just as the sun started to rise. With his right hand he took his phone out of his bag, holding onto the ladder with the left one. 'That's it,' he thought and smiled into the camera. Just then he realised that he couldn't hold onto the ladder any longer. Luckily he managed somehow to hold onto it, but he had to drop his smartphone, which fell to the ground. His body was shaking as he climbed down the tower. He found his smartphone on the ground – broken. Michael knew he would be picking up lunch for the next four weeks, but he didn't care any more.

(583 words)

4 Check out

b) Are the statements true or false? Correct the false ones.

1. Michael has a permanent job at the office.
2. Michael leaves the office to pick up lunch for everyone.
3. Michael, Karen and Curtis are good friends.
4. Karen has to convince Michael to take part in the selfie challenge.
5. Karen and Curtis don't know the city well.
6. Michael climbs a tower to take his selfie.
7. Michael takes the perfect selfie and wins the challenge.

c) Answer the questions in complete sentences. Use your own words.

1. Why is the job at the office difficult sometimes?
2. When and where does Michael want to take his selfie?
3. What happens to Michael's phone?

d) Fassen Sie die Regeln für den Selfie-Wettbewerb auf Deutsch zusammen.

3 Writing

a) Your friend is addicted to his/her smartphone and asks you for advice. Write a recommendation with at least three tips to fight the addiction. Write about 100 words.

b) Choose one of the two tasks (1–2). Write about 160 words.

1. Write a story about the picture below.

2. Write an email to a friend from Hong Kong about travelling. Answer these questions:

- Do you like travelling? Give reasons.
- To which countries have you been so far?
- Where would you like to travel if you had the choice? Why?
- Would you like to visit Hong Kong? Give reasons.
- Should people from Hong Kong visit Germany? Why?

Check out 4

4 Use of language

a) Find words or phrases in the story on page 79 which mean more or less the same (=), or the opposite (↔).

1. to end = ■ (lines 1–10)
2. opportunity = ■ (lines 1–10)
3. country ↔ ■ (lines 10–18)
4. to answer = ■ (lines 24–29)
5. to win ↔ ■ (lines 36–43)
6. confident ↔ ■ (lines 36–43)

b) Explain one of these words from the story on page x. Write complete sentences.

1. internship (line 15)
2. sunrise (line 47)
3. broken (line 63)

c) Write two questions to Michael which Karen and Curtis could ask him on Monday morning. Use different question forms and tenses.

d) Complete these statements by a social media user. Use the passive voice.

1. This cool picture ■ (to send – *simple past*) by my favourite influencer.
2. The last post ■ (to share – not – *will-future*) by anybody. It's too boring.
3. My comment ■ (to publish – not – *present perfect*) because the Chinese government didn't like it.
4. A new Instagrammable restaurant ■ (to open – *will-future*) by a celebrity next week.

e) Rewrite these statements by an influencer. Use the passive voice.

1. More than 50,000 people follow my account.
2. 17,000 people watched my new tutorial.
3. The company asked me to make an advert for its new product.
4. I often like videos by other people.
5. Some people write awful comments.
6. I took my latest selfie in Hong Kong.

f) Complete the text with the correct words. You need to change the words on the right, fill in the missing word if there is a question mark, or choose the correct word if two options are given.

As a foreigner in Hong Kong

When my company asked me to work in Hong Kong for a year, I didn't think twice. ■ (1) abroad had always been my dream.
In Hong Kong I lived in a small apartment in a ■ (2) my company had rented for its foreign workers. I was happy about that because the rent is ■ (3) high in Hong Kong. Also I became friends ■ (4) the others who lived there. Sadly, this was also the ■ (5) of living in a so-called "foreigner bubble" for me. I experienced this community as very ■ (6) and welcoming. There was always someone to talk to, to go out with or to help you with a problem. But it was also like living in a world without ■ (7) contact to the locals. It felt like it was easier to have friends ■ (8) the same cultural background. However, when I met my boyfriend, ■ (9) was born in Hong Kong, I got to know a lot more about the local ■ (10).

1 life
2 to build
3 extreme
4 ?
5 to begin
6 friend

7 much/many   8 ?
9 who/which/whose
10 cultural

 g9kc3c

In this unit you will:
- write a wiki entry about an aspect of California.
- have a debate about a zero-waste snack shop.
- write a blog post about your ideal school.
- have a conversation in a diner.

5 Green California?

High tech meets agriculture

California is loved for its warm sunny climate, beaches, lively cities and easy-going lifestyle. Famous for the glitz and glamour of Hollywood, it is also the site of Silicon Valley, home to the world's most valuable technology companies. In contrast, Central Valley is one of the most productive agricultural regions on Earth. But the state has to deal with the dangers of drought and wildfires.

1 About California ▶ M4 Placemat

a) Work in groups of four. Copy the placemat on a big sheet of paper. Each group member chooses a corner.

b) Each one chooses one picture (A–E). What comes to your mind? Write 4–5 keywords in your corner.

c) Turn the placemat and take notes on another picture until everyone has commented on each picture.

d) In your group, agree on five words for each picture. Write them down in the middle of the sheet.
   ▶ V23 Suggestions

> California is the most diverse state in the US. Minority groups make up more than half of the population. Latinos are the largest ethnic group in California, representing about 40% of the population and providing a cheap workforce for agriculture. Workers from all over the world also bring their knowledge to Silicon Valley and are paid a lot.

82 eighty-two

Starter **5**

e) Use your words from the placemat and start a mind map for the topic "California". Add more words. ► **S7** Sammeln und ordnen

A22 **2 Different aspects** ► **S10** Hörverstehen

a) Copy the table and listen to Zoe, Maya, Aiden and Greg talking about California. What do they talk about? Choose the correct topics.

Person	climate/ earthquakes	people/ diversity	landscape/ agriculture	inequality (poor/rich)	work/studies
Zoe	X	…	…	…	

b) With a partner, choose a person from a). Listen again and take notes about:
- the speaker's image of California.
- the speaker's location: is he/she from California?
- details/keywords for "their" aspects from a).

Collect your results in class.

A23 c) Read what Maria José thinks about California. Take notes.

What do I think about California? I adore it. You know why? Because of Los Angeles and technology. Strange combination, isn't it? I've lived there for five years and I still think LA is the best city to live in. There's Venice Beach and Santa Monica where you can watch lots of attractive people. No celebrities – I must warn you … They hang out in completely different places. And there's Hollywood
5 of course, with the famous Hollywood sign, the theatre where the Oscars take place, the Hollywood Hills, the Universal Studios – all those places that you've seen a thousand times in films and on TV. And last but not least: California is one of the leading states in technological innovations. Just imagine, when you're at the beach you can have your food delivered by small robot cars. Isn't that awesome?

d) Add your notes from b) and c) to the mind map in ex. 1.

3 Your turn A wiki entry ► **S3** Textsorten ► **S16** Schreibstil

a) Choose the aspect of California that interests you most. Write a wiki entry for it with the most important facts. Use your mind map from ex. 1. Write 5–6 sentences.

b) Exchange your text with a partner. Check his/her facts. You can research online. ► **M7** Peer correction

The non-profit Wikimedia Foundation hosts Wikipedia, the free online information platform. Its headquarters are in San Francisco, California. Which sources do you use to find information online?

Now I can write a wiki entry about an aspect of California.

eighty-three **83**

5 Workshop

Having a debate about a zero-waste shop

Step A: Waste not, want not

Despite the water crisis in California, the state is one of the world's largest producers of food. About 40% of California's fresh water is used to grow food (source: *Public Policy Institute of California*).

1 Wasting food at home

a) Americans throw away about 219 pounds of food per person per year which is almost two kilos of food wasted every week. How much food do you and your family throw away every week? Write a waste diary for seven days. Take notes about:

- how often you throw away food,
- what sort of food you throw away,
- why you throw it away.

Talk about it in class. ▶ **G1** Present tenses ▶ **V30** Food

In English-speaking countries you often measure weights with pounds: 1 lb (pound) = 453.6 g

b) Before you read: look at the picture of wonky carrots. What do you think does the word "wonky" mean? Would you buy (and eat) wonky fruit and vegetables? Discuss in class.

2 Beauty standards for food ▶ **S9** Leseverstehen

a) Read the article about "ugly produce". Write down 1–2 keywords for each paragraph. ▶ **H5**

USDA stands for the United States Department of Agriculture. It's responsible for laws about farming and food.

October 12, 2019

Is "ugly produce" the key to our food waste problem?

SAN FRANCISCO – Juan Gonzalez works in the heart of California farm country where about 90% of America's cauliflower is harvested every year. And, for a long time, his farms were also the site of a shocking amount of food waste, he says: 10 million tons per year. That's because so many fruits and vegetables never make it to the stores. […]

"Everybody knows cauliflower as being white. We break the leaves or tie the leaves to keep organic cauliflower white. […] It stops the sun from hitting this head of cauliflower," Gonzalez explained to *CBS News* Kenneth Craig. If the cauliflower is a little too yellow on the top, grocery stores won't take it.

Looking at the USDA guidelines, they separate fruits and vegetables into grades based on things like size and color. Large supermarket chains often follow those strict beauty standards. The result is that 10 million tons of cosmetically imperfect or unharvested food are lost each year.

But one man's trash has become another man's treasure. Ben Chesler saw "imperfect produce" as the perfect recipe and name for a new business model. "The goal was really to improve a part of the food system," Chesler said. "Starting with produce and then moving into the wider food system step by step, we could solve the environmental impact of all the food going to waste. It would be easy to make food more affordable for people." […]

In four years, the doorstep delivery service has expanded to more than 30 markets and more than 200,000 customers. One of the first customers to order vegetables was Caroline Devane in

Workshop 5

Cambridge, Massachusetts. "In my experience, the food has been just as good as grocery store quality. [...] It seems just fine and it's a great price," Devane said. The mother of two said it's not only saving her money, but also trips to the store. "It's nice to think that there's a very small consumer impact I can make just by choosing these vegetables, instead of choosing the very beautiful vegetables at the grocery store," Devane said.

[*Imperfect Produce* isn't the only company to offer this service anymore.] The ugly produce movement has grown into a competitive field with companies like *Misfits Market* and *Hungry Harvest* all fighting for a share. It has also started a debate, with some experts making clear that more than 80 % of food waste each year comes from consumers at homes, businesses and restaurants.

"There's no silver bullet to any of these problems like food waste," Chesler said. Six billion pounds of food never make it to people's homes and mouths – not even in the form of juices or jams. That's after the food banks have taken produce. [...]

On thousands of acres at *Lakeside Organic Gardens*, where Juan Gonzalez's team grows [more] than 50 different vegetable varieties, the efforts to rescue more food have been a game changer.

"Profitability has gone up. Our employees' production numbers have gone up. The fields' harvest numbers have gone up. Everything has gone up," Gonzalez said. "If we could turn all that around, California could even end world hunger … that's how much product gets left behind."

CBS, 2019

b) Read the article again. What do the numbers stand for? Write a sentence for each.

10,000,000   200,000   90   80   50

c) Choose the correct answer.

1. Cauliflower stays white when you …
   a) protect it from the sun.
   b) remove the leaves.
   c) keep it organic.

2. Many fruit and vegetables are wasted because …
   a) they don't get enough sun.
   b) they don't look perfect.
   c) customers don't need them.

3. Ben Chesler's company brings imperfect produce to …
   a) the stores.
   b) the delivery services.
   c) the customers' homes.

4. By buying imperfect produce, the customers …
   a) save money.
   b) eat healthier.
   c) avoid buying bad quality.

5. The biggest part of food waste comes from …
   a) supermarkets.
   b) private homes.
   c) companies fighting for a share.

6. Juan Gonzalez is happy about the ugly produce movement because his workers …
   a) earn more money.
   b) harvest more.
   c) work harder.

d) Write two questions for Juan Gonzalez about food waste. Use different question forms or tenses. Your partner answers the questions. ▶ G1, G5, G6, G7 Tenses

5 Workshop

3 Focus on words

a) Match the words (1–10) from the article on pages 84–85 with their German translations (A–J).

| 1 affordable | 2 competitive | 3 consumer | 4 cosmetically | 5 doorstep | 6 grade | 7 imperfect | 8 profitability | 9 share | 10 treasure |

| A erschwinglich | B äußerlich | C fehlerhaft | D Ertragsfähigkeit | E Türschwelle | F Qualitätsklasse | G Schatz | H Teil | I Verbraucher(in) | J Wettbewerbs-

b) Complete the sentences with words from a).

1. Supermarkets all offer the same ■ perfect fruit and vegetables.
2. We hope to have a greater ■ of the market next year.
3. ■ who care about their health want to know how their food is produced.
4. You've done well to succeed in such a ■ field.
5. All the produce that we sell is of the highest ■.
6. The company wants to improve ■ by reducing costs.

c) Complete the definitions with the words and phrases from the word bank.

game changer | guidelines | make it | silver bullet | standard | turns around

1. If somebody ■ a business, it starts being successful after it has been unsuccessful for a time.
2. A ■ is a person, an idea or an event that completely changes the way a situation develops.
3. A ■ is a fast and effective solution to a serious problem.
4. ■ are a set of rules that are given by an official organisation telling you how to do something.
5. If you succeed in reaching a place in time, especially when this is difficult, you ■.
6. A ■ is a level of quality that most people find acceptable.

d) Find a word or phrase from the article on pages 84–85 which means more or less the same.

1. in the middle of = ■ (lines 2–8)
2. rubbish = ■ (lines 22–31)
3. to find a solution = ■ (lines 22–31)
4. to become = ■ (lines 45–52)
5. discussion = ■ (lines 45–52)
6. types = ■ (lines 57–61)

4 Healthy leftovers ▶ H5 ▶ G15 Prepositions

Complete the text about food waste with the correct prepositions.

Kaitlin Mogentale is ■ Los Angeles and has always cared ■ food waste. It was when she was watching a friend making carrot juice that she realised that her friend was going to throw away the leftover pulp. "There was so little juice, but so much pulp," says Mogentale. "And it smelled so good."
She asked her friend if she could have the pulp and decided she would try to make carrot pulp cookies ■ it. They were delicious! She realised that the many juice bars ■ Los Angeles must be throwing away their leftover pulp. Mogentale decided to set up her company, Pulp Pantry, ■ the goal of turning the hundreds of pounds ■ leftover pulp ■ healthy snacks, like crackers and vegetable crisps, that are all full ■ vitamins, minerals and fibre. Today, Pulp Pantry works ■ large food companies to turn overlooked resources ■ healthy ingredients.

Workshop 5

G ▶ **G25 INFINITIVE AND PARTICIPLE CONSTRUCTIONS INSTEAD OF SUBORDINATE CLAUSES**

a) Complete the sentences from the article on pages 84–85. Use the correct verb forms.
   1. ■ (look) at the USDA guidelines, they separate fruits and vegetables into grades …
   2. ■ (start) with produce and then ■ (move) into the wider food system step by step …
   3. One of the **first** customers ■ (order) vegetables was Caroline Devane …
   4. Imperfect Produce isn't the **only** company ■ (offer) this service anymore.

b) Compare the sentences 1+3 with the sentences from a). Then complete the sentences 2+4. Use the words from the word bank.

   `move` `offers` `start` `when` `that`

   1. **When** you look at the USDA guidelines, they separate fruits and vegetables into grades …
   2. ■ you ■ (start) with produce and then ■ (move) into the wider food system step by step …
   3. One of the first customers **who ordered** vegetables was Caroline Devane …
   4. Imperfect Produce isn't the **only** company ■ ■ this service anymore.

c) Complete the rules. Use the words from the word bank.

   `infinitive` `-ing form` `only` `to` `when`

   1. Instead of a subordinate clause that starts with ■, you can use the ■ of the verb.
   2. After adjectives like 'first', 'last' or '■' you can use '■' + the ■ form of the verb.

5 Focus on grammar ▶ G25 ▶ G25 Gerund

Complete the sentences with the correct form of the verbs.

1. My dad is always the first ■ ■ (come) home in the evening.
2. But today he was late. ■ (come) home, he thought we were all in bed.
3. Then my dad saw my sister and asked: "Are you the only one ■ ■ (be) up?"
4. After ■ (finish) dinner, he wanted to watch a film on TV.
5. ■ (go) to bed, he found out that I still wasn't home.
6. I was the last person ■ ■ (come) home.

6 Food sharing ▶ S12 E-Mail ▶ S17 Mediation
▶ V29 E-mail

Your American friend told you about Kaitlin Mogentale and her snacks. You do some research into food projects in Germany.

a) You find this information on the right and want to tell your friend about it. Write an email. ▶ H5

   • Explain how the system works.
   • Ask if he/she knows about it.
   • Say what you think of it.

b) Would you use food sharing if there was a place like this near you? Give reasons.

Foodsharing

Foodsharing gibt es in Deutschland seit 2012. Über eine Onlineplattform werden Lebensmittel, die Privatleute und Supermärkte übrig haben, verteilt. Inzwischen wird Foodsharing von tausenden von Menschen genutzt. Viele davon sind sogenannte Foodsaver, die die Lebensmittel bei Händlern und auch bei Produzenten abholen. Sie alle sind ehrenamtliche Helfer/innen. Ein Teil der Ware wird an dafür eingerichteten Plätzen in offene Regale und Kühlschränke gebracht und kann dort von Verbrauchern geholt und verwendet werden. Foodsharing hilft, die Menge der Lebensmittel, die im Müll landen, zu reduzieren. Natürlich sind die Sachen nicht immer ganz frisch, aber verdorbene Lebensmittel werden entsorgt.

5 Workshop

Step B: Shopping and packaging

Not only food is wasted. Together, food and packaging make up almost 45 per cent of the rubbish that is dumped in landfill sites in the United States (source: *United States Environmental Protection Agency*).

7 Bag habits ▶ M5 Round robin ▶ V31 Packaging

When you go shopping, what do you use to carry your shopping home in?
Tell the class and give reasons.
Example: I always/usually/never use … because …

8 Single-use culture

a) With a partner, make a list of things that are designed to be used only once, e.g. plastic straws. Use a dictionary. Share your list with the class. ▶ H5

b) Talk about these questions with your partner:
▶ G1, G2, G5, G6, G7 Tenses/Modals

1. Which of the things on your list do you use?
2. Which have you stopped using?
3. Which could you stop using?
4. Which are difficult to stop using?

 In August 2014, California became the first US state to ban single-use plastic bags at large retail stores. In Germany, the use of plastic shopping bags will be banned in supermarkets from 2022.

9 Unnecessary packaging ▶ S10 Hörverstehen

You're going to hear a radio presenter talking to two experts about plastic bag bans in the US.

a) Before you listen: match the definitions with the correct words from the word bank.

| debris | decompose | fabric | no-brainer | reusable bag | single-use plastic | stomach | zero-waste |

1. a container that you can use more than once
2. to be destroyed after death by natural processes
3. producing little or no waste
4. made to be used only once and then thrown away
5. the organ inside the body where food goes after having been eaten
6. a material that clothes are also made of
7. a decision or a problem that you do not need to think about much because it is clear what you should do
8. small pieces that are left when something larger is broken many times

b) Before you listen: guess if the statements are true or false. Give reasons for your decisions.

1. Until today, only one US state has banned plastic shopping bags in grocery stores.
2. It takes plastic between 500 and 1,000 years to decompose.
3. Nearly 31,000 Americans are employed to make plastic bags.
4. Reusable bags have an environmental footprint too.

Workshop 5

A25 c) Listen to the radio show. Did you guess right?

d) Listen again. Choose the correct answer.

1. Which state(s) banned plastic bags in 2020?
   a) California
   b) Connecticut and Delaware
   c) Maine, New York, Oregon, Hawaii and Vermont

2. How many times does a fabric bag have to be used to be more environmentally friendly than a plastic bag?
   a) 14 times
   b) 40 times
   c) 400 times

3. Why has there been a decrease in sales in some shops in areas with plastic bag bans?
   a) Customers buy only what fits in a reusable bag.
   b) Customers are shopping in other areas.
   c) The shops don't have enough employees.

4. How many tons of plastic get thrown into the sea around Los Angeles?
   a) 10 tons a year
   b) 12 tons a year
   c) 100 tons a year

e) Do you think unnecessary packaging should be banned? Why or why not? Collect the pros and cons and write a comment of about 100 words. ▶ H5 ▶ S6 Kommentar ▶ V9 Comment

10 How can we reduce waste?

a) Look at the cartoon and analyse it. Talk to a partner about: ▶ S13 Bildbeschreibung (Cartoon) ▶ V12 Cartoon

1. the situation in the cartoon,
2. its message,
3. your opinion about it.

b) Look back at your answers from ex. 8b). Research online for information on how to reduce waste at home, especially for things that you find difficult to stop using. Make a list of things everyone can do or use. Think of: ▶ S1 Informationen ▶ M2 Think-pair-share

- shopping bags
- food and drinks
- clothes, toys, books, etc. that you don't need any more
- electronic devices, batteries, etc.
- …

eighty-nine 89

5 Workshop

11 Your turn — Organising and having a debate ▶ S18 Sprechen (Diskussion/Debatte) ▶ V8 Discussion ▶ V30 Food ▶ V31 Packaging

Your school plans to have a zero-waste snack shop. Each student can vote for or against it.
You are going to debate the plan.

a) With a partner, collect three arguments for and three against the school's plan. Then decide whether you agree or disagree with it.

b) Organise the debate: choose who is going to be the chairperson and who is going to play the roles of the four main speakers.

c) Prepare for your role with the help of the role cards.

> **S ▶ S18 Sprechen (Diskussion/Debatte)**
> Eine Debatte ist ein Gespräch zwischen Parteien, in dem das Für und Wider einer Sache oder einer Aussage diskutiert wird.
> Die drei Parteien sind:
> 1. der/die Diskussionsleiter/in (*chairperson*),
> 2. der/die Fürsprecher/in
> 3. der/die Gegensprecher/in.
> Argumente können auch von mehreren Personen ausgetauscht werden.
> Am Ende der Debatte wird über die Sache/Aussage abgestimmt.

d) Debate the plan. Then vote in class.

e) Beurteilen Sie in einem Klassengespräch, wie die Debatte gelaufen ist: ▶ M6 Opinion line
- Wurden alle Argumente ausgetauscht?
- Waren die Argumente verständlich?
- Waren alle höflich?
- Was hätte besser sein können?

Chairperson

You introduce the topic. During the debate you signal to audience members when they can speak. At the end you ask everyone to raise their hands for or against.

> **V**
> Today we're discussing …
> First, I'd like to call … to speak for …
> I really must ask you not to interrupt.
> Let's vote now. / May I have your votes for/against …?

Audience

You listen carefully to what the main speakers are saying. Think about your own opinion. You can also take part by raising your hands and making comments or asking questions.

> **V**
> Why do you think …?
> How …?
> What do you mean by …?
> Is it true that …?

Four main speakers

You speak one after the other for and against. Each person has a certain amount of time to speak, present facts and give their opinion. Try to convince other people so that your side will win the vote at the end of the debate. Even if you disagree strongly, always express yourself politely.

> **V**
> I'd like to begin by saying …
> It's important to remember that …
> Another point I'd like to make is …
> I agree with the point that …
> I'm afraid I disagree.
> I think you should vote for/against the statement because …

Now I can have a debate about a zero-waste shop. ✓

Writing a blog post about my ideal school

Reading workshop **5**

My ideal school

In Germany, most students first attend a regular primary school and then one of the secondary schools. However, some schools, like Waldorf or Montessori schools, have different concepts.

1 My school experience ▶ V33 School

 a) Now that you have almost finished school, think about your experience there.
Talk to a partner. You can include these aspects: ▶ H5

- school subjects
- timetable / free study time
- full time / part time
- people: teachers / classmates
- equipment
- amount of tasks / pressure
- fairness
- fun / motivation
- atmosphere

b) What is your opinion on your school experience? What did you like?
What could have been better? ▶ M6 Opinion line ▶ V15 Opinion

2 A different kind of school ▶ S9 Leseverstehen

a) Read Daniel's blog post about his school. Match the subtitles (A–H) with the paragraphs (1–6).
There are two subtitles more than you need.

A Questions to the readers
B How to use tablets in school
C No technology allowed
D Different opinions
E Catching balls and counting numbers
F Many with technological background
G Here we eat at fast-food chains
H Living close to Silicon Valley

> The first Waldorf school was opened by Rudolf Steiner in 1919 in Stuttgart, Germany. Today, Waldorf has become one of the largest independent school movements in the world, with about 1,200 schools in about 70 countries. Most Waldorf schools are in Germany, followed by the USA.

A26

Why do I go to a tech-free school in Silicon Valley?

1 Hi there,
My name is Daniel, I'm 16 years old, and I come from California. My family lives next to Silicon Valley, where my dad works as an IT specialist. I'm almost finished with my school time here at the Waldorf school of Peninsula, which is close to Silicon Valley. And this school is special.

2 Why is it special? At my school, no technology is allowed because they believe it damages your imagination, your attention span, and interactions between people. Parents are also recommended to

▼

ninety-one **91**

5 Reading workshop

set rules for its usage at home. I mean, I basically grew up with all kinds of technology, but my dad decided that he wanted to set another focus in my life. He even spends $35,000 a year to send me there! The Waldorf school still works with blackboard and chalk. In the Waldorf primary school there are no screens at all. We students learn a lot of artistic and practical skills.

3 About 75% of my classmates have parents who work for a technology company, so at first I found it strange to go to a school which is against technology. Over the years, I found out that they aren't totally against technology; they just want to set limits on its usage. Jennifer Mayer, one of my high school teachers, said that it's like a parent working at a fast food chain. You don't ban it but don't have it for every meal. Today, scientists are very worried about a growing social media addiction. That's why I think it's important to be critical of technological developments.

4 So, what does a normal school day look like? In primary school, my teacher started every day by pointing at a blackboard with colorful musical scales and motivating us to sing along. We sat at wooden desks, used paper and colorful pens, and there were lots of books and green plants. Mr. Miller kept us moving around while we mixed math and grammar. For example, we caught balls while counting numbers in Farsi, German, Spanish, and Mandarin. I really liked it because I sometimes find it hard to focus and I have a lot of energy

to burn. There are no standardized tests for a long time, which takes away some of the pressure. The content we learn goes along with our physical and intellectual development. For example, at 13 I learnt about historic revolutions because I was starting to question my parents, and it's good to know the consequences of historical events. I did gardening to learn how to use my hands too. Right now, I'm preparing a discussion about poverty because more and more people in California don't have enough money. That's unfair!

5 What does my family think about it? My dad said, "When I was at school, there wasn't the same technology as there is today – who knows what we will be dealing with tomorrow! That's why I want you and your sister to be able to deal with an unknown world in the future. You need creativity to overcome its challenges." My mom said: "I'm glad about your school because you learn how to answer your own questions there." And my little sister answered: "Sometimes, when I'm tired, I don't want to move around. I just want to listen and do nothing." What do I think about it? I like my school building, my teachers (at least most of them) and my classmates. I worry that my different education hasn't prepared me very well for my job training in robotics because I've learnt very differently compared to a regular high school. Waldorf school isn't my ideal school but I am happy with what I've learnt here.

6 What do you think about my school? What would your ideal school look like? I look forward to your comments!

Reading workshop 5

b) Read the blog post again. Are the statements true or false?

1. Daniel's father works as an IT assistant at Google.
2. According to Waldorf schools, technology isn't good for one's imagination.
3. In the first years of Waldorf school, students don't use screens.
4. Almost three-quarters of Daniel's classmates grew up in households with parents working in IT.
5. Scientists are afraid that people will become more and more addicted to social media.
6. Students shouldn't move while they are learning about grammar or maths.
7. Gardening is one of the subjects in a Waldorf school because it's practical.
8. Waldorf school is Daniel's ideal school because he is well prepared for his future job.

c) Name at least three aspects that are different between your school and Daniel's school.
Example: In Daniel's school they don't have tests for a long time, but we have tests from the beginning.

d) Why did Daniel's parents send him to a Waldorf school? What did they want him to learn? Find the sentences in the blog post and express them in your own words. ► H5

e) What is your opinion on Daniel's school? Would you like to attend it? Give reasons.
► M5 Round robin ► V15 Opinion

3 Focus on words

a) Write down a word from the same word family for each underlined word from the blog post on pages 91–92.

b) Explain these words from the blog post. Write complete sentences.

1. screen (line 15) 2. scientist (line 25) 3. blackboard (line 30)

c) Complete Daniel's blog post about his ideal school. Use the correct words. You need to change the words on the right, fill in a word if there is a question mark, or choose the correct word if two words are given.

| At my ideal school, students who have problems in a subject would get a free tutor ■ (1) helps them so the student can improve ■ (2). The tutor is an older ■ (3). This way the older student would also learn something. At the end of each month, the tutor and the teachers should tell the student what they are good ■ (4) and what they need to focus on. The school building could be very ■ (5) because right now my school looks ■ (6). I would allow technology and every student would get a tablet ■ (7) free. However, there would be ■ (8) time during the day for students to research online. | 1 who/which
2 themselves/themself
3 study
4 ?
5 colour
6 bored/boring
7 ?
8 some/any |

4 Your turn My ideal school ► S8 Blogpost ► S16 Schreibstil ► G16 Conditional clauses (type II) ► V33 School

a) Think about your ideal school.
What is special about it? What is different from your school? ► S7 Sammeln und ordnen

V | I wish for a school that …
My ideal school is / should …
The government / Teachers should …
There aren't …
I think it's important that …
I would change … because …

b) Write a blog post and answer Daniel's last question.

c) With a partner, exchange your blog posts.
What do you think about your partner's idea(s)? Give feedback. ► M7 Peer correction ► M10 Tip-top

Now I can write a blog post about my ideal school.

5 Speaking workshop

Having a conversation in a diner

Talking about food

1 You are what you eat
▶ **S18** Sprechen (Monolog) ▶ **V30** Food

a) What is your favourite food?

b) Look at the food pyramid: ▶ **H5**
   1. What kind of food from the pyramid do you usually eat in a day?
   2. Do you think your eating habits are healthy? Give reasons.
   3. What would you like to change?

2 At the diner ▶ **S18** Sprechen (Dialog: Rollenspiel)
▶ **V34** Restaurant

a) At a diner in Los Angeles, you talk to the waiter/waitress. With a partner, choose a role and practise the conversation. ▶ **M9** Read and look up

Partner A: Waiter/Waitress

1. Welcome the customers and ask if they have a reservation.
3. Show the customers to their table and ask them for their drink orders.
5. Ask for the food orders.
7. Suggest a dish and take the orders. Bring the food and ask if everything is OK.
9. Say sorry for the mistake and offer a drink/dessert for free.
11. Tell the customer the amount. Then thank them for their visit and say goodbye.

Partner B: Restaurant customer

2. Say that you have a reservation for ■ people for ■ o'clock.
4. Order drinks.
6. Ask for dish recommendations and order the dishes.
8. Give feedback on the dishes.
   There was one dish you didn't like.
   Give reasons.
10. Accept the offer and ask for the bill.
12. Pay the amount and say goodbye.

b) Act out the conversation in front of the class. The others give feedback. ▶ **M10** Tip-top

94   ninety-four

Now I can have a conversation in a diner.

Video lounge 5

Californian national parks

1 Natural beauty

Match the pictures of the national parks (A–C) with the texts (1–3) that describe their landscape. You can use a dictionary.

A — Joshua Tree National Park

B — Death Valley National Park

C — Yosemite National Park

1 The park is situated east of the Sierra Nevada. There are two valleys separated by a 3368 m high mountain range. The lowest point is 86 m below sea level. The landscape includes salt-flats, sand dunes and soft rocks. Part of it is the hottest and driest place in North America.

2 The park is situated in the western Sierra Nevada. It has many different plants and animals. Its landscape includes cliffs, waterfalls, clear rivers, giant trees, lakes, mountains, meadows and glaciers. Almost 95% of the park is wilderness.

3 The park is situated in southeastern California and is named after a plant which grows in the Mojave Desert. There are hills of rocks which are broken up into boulders. The eastern part is dominated by bushes and cacti.

2 Presenting a national park ► S4 Präsentation
► V1 Presentation

a) Choose a national park from ex. 1. Go online and look for videos which give information about this park. Take notes about: ► S1 Informationen
► S5 Hörsehverstehen ► V22 Sightseeing

1. location/size
2. landscape/climate
3. sights/activities
4. visitor information

b) Prepare a slide show. Find 7–10 photos of the national park which show different aspects. Put them in the order you would like to present them. ► S11 Visualisierung

c) Use your notes from a) and write a short text for each photo. Give background information about it.

d) Present your slide show to the class. ► M10 Tip-top

e) Which national park would you like to visit? Vote in class.

S ► S4 Eine Präsentation halten
- Zeigen Sie pro Aspekt nur ein Bild.
- Die Bilder passen zum Gesagten.
- Die Bilder haben eine gute Qualität.
- Lassen Sie den Zuhörern genug Zeit, die Bilder zu betrachten.

V
… is located/situated in …
As you can see in the picture, there is/are …
There are wild animals such as …
In summer/winter it gets hot/wet/dry/cold/windy/…
The highest/lowest/average temperature is …
The highest/lowest point is …
The best time to visit the park is …
The entry costs … and it's open from … to …
You should pack …
You can get there by …

5 Check out

Check out: California

1 Listening

a) Listen to the weather reports for different regions in California at different times of the year. Match the reports (1–6) with the photos (A–F).

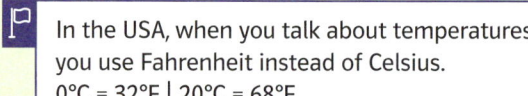
In the USA, when you talk about temperatures, you use Fahrenheit instead of Celsius.
0°C = 32°F | 20°C = 68°F

b) Listen again. Are the statements true or false?

1. On January 14th, people in the Big Sur area should stay at home.
2. On June 25th, the beaches in Los Angeles will be empty.
3. On July 27th, it will be windy in Death Valley.
4. On August 25th, the weather will be the same across all of the San Francisco Bay area.
5. On August 30th, the weather around Mariposa will help to get the wildfires under control.
6. On November 12th, visitors to Yosemite National Park won't be able to use all of the roads in the park.

c) Complete the sentences with the missing word(s).

1. On January 14th, there will be strong wind and ■ in the Big Sur area.
2. On June 25th, temperatures will reach ■ °F in Los Angeles.
3. On July 27th, it will be hot and ■ in Death Valley.
4. On August 25th, the wind in the San Francisco Bay area will come from the ■.
5. On August 30th, temperatures around Mariposa will reach ■ °F.
6. On November 12th, there will be ■ in Yosemite Valley.

Check out 5

2 Reading

a) Read the news report. Choose the best heading (A–F).

A What to do when you see a wildfire
B The benefits of wildfires
C Wildfires are becoming a big danger in California
D How to prevent a wildfire
E The work of California's firefighters
F The effects of climate change on the growing plants

by Marc Staffa/May 20th 2021

LA – Wildfires aren't new to California and other parts of the world. They keep happening on a regular basis as natural events. Some plants even need
5 these fires, as they grow on the ground which is rich in nutrients once the fire has gone. California's sequoia trees, for example, are so tall and strong that the fires usually don't destroy them, but lower plants under these trees. And these plants are
10 important because they let new sequoia trees grow without competition from other plants.
What has increased over the past years, however, is the violence of the fires and the duration of the fire season. Scientists link this alarming
15 development to climate change. Extreme weather conditions caused by climate change can speed up the creation of wildfires. It isn't surprising that long periods of high temperatures and no rain increase the danger of wildfires as the plants and
20 the soil dry out. A small spark, for example from lighting a cigarette, and winds from the wrong direction can then be enough to cause a huge fire. But what is it like to experience a wildfire? Some Californians shared their experiences with us:

25 **Daniel, 54:** When we heard that the fires were getting close to our town, my family and I put our most important things into our car to be ready in case we were evacuated. Those were terrible days. We were so scared to lose our home and every-
30 thing we'd built up over the years. But the firefighters did an amazing job. They worked day and night and saved our town. Everybody here was so grateful that we put up signs along the road to thank them. We were lucky, but lots of other
35 Californians weren't.

Wildfires close to a village

Sheela, 25: I was on a camping trip with some friends when suddenly the area around our campground was surrounded by fire. We couldn't get away because the only road was blocked by fallen trees. We really thought we would die. It was
40 so hot and there was smoke everywhere, so we could hardly breathe. Our last option was to get into a small lake and wait for help. You can't imagine how we felt when a helicopter finally arrived to fly us out.
45

Eric, 40 and Jane, 42: When we heard about all the people that had to be evacuated because of the wildfires, we knew we had to do something to help. As we have enough space, we invited people to sleep in our house and cooked meals for them.
50 That was the least we could do for those who had to leave everything behind. This time we weren't in danger, but you never know – next time it could be us who need help.

(457 words)

5 Check out

b) Complete the sentences. Use your own words.

1. It isn't new that …
2. Sequoia trees aren't usually destroyed by wildfires because …
3. When lower plants burn down, sequoia trees can …
4. Over the past years there have been …
5. Scientists think that climate change and the increase …

c) Are the statements true or false? Correct the false statements.

1. Daniel and his family had to live in their car because of the fires.
2. Daniel and his family lost their home to the fire.
3. Sheela and her friends were trapped by the wildfire at a campground.
4. Sheela and her friends waited in their car for help.
5. Eric and Jane were evacuated and left everything behind.

d) Fassen Sie die Gründe, die im Artikel für das Entstehen von Waldbränden im Zusammenhang mit dem Klimawandel genannt werden, auf Deutsch zusammen.

3 Writing

a) Write a comment on the following statement: "It is possible to live without producing any waste." Write about 100 words.

b) Read the job advert below. Choose one of the two tasks. Write about 160 words.

VOLUNTEER AT A FARMERS' MARKET IN SAN DIEGO

We are looking for volunteers to help at our farmers' market, which takes place every Friday from 1 p.m. to 6 p.m. Our main goals are sustainability, and fair conditions for our farmers. We aim to reduce waste, sell "ugly produce" and organize workshops for children to learn about sustainability and healthy eating habits.

Tasks:
– help out at different food stalls
– set up and clear away the stalls
– give advice to the customers
– organize and carry out workshops

Requirements:
– be able to work on two Friday afternoons a month
– motivation and flexibility
– passion for sustainability and a healthy lifestyle
– speak English and another language

Please send a short letter of application to Olivia Martinez.

1. Write a letter of application for the volunteer position at the farmers' market.

2. Imagine you're volunteering at the farmers' market. Write a blog post in which you want to convince others to apply too. Write about a normal day at the market and say why you decided to volunteer there.

Check out 5

4 Use of language

a) Find words or phrases in the news report on page 97 which mean more or less the same (=), or the opposite (↔).

1. to get bigger ↔ ■ (lines 2–24)
2. high = ■ (lines 2–24)
3. to allow = ■ (lines 2–24)
4. to decrease ↔ ■ (lines 2–24)
5. period of time = ■ (lines 2–24)
6. tiny ↔ ■ (lines 2–24)
7. far away from ↔ ■ (lines 25–35)
8. thankful = ■ (lines 25–35)
9. to welcome = ■ (lines 46–54)
10. to be awake ↔ ■ (lines 46–54)

b) Explain one of these words from the news report. Write complete sentences.

1. to be evacuated (line 28)
2. firefighter (line 31)
3. suddenly (line 37)

c) Write two questions you could ask Daniel, Sheela, Eric or Jane about their experiences with wildfires in California.

d) Rewrite the sentences with infinitive or participle constructions.

1. I was the first of my friends who became a vegan.
2. When I turned vegan, I made sure to eat a lot of fruit, vegetables and nuts.
3. Food is only one aspect that is part of a vegan lifestyle.
4. When I adopted the vegan lifestyle, I also stopped buying clothes made from leather, for example.
5. I think giving up animal products is the best thing you can do for yourself and for the environment.
6. When I avoid animal products, I help to reduce people's carbon footprint.

e) Complete the text with the correct words. You need to change the words on the right, fill in a word if there is a question mark, or choose the correct word if two or three words are given.

Working culture in Silicon Valley

The term Silicon Valley seems to be highly ■ (1) with high tech, ■ (2) and getting in touch with other people who also work in IT. The region, which is located in the southern part ■ (3) the San Francisco Bay Area in California, is home to ■ (4) of the world's ■ (5) high-tech companies and thousands of start-up companies.
The big companies in Silicon Valley have set new standards in working culture with their ■ (6) offices and the huge universities close by.
■ (7) companies offer their workers free snacks or even 5-star food, ping-pong tables, free fitness classes and massages. Employees should feel at home and ■ (8) with their company. That's why the companies create a nice working environment, ■ (9) also make sure their ■ (10) have a good work-life balance, which means that they don't work too much and have enough free time.

1 connection
2 innovative
3 ?
4 much/many
5 to lead
6 modernity
7 Some/Any
8 identification
9 so/but/because
10 to employ

1 Advanced texts

A very unusual job

If you're a person who likes adventures, maybe you don't want a "normal" job like a mechanic or nurse. There are many unusual jobs in the world of work.

1 What kind of job?

Before you read: look at the pictures (A–B). Think of any unusual jobs that could be connected to them. Give reasons.

Example: I think picture A shows … because they are wearing ….

Briton lands 'world's best job' as caretaker of Australian island

SYDNEY - A British charity worker today got what has been described as the "best job in the world" when he was given a A$150,000 (£73,000) contract to serve as the caretaker of a tropical Australian island.

Ben Southall, 34, won against almost 35,000 worldwide applicants[1]. He now has the chance to swim, explore and relax on Hamilton Island, in the Great Barrier Reef, for six months while writing a blog to promote[2] the area.

Southall won the six-month job after spending three days swimming, snorkelling, diving[3] and lounging with 15 other finalists under the eyes of Queensland Tourism officials who tested the candidates. The finalists also had to demonstrate their blogging abilities[4] and take swimming tests.

"I hope I can sell the reef as much as everybody is expecting," said Southall before he was taken away for interviews with local and international media.

In his 60-second video application Southall rode an ostrich[5], ran a marathon, hiked through Africa and kissed a giraffe. He described himself as "the adventurous, crazy energetic one". But he seemed surprised by his own success. "Wow … to all of the candidates that stand behind me – everyone there is an absolute winner," he said.

The job is part of a A$1.7m tourism campaign to advertise north-eastern Queensland. A very successful one. The state's premier, Anna Bligh, flew to Hamilton Island and announced that Queensland Tourism generated[6] about A$100m in publicity[7] with the competition so far.

Steve McRoberts presented Southall with a dive suit and flippers and urged him to wear them every day while the 15 other candidates, who included students, journalists, TV presenters, photographers, a receptionist, radio DJ, teacher, and an actor, hugged him and cheered.

When Southall begins the job, he will travel all around the Great Barrier Reef, write blogs and be interviewed by the media. The rest of the time he will relax in a three-bedroom luxury villa and drive a buggy to explore the island.

The contest[8] for the dream job attracted some controversy after being announced in January. Its website crashed because of a huge amount of visitors, so many hopeful applicants could not upload their video applications. At least two finalists caused trouble: one woman had connections to the adult entertainment industry, and a man introduced himself as Osama bin Laden and posted a YouTube video saying why he was the best man for the job.

Southall plans to bring his Canadian girlfriend with him to the island when he starts work on 1 July.

(427 words)

Toni O'Loughlin, *The Guardian*, 2009

1 applicant – *Bewerber*; 2 to promote – *anpreisen*; 3 to dive – *tauchen*; 4 ability – *Fähigkeit*; 5 ostrich – *Vogelstrauß*; 6 to generate – *erzeugen*; 7 publicity – *Werbung*; 8 contest – *Wettbewerb*

Advanced texts 1

 The Great Barrier Reef is the largest coral reef in the world. But it is in danger from pollution, climate change and tourism. The reef has lost more than half of its corals since 1985. Is there a similar danger in Germany?

2 Reading for gist ▶ S9 Leseverstehen

Where can you find the answers to the questions? Match the questions (1–7) with the paragraphs. There are three more paragraphs than questions.

1. How long will Ben stay?
2. What did Ben do in his application?
3. What are Ben's tasks?
4. How many applicants were in the contest?
5. Who advertised the job?
6. What did Ben win?
7. Who will Ben bring with him?

3 Reading for detail ▶ S9 Leseverstehen

a) Write questions for the other three paragraphs.

b) Answer the questions from ex. 2. Use your own words.

c) Fassen Sie Bens Job auf Deutsch zusammen.

4 Focus on words

Match the underlined words (1–8) with their synonyms from the word bank.

| advertise | characteristics | adventurous | keeper | opportunity | press | show | gave |

1. serve as the caretaker
2. he now has the chance to swim
3. a blog to promote the area
4. demonstrate their blogging abilities
5. the crazy, energetic one
6. his most impressive qualities
7. McRoberts presented Southall with a dive suit
8. interviewed by the media

5 A step further: Unusual jobs in Germany ▶ S14 Zeitungsbericht

a) Think of an unusual job in Germany. Here are some ideas: roller coaster tester, dogsitter, horoscope author, LEGO builder, crime scene cleaner, treasure diver.
Research online and take notes about:

1. why it's special
2. the workplace
3. the tasks
4. the skills needed
5. how to apply
6. the wage

b) Write an article about someone who does this job. Include all the aspects from a).

 The best/most interesting/strangest part of the job is …
… needs to have/to be …
… spends a lot of time …
… gets paid …
It's an amazing opportunity to …
People don't realise that it's very hard to …

one hundred and one 101

2 Advanced texts

A new way of job hunting

1 How to find a job online

a) Before you read: what does "job hunting" mean? Talk about it in class.

b) Look at the title of the article. What do you think it is about? Take notes.

Don't ruin your career in 140 characters: social media job hunting tips

Who could have predicted[1] a decade ago that social media would have such a grip on our lives? The rise of social media can be seen as both a godsend and a threat[2] to jobseekers. Why? Because not everyone is sure how to use it. HR departments[3] no longer have the time or resources to plough their way through hundreds of CVs. They want to be able to see if the applicant is worth bringing in for an interview. Social media, if used correctly, can propel a job application to the top of the pile[4] – simply by being different and innovative.

Social media makes it very easy to see what makes a prospective employee tick – giving employers a view of that candidate before they actually meet them.

How to do it right
So, how do you make sure that you create the right impression? The first thing you should do is set up a profile on professional networking sites such as LinkedIn to give yourself a better chance of being noticed. Get your name out there. You may find that you connect with people who end up on your interview panel or who have the power to shortlist[5] you for a position.

Facebook and Twitter can also reap great rewards if harnessed correctly. Don't be afraid to show your personality, comment on industry trends and news, and follow the right people in that sector to try and attempt[6] interaction. [...] Don't be downhearted if you're not followed by those you're following or if your attempts to start a conversation with an industry bigwig[7] are ignored. Interaction through social media will happen, but don't try and force it.

How to do it wrong
Facebook and Twitter can be great when it comes to showing off your talents, but there is nothing more stupid than thinking employers won't check you out before deciding whether or not you're worth an interview.

Take these things into consideration: there is a difference between showing personality and pushing out photos of you and your mates partying. They might not go down so well with your potential future boss. Clean up your profile – it's a given that companies check social media these days. Use the internet to promote yourself and your talents. Don't let stupidity scupper[8] your chances of success.

Similarly, offensive language is a no-go. [...] Do you really want to lose sight of your dream job just because of a risqué, off-the-cuff remark to one of your friends on Facebook or Twitter? Depending on what role you're after, it might also be wise to steer clear of posting anything too political. While no employer can discriminate against you on political grounds, everyone has different views on what goes on in the world [...]. While the majority of employers don't like CVs with photos, it makes sense to get a shot done for your social media platforms that looks professional. More employers are using social media to screen prospective employees, with Facebook, Twitter and LinkedIn being among the most popular. So, before you post ask yourself: do you really want 140 characters ruining your career?

(531 words)

Chris Smith, *The Guardian*, 2015

1 to predict – vorhersagen; **2 threat** – Bedrohung; **3 HR department** – Personalabteilung; **4 pile** – Stapel; **5 to shortlist sb** – jmdn. in die engere Auswahl nehmen; **6 attempt** – Versuch; **7 bigwig** – hohes Tier; **8 to scupper** – vereiteln

Advanced texts **2**

2 Reading for gist ▶ S9 Leseverstehen

Find out if your ideas from ex. 1b) were right. Then explain the meaning of the title. Write 2–4 sentences.

3 Reading for detail ▶ S9 Leseverstehen

a) What online behaviour can have a negative effect on job hunting? Make a list.

b) What can applicants do on social networking sites to "be seen" by potential employers? Write down four pieces of advice.

c) Would you use social networking sites to look for a job? Give reasons. Talk to a partner.

4 Focus on words

a) Match the phrasal verbs (1–5) with the verbs which have more or less the same meaning (A–E).

1	to bring in (line 10)	A	to demonstrate
2	to set up (line 21)	B	to continue
3	to end up (lines 24–25)	C	to land
4	to show off (line 39)	D	to introduce
5	to go on (line 60)	E	to create

b) Write definitions for these words. Write complete sentences.

1. to ruin (line 1)   2. jobseeker (line 5)   3. reward (line 27)

5 A step further: Analysing a cartoon ▶ S13 Bildbeschreibung ▶ V12 Cartoon

a) Describe the cartoon.

b) Explain its message. What does the author want to say with the cartoon? Which topic/problem does it present?

c) Give your opinion. Do you like the cartoon? Do you agree with it? Give reasons.

3 Advanced texts

Living in two or more worlds

1 Choosing where and how to live

Before you read: if you could decide where you wanted to live, where would it be? Why? What would you have to do to make this dream possible?
▶ **M2** Think-pair-share

A book review for *Born a Crime*: Stories from a South African Childhood

Trevor Noah is regarded[1] as one of South Africa's biggest exports: the boy from the township who made it big in the US and ended up hosting The Daily Show, one of the most influential satirical news programmes on American television.

But [...] Noah [and] South Africa's black citizens [...] are trapped by the legacies[2] of colonialism [and] apartheid and face poverty, hunger, violence, bullying[3], racism and limited opportunities.

But there was an extraordinary buffer between this brutal world and Noah, as his autobiography, *Born a Crime: Stories from a South African Childhood*, makes clear.

"For my mother. My first fan. Thank you for making me a man," Noah writes in the book's dedication. [Without] his mother, Patricia Nombuyiselo Noah, and the rebellious spirit that enabled[4] her to face down a hostile [...] world, Noah would not have ended up where he is. Noah was "born a crime" because his Xhosa mother had [...] a child with a white Swiss-German, which was illegal at the time. And while Noah was born in 1984, [during the last days of] apartheid, the world [...] was riven[5] with the deep [wounds] of history.

"The fact that I grew up in a world run by women was no accident," Noah writes. "Apartheid kept me away from my father because he was white, but for almost all the kids I knew in my grandmother's neighbourhood in Soweto, apartheid had taken away their fathers as well, just for different reasons.

"Their fathers were off working in a mine somewhere, able to come home only during the holidays. Their fathers had been sent to prison. Their fathers were in exile, fighting for the cause[6]. Women held the community together."

Noah writes of his profiling[7] as white in a black world with [great] insight[8] and humour. "There were so many perks[9] to being 'white' in a black family, I can't lie. I was having a great time," he writes. Only the young Noah did not think this special treatment was because he was light-skinned, but because he was special. "It wasn't 'Trevor doesn't get beaten because Trevor is white'. It was 'Trevor doesn't get beaten because Trevor is Trevor'," he writes.

In the end, Noah chose to be black, a state of mind that had so much more to do with his lived experience than someone else's notion[10] of who he was, and is.

"I soon learned that the quickest way to bridge the race gap was through language. Soweto was a melting pot[11]: families from different cultural groups, and thus different [home countries]. Most kids in the township spoke only their home language, but I learned several languages because I grew up in a house where there was no option but to learn them."

The book is essential[12] reading not only because it is a personal story of survival, [...] but because it does more to expose[13] apartheid – its legacy [...], its small-minded[14] stupidity and its damage – than any other recent[15] history book [...].

(510 words)

Marianne Thamm, *The Guardian*, 2016

---

1 be regarded as – *gelten als*; **2 legacy** – *Erbe*; **3 to bully** – *mobben*; **4 to enable** – *befähigen*; **5 to rive** – *spalten*; **6 cause** – *hier: Angelegenheit*; **7 profiling** – *Diskriminierung anhand von bestimmten Merkmalen*; **8 insight** – *Einblick*; **9 perk** – *Vorteil*; **10 notion** – *Ansicht*; **11 melting pot** – *hier: multikulturelle Gemeinschaft*; **12 essential** – *notwendig*; **13 to expose** – *enthüllen*; **14 small-minded** – *kleingeistig*; **15 recent** – *neuste*

Advanced texts 3

2 Reading for gist ▶ S9 Leseverstehen

Which topics (1–8) does the article not mention?

1. strong women
2. importance of Noah's father in his life
3. absent fathers
4. disadvantages of being white in Soweto
5. Nelson Mandela's role in apartheid
6. Noah's grandfather's influence
7. the importance of languages
8. effects of apartheid on South Africa's blacks

3 Reading for detail ▶ S9 Leseverstehen

a) Find the lines in the article where the topics from ex. 2 are mentioned.

b) Answer these questions in complete sentences. Use your own words.

1. What is Noah's occupation?
2. Who wrote the book *Born a Crime*?
3. How old was Noah when Nelson Mandela was released from prison?
4. Where was Noah's father from?
5. Why was Noah's birth a crime?
6. What did Noah have in common with other children in Soweto?

4 Focus on words

a) Match the expressions (1–5) with their explanations (A–E).

1. to make it big
2. to have the odds stacked against you
3. to fight for the cause
4. to have perks
5. to bridge the gap

A. to have poor chances
B. to have advantages
C. to connect two sides
D. to be very successful
E. to work hard for a certain idea

b) Explain these words. Write complete sentences.

1. autobiography (line 13)
2. rebellious (line 19)
3. to live in exile (line 38)

5 A step further: Giving a statement ▶ S6 Kommentar

a) What do you think: what does Trevor Noah say in his quote? ▶ M2 Think-pair-share

> „We tell people to follow their dreams but you can only dream of what you can imagine, and depending on where you come from, your imagination can be quite limited."

b) Give your opinion on the quote from Trevor Noah. Write a statement of about 100 words. ▶ V15 Opinion

4 Advanced texts

Escaping social media

More and more people realise that an overuse of media isn't good for them. They try to get control of their life again.

1 Digital detox

Before you read: describe the picture. Guess what "digital detox" means. ▶ M2 Think-pair-share

Growing social media backlash among young people, survey shows

[…] Almost two-thirds of schoolchildren would not mind if social media had never been invented, a survey has indicated.

5 The study provides evidence of a growing backlash among young people disillusioned with the negative aspects of the technology, like online abuse and fake news.
As well as the 63% who would not care if it did not 10 exist, even more pupils (71%) said they had taken temporary digital detoxes to escape social media.

The survey of about 5,000 students at independent and state schools in England was commissioned[1] by Digital Awareness UK and the 15 Headmasters' and Headmistresses' Conference (HMC), which represents the headteachers of independent schools around the world.

Many respondents indicated that social media was having a negative impact on their emotional 20 well-being.
A total of 57% said they had received abusive[2] comments online, 56% admitted to being on the edge of addiction and 52% said social media made them feel less confident about how they 25 look or how interesting their life is. […]
While more than 60% believed friends showed a "fake version" of themselves on social media, 85% of pupils questioned denied they were guilty of that themselves.

The feedback was not all negative, with students 30 identifying memes, filters/lenses and storytelling features, like for example Snapchat stories, among the things they like about social media.

Asked to recommend improvements, students named less advertising (71%), less fake news 35 (61%), more creative content (55%) and greater privacy (49%).
One in three of those surveyed[3] said they would like to see social media provide more opportunities to earn an income. […] 40

Charlotte Robertson, the co-founder of Digital Awareness UK, said: "We speak to thousands of students on a daily basis about safe internet use and while it's a matter of concern[4] to see the emotional impact social media is having on 45 young people's health and well-being, it's encouraging to see that they are also employing smart strategies such as digital detoxing to take control of their social media use. […]
"This research is a real wake-up call for all of us 50 working in social media to ensure that we listen to the needs of young people, who will dictate the direction in which the industry moves." […]

(378 words)

Charlotte Robertson, *The Guardian*, 2017

1 to commission – *beauftragen*; **2 abusive** – *beleidigend*; **3 to survey** – *befragen*; **4 matter of concern* – *Grund zur Sorge*

Advanced texts 4

2 Reading for gist ▶ S9 Leseverstehen

a) Find headings for the six paragraphs of the article.

b) Summarise the article in 3–5 sentences. Use your own words.

3 Reading for detail ▶ S9 Leseverstehen

a) Match the percentages (1–5) with what they stand for (A–E).

1	71%	A	… admitted to being on the edge of addiction
2	63%	B	… had received abusive comments online
3	57%	C	… had taken temporary digital detoxes to escape social media
4	56%	D	… said social media made them feel less confident
5	52%	E	… would not care if social media did not exist

b) Finish the sentences. Use your own words.

1. The study shows …
2. The HMC is …
3. Memes and storytelling features are …
4. Less advertising and less fake news are suggestions …
5. The survey is a wake-up call to the social media industry to …

4 Focus on words

a) Match the German words (1–6) with the underlined words in the article.

1. Beschimpfung[en]   3. Gegenreaktion   5. Wohlbefinden
2. Proband(in)   4. Warnruf   6. Privatsphäre

b) Find a word or phrase in the article which means more or less the same as the words in **bold**.

1. They speak to thousands of students **every day**.
2. Students **strongly recommended** that social media had greater privacy.
3. **It gives me hope** to see that young people are taking control of their social media usage.
4. A large number of students said that they had taken **brief** digital detoxes.
5. More than half of the students said social media made them feel less **secure** about how they look.
6. 56% admitted that they were **very close to** addiction.

5 A step further: Evil social media? ▶ S6 Kommentar ▶ V9 Comment

a) With a partner, collect arguments for and against the use of social media.

b) Write a comment of about 130 words. Answer this question: Is social media social?

5 Advanced texts

California's drought

California is the world's fifth largest supplier of food. Much of the produce comes from the Central Valley, which is getting drier and drier as a consequence of climate change.

1 What is drought?

With a partner, describe the situation in the picture. Use the words from the word bank.

| plants | green leaves | dry earth |

| hot climate | little rain | drought |

'Without water we can't grow anything': can small farms survive California's landmark water law?

For the first time in history, the state is regulating the groundwater that fuels[1] its massive agriculture industry. Now the smallest farms face the biggest threat.

5 Nikiko Masumoto began her farming career in the summer of 2011, just as California was entering its worst drought in recorded history. Masumoto is the fourth generation of her family to farm this land in Del Rey: 80 organic acres of stone fruit in
10 eastern Fresno county in California's fertile Central Valley. [...]
For four years in a row, the farm survived only on the water it could draw from underground. And as the drought persisted[2], the perfect peaches grew
15 less perfect – smaller, malnourished. The farm lowered its wells and pumped more so Masumoto could keep the trees alive.
The farm made it through by way of grit[3] and preparation. But even with plenty of both, said
20 Masumoto, "surviving is a real question."
At 34, Masumoto is roughly half the age of the average farmer. Where her neighbors are thinking about retirement, she is thinking about how climate change and dwindling underground
25 water reserves are going to affect the rest of her life, and her family's legacy.

"I'm at the beginning of my career. I hope to be farming for another 40, 50 years," she said.
"I think there's going to be another catastrophic drought. What are we going to do?" 30
The Central Valley is America's fruit bowl, and the heart of California's $50bn agriculture industry. But the 2011–2017 drought [...] forced the state to grapple[4] with regulating the one thing fueling much of it: groundwater. 35
Rights to California's uniquely unregulated groundwater have always come along with ownership of the land above. Groundwater allowed farmers to make it through dry times and to plant in parched[5] places far from natural 40
rivers. [...]
Hoping to bring overtaxed groundwater basins back into balance, the California legislature passed the Sustainable Groundwater Management Act (Sgma) in 2014 to begin 45
regulating groundwater for the first time in the state's history.

Advanced texts 5

The law, which [...] set a 2040 deadline for sustainability, stands to reshape California
50 agriculture and the Central Valley's way of life. The Public Policy Institute of California estimated[6] between 500,000 and 780,000 acres would have to be fallowed[7] in order for the state's natural aquifers to come back into balance. [...]

Farmers with means[8] plan for survival by seeking[9] 55 other water rights or planting more water-intensive but high-priced crops. Those without may be faced with fallowing their fields or getting out of the growing game altogether. [...]

(434 words)

Susie Cagle, *The Guardian*, 2020

1 to fuel – *am Leben halten*; **2 to persist** – *andauern*; **3 grit** – *Schneid, Mumm*; **4 to grapple with** – *zu kämpfen haben mit*; **5 parched** – *vertrocknet, verdorrt*; **6 to estimate** – *schätzen*; **7 to be fallowed** – *brach liegen lassen*; **8 means** – *finanzielle Mittel*; **9 to seek** – *suchen*

2 Reading for gist ▶ S9 Leseverstehen

Who is Nikiko Masumoto? Write down what you know. Make notes.

 An **acre** is a unit for measuring an area of land.
1 acre = 4,047 square metres.

3 Reading for detail ▶ S9 Leseverstehen

Answer the questions in complete sentences.

1. Where did Masumoto get water from during the drought?
2. What do Masumoto's neighbours think about?
3. Who does the groundwater belong to in California?
4. How does California hope to rebalance the overused groundwater reservoirs?
5. How will wealthy farmers survive the Sustainable Groundwater Management Act?
6. How will farmers who have no savings be affected by the new groundwater regulations?

4 Focus on words

a) Find a word or phrase in the article which means more or less the same (=), or the opposite (↔).

1. to leave ↔ ■ (lines 5–11)
2. to kill ↔ ■ (lines 12–17)
3. a lot of = ■ (lines 18–26)
4. the middle of = ■ (lines 27–41)
5. wet ↔ ■ (lines 27–41)
6. expensive = ■ (lines 51–59)

b) Explain the following words. Write complete sentences.

1. malnourished (line 15)
2. legacy (line 26)
3. overtaxed (line 42)

5 A step further: Giving a statement ▶ S6 Kommentar

Give your opinion on the following quote. Write a statement of about 100 words. ▶ V15 Opinion

> It would be better if all of us gave up a little comfort to try to stop climate change, instead of waiting and hoping that climate change won't happen.

H 1 Helping hand

Unit 1

Starter

2 Young Aussies ▶ **S5** Hörverstehen ▶ page 11

b) Listen to Georgina (age 17) and her cousin Peter (age 22) on the phone.
Who talked about these rights and obligations: Georgina or Peter?

1. Right: driver's licence at 16
2. Obligation: have parents' permission to travel
3. Right: travel outside the US when I'm 18
4. Obligation: one parent must be in the car
5. Obligation: put black and yellow stickers on car
6. Right: full license after three years of practice
7. Right: same rights as Australian workers
8. Right: buy alcohol and cigarettes
9. Obligation: act responsibly
10. Right: the police protect and respect us

Workshop

4 The parts of speech ▶ **S19** Wortarten ▶ page 14

Complete the text. Use words from the table in on page 14. The first letter is already given.

I couldn't find any job that interested me. Then one of my teachers i■ (1) me to
c■ (2) my dream job. After I had made the d■ (3) to try, I was sure that I could be s■ (4).
I've always been happiest when I can be c■ (5) – with wood, paint, glass and paper.
So when I was done with school, I d■ (6) to open a shop filled with my own c■ (7) –
paintings, furniture, and books. The first six months were difficult and I was sure
I was going to f■ (8). But now people tell me that the shop is very i■ (9) for them
and I even offer art classes in the evening. They're a huge s■ (10)!

d) Complete the sentences with the correct prepositions. Use the prepositions from the word bank.

`by   in   of   on   on   to`

1. My goal at the moment is to succeed ■ school.
2. I want a job where I can take care ■ other people.
3. My decision is based ■ my experience during my internship.
4. I've been inspired ■ my mother who is a nurse.
5. I wish I had listened ■ my own feelings sooner.
6. It's important to spend time ■ big decisions like this.

8 Where do they work? ▶ **S10** Hörverstehen ▶ page 18

c) Listen again. Which positive aspects about their job do the speakers mention? Which negative ones? Copy and complete the table with the information from the word bank.

`freedom   colleagues are friendly and happy   long flights   loves all the products`

`doesn't enough time to chat   stressful   on feet all day   sits at the desk all day`

`time goes by fast   team work   talks to customer and helps them   can be creative`

`job is his/her hobby   moves around all day   sees a lot of different places   tried after work`

`always busy   meets interesting people`

Helping hand H1

	positive	negative
hairdresser	...	...
mechanic	...	...
flight attendant	...	...
receptionist	...	...
nurse	...	...
shop assistant	...	...

Reading workshop

3 Two different lives ▶ **G21** Quantifiers ▶ page 21

a) Copy the table. Match the positive and negative aspects with the characters (Jane or John).

grows up in a rich area   parents are proud   parents expect good marks   gets help with homework

goes to mordern school   helps with his brother and sister   good connections

has no time to study and fails the exam   has lots of free time   parents don't have time

parents pay for university   needs to work to pay for university   good school equipment   big classes

dependant on parents   has work experience   father gives motivation

	positive aspects	negative aspects
Jane	...	...
John	...	...

c) Describe and compare their lives. What do they share? What is different?
Complete the text with the words from the word bank.

advantages   anything   because   confident   difference   earn   enough   equipment   failed

finished   however   motivated

Both of the children's parents would do ■ (1) for their children. ■ (2), John's parents don't have ■ (3) time to help him with his homework because they both work two jobs. Jane has more ■ (4) at her school than John does. The school has modern ■ (5) and the teachers are ■ (6). Both Jane and John go to university, but there is a big ■ (7) here too. John has to ■ (8) money to pay the university fees while Jane has lots of free time. ■ (9) John didn't have enough time to prepare for his exam, he ■ (10). When Jane ■ (11) university, her father helped her to get a good job. John's father is ■ (12) that his son will still be happy.

H 2 Helping hand

Unit 2

Starter

1 Highlights of Ireland ▶ page 28

b) What would you recommend to visit, try or do in Ireland? Complete the recommendations for each picture (A–E) on page 28. Use the words from the word bank. ▶ **V7** Recommendation

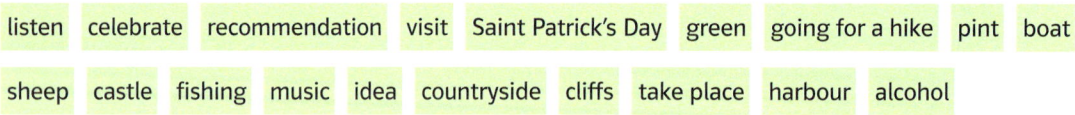

1. Listen again. Make sure you ■ with the locals! ■ is on 17th March. You should wear something ■ that day!
2. I recommend ■ on the ■. You can see the ■ living there.
3. My advice is to go ■! You have to take a ■ from the ■ to catch some fish.
4. My ■ would be to drink a ■ in a local pub and to ■ to the traditional ■. Of course, you can only drink ■ if you are already 18 years old.
5. It is a good ■ to ■ an old ■ in Ireland. They are usually in the beautiful lush green ■.

2 People's experiences ▶ page 29 ▶ **S10** Hörverstehen

d) Listen again. What are the pros and cons of working in another country?
Copy the table and complete it with the arguments.

- You can improve your language skills.
- People can't understand your traditions.
- At first, it can be difficult to understand the new language.
- You become more independent and open-minded.
- You can call two different countries home.
- You can make new friends from all around the world.
- You might earn more money than back home.
- You miss your family and friends back home.

Pros	Cons
• You can gain work experience abroad.	…

Workshop

2 What's the job about? ▶ page 31 ▶ **S9** Leseverstehen ▶ **V10** Job adverts

b) Read the adverts on page 30 again. The requirements, interests and types of contract from the adverts in the table are in the wrong places. Copy the table and correct it.

Job	Requirements	Interests	Type of contract
apprentice electrician	basic computer skills, very polite, knows how to dress formally, strong communication skills (at least grade B in English), can do multi-tasking	(free ride) bikes	contract for one year
office assistant	great communication skills, basic technical know-how, at least grade C in maths, 18 years old	construction	fixed-term
retail assistant	be strong, not afraid of narrow and dark spaces, quick learner, driving licence	travel, languages, fashion	permanent

Helping hand H 2

6 Laura's letter of application ▶ page 34 ▶ **S9** Leseverstehen ▶ **S20** Bewerbung

b) Read Laura's email on page 33 again. Complete the answers with the missing information.

1. Which school does Laura go to?
   Answer: Laura goes to a ▪ in Dublin.
2. What is she doing at school?
   Answer: She is doing a ▪ course.
3. What experience does she have?
   Answer: She has a ▪ in a supermarket.
4. Which skills and interests qualify her for the job?
   Answer: She is ▪ and helpful with customers. She is a team player and she likes ▪ her ▪.
5. Which document did Laura add to her application?
   Answer: Laura attached her ▪ to her application.

c) How do you say that in English? Match the German sentences (1–5) with the English translations (A–E).
▶ **G14** Pronouns ▶ **G17** Articles ▶ **V14** Letter of application

1 Ich möchte mich auf die Stelle als … bewerben.
2 Meine Fähigkeiten qualifizieren mich für die Stelle.
3 Meinen Lebenslauf lege ich bei / hänge ich an.
4 Ich würde mich über die Möglichkeit freuen, für Ihre Firma zu arbeiten.
5 Ich freue mich darauf, von Ihnen zu hören.

A Please find attached my CV.
B I look forward to hearing from you.
C I would welcome the opportunity to train in your company.
D I would like to apply for the … position.
E My skills qualify me for the job.

Reading workshop

A

B

1 Then and now ▶ page 36 ▶ **G1, G5** Present/Past tenses

b) Look at the two pictures of College Street in Dublin on page 36. One was taken in 1919 and the other photo was taken in 2020. Describe the two pictures. Then compare them. What has changed? Work with a partner. Use the words from the word bank and the phrases from the box. ▶ **S9** Bildbeschreibung ▶ **V13** Pictures

horse and carriage · elegant clothes · asphalt · advertising · cobblestone · sit on the roof · tram · police officer · double-decker bus · traffic lights

V
Both of the pictures show …
In both photos you can see …
The picture on the left is/has …, while the picture on the right is/has …
The photo from 1919 shows …, but the photo from 2020 shows …
The pictures tell us that College Street was … in 1919, but by 2020 it had become …

H 2 Helping hand

Reading workshop

1 Questions in a job interview ▶ page 41 ▶ S10 Hörverstehen

A8 c) Listen to the phone interviews. What do the candidates answer?
Match the answers with the correct candidate. Who will get the job?
Discuss in class.
Example: 1. a) Laura, …

1. Can you tell me something about yourself?
   a) at a college, loves mountain biking and travelling
   b) has a part-time job in a shop, likes running
   c) takes part in racing bike competitions, loves hiking

2. Which school subjects do you like?
   a) maths (B) and Spanish (B)
   b) English (A) and maths (B)
   c) physical education (A) and physics (B)

3. What are your skills?
   a) technical know-how
   b) great communication skills
   c) good at languages

4. Are you over 18 years old?
   a) no, 17 years
   b) yes, 19 years
   c) yes, 18 years

5. Why should we choose you for the job?
   a) experience in a workshop, is reliable
   b) knows everything about bikes, is motivated
   c) work experience in retail, team player, can fix bikes

6. When can you start work?
   a) in 2 weeks
   b) in 6 weeks
   c) now

Helping hand **H 3**

Unit 3

Starter

1 This is South Africa ▶ page 46 ▶ **M2** Think-pair-share

c) How is the title "rainbow nation" reflected in the pictures on page 46?

> **V** Picture X shows …
> You can see people with different …
> In some of the pictures you see …
> The pictures show a variety of …
> skin colours | colourful houses | nationality | lifestyles | fashion

2 People of South Africa ▶ page 47 ▶ **S10** Hörverstehen

c) Listen again. Choose the correct answers.

1. Which sport does Lionel play?
   a) football
   b) boxing
   c) rugby

2. What did Mandela do after the World Cup in 1995?
   a) became president
   b) wore Springbok cap and shirt
   c) named the team "Springboks"

3. What happened after the 2019 World Cup?
   a) everybody celebrated
   b) apartheid ended
   c) The team name was changed

4. Which is still the typical sport for black people in South Africa?
   a) hockey
   b) football
   c) rugby

5. What is the benefit of rugby and sports?
   a) It makes your relaxed.
   b) It brings happiness.
   c) It brings people together.

Workshop

1 A timeline of South African history ▶ page 48

b) Look at the four pictures (A–D) of important events in German history. Match the pictures (A–D) with the German events (I–IV) and the dates (I–IV).

A

B

C

D

1 1939   I   Germany becomes one country again after being separated into East and West Germany.
2 1961   II Hitler and the Nazis start the Second World War together with Italy and Japan.
3 1990   The war lasts until 1945.
4 2005   III Angela Merkel becomes the first female Chancellor of Germany.
           IV A fence was built in the German capital, later followed by the Berlin Wall.

H 3 Helping hand

4 More pictures ▶ page 50 ▶ **S13** Bildbeschreibung ▶ **G1** Present progressive ▶ **V11** Pictures

Look at the pictures (A–D) and read their descriptions (1–4). Complete the descriptions with the words from the word bank. You need to use the correct tense with the verbs.

A

B

C

D

| to perform | sea | exciting | dangerously | ballet dancer | sports clothes | goal | costume | elephant |

| view | tourist | to celebrate | Table Mountain | Cape Town | victory | interest | in the background |

| goalkeeper | to take a close-up picture | angry | during a safari | to pose |

1. The picture shows a match between the German and South African women's football teams. A German player has just scored a ■. This is very ■ for her. She and her teammates ■ their ■. The South African ■ is very ■ about the goal and she is hitting the ground.
2. In picture B you can see a ■ in the foreground who ■ of an elephant ■. The ■ is coming ■ close to the man.
3. Here we see a South African ■. She looks very elegant. She ■ a dance and wearing a ■. A school class is sitting ■. The class is watching with ■.
4. In picture D, a girl ■ on top of ■. She is wearing ■ and enjoying the ■ over ■. In the background you can see the ■.

6 Focus on words ▶ page 52

b) Match the words (1–3) with their definitions (A–C).

1 uprising   A This is a noun which shows that you aren't happy.
2 to bleed   B It's when the people stand up for their rights against the government.
3 dissatisfaction   C If someone loses blood, for example after an accident.

Helping hand H 3

Reading workshop

4 **What happened after the loud noise** ▶ **S15** Geschichte ▶ **S16** Schreibstil
▶ **G20** Conjunctions ▶ **V5** Story ▶ page 56

a) One part (***) in the story on pages 54–55 is missing. What happened in the one hour between the loud noise and the rest of the run? Complete the text with your own words.
▶ **V5** Story ▶ **V19** Conjunctions

The loud noise I heard was a ■ (1) shouting at me. He told me to come to his ■ (2) because it was ■ (3) there. At first I couldn't ■ (4) anything because there was dust everywhere in the air. Soon there was the smell of sweaty ■ (5). The next thing I heard was a ■ (6) trumpet call – elephants! These gigantic animals didn't ■ (7) like the zebras; they weren't in a ■ (8). Afterwards I realised that the animals were not ■ (9) in me or the ranger. They only wanted their water.

5 **Focus on words** ▶ page 57

d) Complete the sentences with the correct word from the same word family.

1. I ■ (admirable) Nelson Mandela for his determination.
2. The runner was very ■ (to know) a lot about the surrounding nature. He could explain everything in this area.
3. It is ■ (possible) to run this marathon without preparation.
4. One of the rangers seemed ■ (friend) when I asked him for help. He didn't help me at all.

one hundred and seventeen **117**

H4 Helping hand

Unit 4

Starter

1 Things to do in Hong Kong ▶ page 64 ▶ **G1, G5, G6, G7, G11** Tenses

b) Complete the questions for the pictures (A–E) with information from the word bank.

selfie   sightseeing   skyline   tourist attractions   virtual reality

1. Where can you play ■ games in Hong Kong?
2. Where is a good spot to take a ■?
3. What is one of the most popular ■ in Hong Kong?
4. What can you do in Hong Kong apart from going ■?
5. Where is a good place to view Hong Kong's ■?

c) Now answer the questions in complete sentences. Use the names and phrases below.

1. AME Stadium   **2.** Victoria Peak   **3.** The Monster Building   **4.** go shopping   **5.** Victoria Harbour

2 Top selfie spots in Hong Kong ▶ page 65

c) Match the sentences (1–5) about Hong Kong's attractions with the pictures (A–E).

1. When you cross Victoria Harbour on the Star Ferry, you have a great look at Hong Kong's skyline.
2. The Big Buddha is one of the largest Buddha statues in the world and took 12 years to complete.
3. Located in Kowloon, Temple Street Night Market is the place to go to find everything from clothing to electronic devices and household goods.
4. The Man Mo Temple temple was built for Man, the god of literature, and Mo, the god of war.
5. The park in central Hong Kong is a real oasis in the jungle of skyscrapers and one of the most peaceful places to visit in the city.

Helping hand H 4

d) Which sights would you like to see? Where would you take a selfie?
Tell your classmates. ► M5 Round robin

> **V** If I went to Hong Kong, I would like to see … /
> I would go to …
> I would love to see/visit …
> One of the most popular/famous attractions is …
> Hong Kong is famous for …
> I would take a selfie/loads of selfies at …
>
> at the top of | in front of | next to | under

Workshop

2 Screen time ► page 66 ► **S10** Hörverstehen

b) Listen again. Copy the table. Complete it with information from the word banks.

Phone use per day: 10 h 53 m   8 h 19 m   30 h 12 m   26 h 32 m

Most used feature: game   streaming app (series)   social media platform   picture sharing app

Pickups: 18   20   45   122

	Davis	Clara	Suki	Vic	Chan
Phone usage per week	20 h 47 m	…	…	…	…
Most used feature	music streaming app	…	…	…	…
Pickups	21	…	…	…	…

4 People's feelings ► page 66 ► **G13** Adjectives and adverbs ► **V29** Feelings

a) Read Loony_Luke's post on pages 67 again. Find three English adjectives which show Luke's feelings about students' phone usage.

  1. schockiert   2. beunruhigend   3. alarmierend

b) Copy the table and add more adjectives that describe feelings.

afraid   amazed   angry   annoyed   anxious   loved   calm   carefree   cheerful   bad

desperate   embarrassed   excited   scared   happy   hopeful   interested   miserable   nervous

sad   stressed   surprised   uncomfortable   crazy   tired   exhausted

positive	negative	neutral
helpful, …	shocked, …	…

H 4 Helping hand

7 Signs of smartphone addiction ▸ page 72 ▸ V8 Discussion

d) Why do you think it is difficult for people to stop using their smartphones? Discuss in class.

> **V**
> The main problem is …
> In my opinion …
> I (don't) think that …
> Personally, I believe/feel (that) …
> I'm (not) convinced that …
> On the one hand …, on the other hand …
> I'm not sure if …
>
> rely on | to be addicted to | to be (un-)aware of | to spend (much/little) time on | to limit | to change (habits/behaviour) | to cause conflicts/stress/fear | to contact | well-being

Reading workshop

2 A traditional way of life ▸ page 73 ▸ S9 Leseverstehen

b) Read the article on pages 73–74. Choose the sentence that best sums up the influencer's message.

1. People need content about beautiful countryside and ancient traditions.
2. Success doesn't have to mean living the big city dream.
3. Chinese traditions are trendy and creative.
4. A simple, natural life in the country is beautiful.

Helping hand H 5

Unit 5

Workshop

2 Beauty standards for food ▶ page 84 ▶ **S9** Leseverstehen

a) Match the keywords from the word bank with the right paragraphs of the text on pages 84–85.
There are two keywords for each paragraph.

beauty standards cauliflower competitive consumer impact delivery service environmental impact

food waste game changer grocery stores guidelines harvested imperfect produce movement

organic produce profitability to rescue end world hunger

4 Healthy leftovers ▶ page 86 ▶ **G15** Prepositions

Complete the text about food waste with the correct prepositions from the word bank.
You will need three of the prepositions more than once.

about across from into of with

Kaitlin Mogentale is ■ (1) Los Angeles and has always cared ■ (2) food waste. It was when she was watching a friend making carrot juice that she realised that her friend was going to throw away the leftover pulp. "There was so little juice, but so much pulp," says Mogentale. "And it smelled so good."
She asked her friend if she could have the pulp and decided she would try to make carrot pulp cookies ■ (3) it. They were delicious! She realised that the many juice bars ■ (4) Los Angeles must be throwing away their leftover pulp. Mogentale decided to set up her company, Pulp Pantry, ■ (5) the goal of turning the hundreds of pounds ■ (6) leftover pulp ■ (7) healthy snacks, for example crackers and vegetable crisps, that are all full ■ (8) vitamins, minerals and fibre. Today, Pulp Pantry works ■ (9) large food companies to turn overlooked resources ■ (10) healthy ingredients.

H5 Helping hand

6 Food sharing ▶ page 87 ▶ S12 E-Mail ▶ S15 Mediation ▶ V29 Email

a) You find this information on the right and want to tell your friend about it. Write an email.

- Explain how the system works.
- Ask what he/she knows about it.
- Say what you think of it.

Write an email. Use the phrases in the box.

> **V** Dear … / Hi …
> I wanted to tell you about …
> Food sharing helps to reduce …
> Food sharing is used by …
> The way it works is …
> Leftover food is given to …
> Do you know anything about …?
> Did you know that …?
> What interested me most is (the fact that) …
> Personally, I believe/feel (that) …
> I think that this is …
> See you, …

Foodsharing

Foodsharing gibt es in Deutschland seit 2012. Über eine Onlineplattform werden Lebensmittel, die Privatleute und Supermärkte übrig haben, verteilt. Inzwischen wird Foodsharing von tausenden von Menschen genutzt. Viele davon sind sogenannte Foodsaver, die die Lebensmittel bei Händlern und auch bei Produzenten abholen. Sie alle sind ehrenamtliche Helfer/innen. Ein Teil der Ware wird an dafür eingerichteten Plätzen in offene Regale und Kühlschränke gebracht und kann dort von Verbrauchern geholt und verwendet werden. Foodsharing hilft, die Menge der Lebensmittel, die im Müll landen, zu reduzieren. Natürlich sind die Sachen nicht immer ganz frisch, aber verdorbene Lebensmittel werden entsorgt.

8 Single-use culture ▶ page 88

a) With a partner, make a list of things that are designed to be used only once, for example plastic straws. Match the English words (1–10) with their German translations (A–J). Share your list with the class.

1 plastic wrap | **2** plastic bags | **3** plastic coffee-cup lids | **4** plastic cutlery | **5** plastic party cups | **6** plastic plates | **7** plastic straws | **8** plastic water bottles | **9** plastic packaging | **10** takeaway containers

A Frischhaltefolie | **B** Plastikdeckel | **C** Einwegplastikflaschen | **D** Einwegplastiktüten | **E** Mitnahmeschalen | **F** Plastikbecher | **G** Plastikbesteck | **H** Plastikteller | **I** Plastikverpackungen | **J** Trinkhalme

Helping hand H 5

9 Unnecessary packaging ▶ page 89

e) Do you think unnecessary packaging should be banned? Why or why not?
Copy the table and complete it with the arguments below.

f) Write a comment of about 100 words. ▶ S6 Kommentar ▶ V9 Comment

Pros	Cons
…	…

it takes centuries for plastic bags to decompose   light but strong   low production costs   only used once

food safety and hygiene   gets into the ocean and into our food chain   animals get trapped or eat it

decrease in sales   many employees in packaging industry   production with high carbon footprint

Reading workshop

1 My school experience ▶ page 91

a) Now that you have almost finished school, think about your experience there.
Talk to a partner. Use the phrases in the box. ▶ V33 School

> **V** The best/worst thing about school is that … because … / I (don't) like about my school that …
> There is a … atmosphere in the school.
> Some of the pupils are …
> There is a lot of pressure/support when it comes to …
> My favourite subject(s) is/are …
> (Most of) the teachers are motivating | annoying | strict | fair | understanding | helpful.
> The school has excellent | modern | old-fashioned facilities and equipment.
> You can take part in … / I'm a member of the … football team | orchestra | choir | chess club.

2 A different kind of school ▶ page 93 ▶ S9 Leseverstehen

d) Why did Daniel's parents send him to a Waldorf school? Are the statements true or false?

1. Technology is allowed at the Waldorf school in Peninsula.
2. The school believes technology is good for children's imagination.
3. Daniel's father wanted to give his son a different focus in life.
4. Daniel's father wants his children to be able to deal with an unknown world in the future.
5. Daniel's father believes people need creativity to overcome life's challenges.
6. Daniel's mother thinks the school should answer Daniel's questions.

M Mediation

Unit 1

Sie machen mit Ihren Eltern Urlaub in Australien und besuchen den *Taronga Zoo* in Sydney. Sie stehen vor dem Terrarium einer Trichternetzspinne *(funnel-web spider)* und sprechen mit dem Tierpfleger.
► **S17** Mediation

a) Geben Sie die Informationen des Tierpflegers (A–D) auf Deutsch Ihren Eltern wieder.

b) Geben Sie die Fragen Ihrer Eltern (1–4) auf Englisch dem Tierpfleger wieder.

Mum:	Schaut euch mal diese Spinne an. Ich glaube, ich habe in unserem Reiseführer etwas über sie gelesen. Frag mal den Tierpfleger da drüben, wie diese Spinne heißt.	
You:	… **(1)**	
Zookeeper:	It's called a funnel-web spider. It's one of the most dangerous animals in Australia.	
You:	… **(A)**	
Mum:	Über diese Spinne habe ich gelesen! Ist es wahr, dass sie in und um Sydney lebt?	
You:	… **(2)**	
Zookeeper:	That's right. People here sometimes even find it in their homes.	
You:	… **(B)**	
Dad:	Oh, ich hoffe, wir finden so eine Spinne nicht in unserem Hotel. Was muss ich tun, wenn mich so eine Spinne beißt?	
You:	… **(3)**	
Zookeeper:	If the funnel-web spider bites you, you must go straight to hospital. If you don't, you probably won't survive.	
You:	… **(C)**	
Dad:	Sterben viele Menschen am Biss dieser Spinne?	
You:	… **(4)**	
Zookeeper:	No. We know that from 1927 to 1981, thirteen people died from this spider's bite – and since 1981, no more deaths have been reported. So we are lucky!	
You:	… **(D)** I was really worried but now I don't have to worry any more! Thank you!	

Mediation

Unit 2

Sie helfen Ihrem Vorgesetzten dabei, sich auf ein Geschäftsmeeting in Irland vorzubereiten. Zu diesem Zweck haben Sie im Internet Verhaltensregeln recherchiert. ► **S17** Mediation

a) Lesen Sie den ersten Teil des Artikels (A) und beschreiben Sie Ihrem Vorgesetzten auf Deutsch grundlegende Aspekte der irischen Mentalität. Schreiben Sie 2–3 Sätze.

b) Lesen Sie den zweiten Teil des Artikels (B) und die Notiz Ihres Vorgesetzten. Beantworten Sie dessen Fragen in Stichworten auf Deutsch.

> Was muss ich beim Vereinbaren eines Geschäftstreffens beachten?
> Ich bin nicht sicher, wie viel Zeit ich für das Meeting ansetzen soll. Haben Sie Informationen zur Zeitplanung gefunden?
> Was muss ich im Gespräch mit meinen irischen Geschäftspartnern beachten?
> Sollten wir danach noch in den Pub gehen, wie wird das mit der Rechnung gehandhabt?

Dos and don'ts in Ireland

A Irish mentality

Politeness: In Ireland it may well happen that someone says 'sorry' to you if you run into them. The Irish are very polite. Some foreigners might think this politeness is too much and have problems understanding the message. However, you should adopt this polite behaviour – for example say the word 'sorry' more often than you might say it at home and say 'hello' when you enter a room.

Humour: The Irish have a strong sense of humour and their behaviour is often less formal than you might be used to from your home country. They really love to make jokes.

Pride: The Irish are very proud of their identity. Pay attention to the difference between Ireland and Northern Ireland and never call an Irish person English or British. This would make Irish people really angry because they had a difficult history with Britain. The Irish want to be seen as what they are – modern Europeans.

B On business in Ireland

Business meetings: You should invite for a business meeting at least two weeks before and call the day before to confirm that you will be there. During the meeting you should plan enough time for discussions and small talk because the Irish people like to talk. It will also be helpful if you know one of your business partners who can introduce you to their colleagues.

Business communication: The Irish don't like dramatic emotions – especially not in business situations. Loud, aggressive or arrogant behaviour isn't accepted. The same is true for physical contact. Keep an arms-length distance from your business partners to guarantee them their personal space. It is important to keep eye contact in conversations as people who avoid doing so may be seen as less reliable.

After work – in the pub: After a successful meeting, you might get invited to join your business partners at the pub. In an Irish pub it is a custom to buy drinks for each other. If you get invited to a round of drinks, you should definitely buy a round yourself.

M Mediation

Unit 3

Ein deutscher Fernsehsender interviewt einen südafrikanischen Fußballspieler, der als Neuzugang bei einem Verein in der Bundesliga spielt.
Sie helfen bei den Übersetzungen. ▶ **S17** Mediation

a) Geben Sie die Antworten des Fußballspielers (A–C) auf Deutsch wieder.

b) Übersetzen Sie die Fragen des Reporters für den Fußballspieler auf Englisch (1–4).

Reporter:	Danke, dass Sie sich heute Zeit für ein Interview genommen haben. Sie spielen zum ersten Mal bei einem deutschen Verein. Wie gefällt es Ihnen in Deutschland?	
You:	… (1)	
Player:	Everyone is really nice and helpful, and I felt I was part of the team from the first minute. The coach and the rest of the team have helped me a lot to settle in.	
You:	… (A)	
Reporter:	Am Samstag spielen Sie Ihr erstes Spiel. Wie haben Sie sich darauf vorbereitet?	
You:	… (2)	
Player:	I've been training hard together with the team. I still need to work on my tackle and I need to work on my German! However, I've joined a German class so soon I'll be able to speak German like a German.	
You:	… (B)	
Reporter:	Sie engagieren sich in der Freizeit gegen Rassismus im Fußball. Können Sie uns mehr darüber erzählen?	
You:	… (3)	
Player:	Sadly, racism is still a problem in the world of football. There are situations when fans make monkey sounds at black players. This is extremely embarrassing. And sometimes you can feel racism among team members or even the big bosses. I'm part of a project that wants to make fans and the club realise the problem and finally end racism in football.	
You:	… (C)	
Reporter:	Toll! Ich bin sicher, Sie werden hier in unserer Stadt noch viele weitere Unterstützer finden. Viel Erfolg dabei und natürlich auch bei Ihrem ersten Spiel am Samstag. Danke für das Interview.	
You:	… (4)	

Mediation

Unit 4

Sie haben einen Zeitungsartikel über die Proteste und Aktivisten in Hong Kong gelesen und möchten im Englischunterricht darüber berichten, da sie über Demonstrationen wie *Fridays for Future* und *Black Lives Matter* sprechen. Lesen Sie den Artikel und beantworten Sie die Fragen auf Deutsch. ► S17 Mediation

1. Über welche Formen des digitalen Aktivismus spricht der Artikel?
2. Inwiefern haben die Aktivisten in Hongkong auf Cybersicherheit und Anonymität geachtet?

The Cyber News   25th February 2021

Activism on social media

HONG KONG – Social media has played a big role in the protests in Hong Kong that started in June 2019. These protests started against a law that would have allowed people to be handed over from Hong Kong to China and developed into a democracy movement fighting against China's growing influence on the region.

Activism happens when a group of people demonstrate or campaign for a topic to bring about political or social change. There are different forms of activism on social media. For example, activists use social media platforms to exchange information and plan demonstrations or to collect money. There's also a quieter form of activism, for example using specific hashtags or posting pictures. This was, for example, the case when people posted black squares on their social media accounts in support of the *Black Lives Matter* movement. In Hong Kong, however, the protesters used social media in a new way, paying a lot of attention to anonymity and cybersecurity.

Just like other protest movements, they also used communication apps to organise the time and place of protests, but they often used some sort of code language, for example inviting people to a "picnic" instead of a demonstration. They also used an app that allowed them to communicate via Bluetooth without Internet connection. This way the Chinese government couldn't read their messages. Messages are safe this way because the information sent is protected against spying by the government. Also, the protesters didn't use their real names, but usernames, bought pre-paid SIM cards and deleted their chats as soon as they could. This created anonymity because if the government did find and open a message, they still couldn't tell who wrote it.

As a form of a quieter protest, the activists of Hong Kong took part in computer games in which they added characters with gas masks (a symbol of the protests in Hong Kong) or posters with the words "Free Hong Kong". These games can't easily be controlled by the Chinese government, which is why they are seen as a more secure space for protests.

Katy Murry

Mediation

Unit 5

Lesen Sie die E-Mail Ihres Freundes und den Blogpost. Beantworten Sie die E-Mail, indem Sie von den Schattenseiten in Kalifornien berichten und Ihrem Freund Ihre Meinung zu seiner Idee sagen.
► **S17** Mediation

Betreff: Ich gehe nach Kalifornien

Hallo Rose,

Ich würde gerne nach der Schule im sonnigen Kalifornien leben. Das Leben scheint dort so entspannt und locker zu sein. Es gibt viele gut bezahlte Jobs, die Menschen leben in traumhaften Häusern und überall sind Strände und Palmen. Was hältst du von meiner Idee? Bist du dabei?

Viele Grüße, Mike

Living a great life in California?

What is the first picture that comes to your mind when you think of California? Let me guess: Happy people enjoying the sun while playing beach volleyball or training their muscles at Venice Beach? The Hollywood sign and the glitz and glamour of the movie industry? Or high-tech companies with their modern universities in Silicon Valley? These are typical thoughts about the Californian dream of a relaxed lifestyle in the sun, freedom for each person's wishes, rich people and innovation. But does this dream still show the reality of the so-called 'Golden State' today?

Villas at the beach in Malibu

Homeless tents in Los Angeles

In fact, reality looks much different to many people living in California. The gap between the rich and the poor in California is becoming wider and the difference between the two groups is becoming more and more extreme. While the super-rich live in their villas, for example in Malibu, lots of streets of L.A., San Francisco and other cities are full of tents with homeless people – among them families with small children and many people addicted to drugs and alcohol. There are different reasons for this situation. One of them is that the rent in the big cities such as L.A. and San Francisco has become extremely high so that a lot of people can't pay it any more and lose their homes. Also, the wildfires during the last couple of years have destroyed the homes of many families – some couldn't rebuild their houses and had to move to the street. Also, the Covid-19 pandemic, which has hit California quite hard, has caused more financial problems among many citizens.

But not only for the less rich has the Californian dream come to an end. Even among people with higher incomes, moving to California has become less popular. For example, homeowners decide to sell their properties because the money they get for them is enough to lead a financially independent life in another part of the USA. The wildfire season, which has become very long, and the heavy traffic in the cities doesn't help either.

Still, the old image of California has survived in our minds, and the future will show whether California can keep up with the dream or whether this image belongs in the past.

S1 Informationen beschaffen Finding information

Das Internet ist eine wertvolle Quelle für Informationen, die Sie für Referate, Präsentationen oder für die Vorbereitung auf eine Diskussion brauchen.

1. Gezielt Informationen suchen

- Überlegen Sie, welche Informationen Sie benötigen und finden Sie klare und präzise Suchwörter.
- Eine Kombination von 2–3 Wörtern ist oft sinnvoller als nur ein Wort. Folgende Eingabearten sind bei den meisten Suchmaschinen möglich:
  - Mehrere Wörter ohne Anführungszeichen
    Beispiel: Las Vegas casinos
    Ergebnis: Alle Texte, in denen entweder Las oder Vegas oder casinos vorkommen, werden angezeigt.
  - Mehrere Wörter mit Anführungszeichen
    Beispiel: „Las Vegas casinos"
    Ergebnis: Es werden nur Texte angezeigt, in denen genau diese Wortfolge vorkommt.
  - Wenn Sie zu wenige Treffer bekommen, überprüfen Sie die Schreibweise, verwenden Sie weniger Begriffe oder versuchen Sie es mit einer Frage:
    Beispiel: „How many casinos are there in Las Vegas?"
  - Wenn Sie zu viele Treffer bekommen, verwenden Sie spezifischere Begriffe oder fügen Sie Stichwörter hinzu.
- Verwenden Sie bei Ihrer Recherche die englische Variante der Suchmaschine und arbeiten Sie mit englischen Seiten.
- Verwenden Sie bei unbekannten Wörtern ein digitales oder gedrucktes Wörterbuch.
- Wenn Sie nach einzelnen Wörtern auf einer Seite suchen möchten, können Sie auch Strg+F drücken. Es erscheint dann ein Suchfeld, in das Sie das betreffende Wort eingeben können.
- Vorsicht bei der Nutzung von Übersetzungsmaschinen; durch die wortwörtliche Übersetzung fehlt oft der Zusammenhang, so dass der Sinn nicht immer klar wird.

2. Informationen prüfen und auswählen

- Folgende Fragen können hilfreich sein:
  - Wer hat die Webseite veröffentlicht? (z. B. kommerziell oder nicht kommerziell, Privatperson oder öffentliche Institution, usw.)
  - Welches Interesse steckt hinter der Webseite? (Soll z. B. etwas verkauft werden?)
  - Werden Fakten dargelegt oder Meinungen?
  - Sind die Informationen aktuell? (Wann wurde die Webseite zum letzten Mal aktualisiert? Von wann sind die Jahreszahlen/Statistiken? An welchem Datum wurde der Onlineartikel veröffentlicht?)
- Vergleichen Sie immer verschiedene Internetseiten und überprüfen Sie, ob die Informationen und Fakten übereinstimmen.

3. Die gefundenen Informationen wiedergeben

- Verwenden Sie Ihre eigenen Worte und kopieren Sie nicht einfach.
- Geben Sie immer an, woher Sie die Informationen haben und zitieren Sie die Quelle korrekt. Nennen Sie dafür den Autoren, die Quelle, das Erscheinungsdatum und den Link der Seite bei einer Onlinequelle.
- Machen Sie Zitate durch Anführungszeichen kenntlich.

S Skills

S2 Diagramme analysieren — Analysing charts

Diagramme fassen komplexe Sachverhalte in einfacher Form zusammen. Welche Art von Darstellung gewählt wird, hängt davon ab, welche Information veranschaulicht werden soll. Je nachdem welche Information man zeigen will, wählt man ein anderes Diagramm.

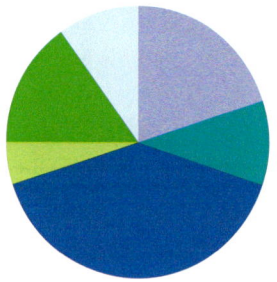

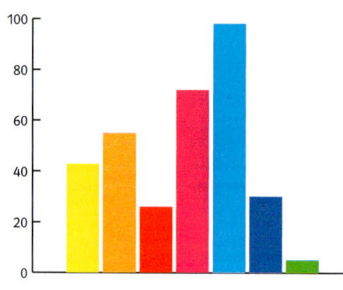

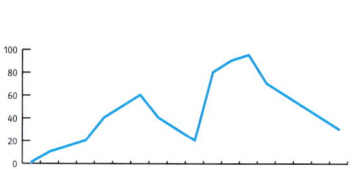

Mit einem Kuchen- oder Kreisdiagramm (*pie chart*) werden **Prozentanteile** verdeutlicht. Die einzelnen Stücke stellen die Anteile am ganzen Kreis (= 100 %) dar.

Säulen- oder Balkendiagramme (*bar chart*) verwendet man, um **Zahlen** direkt miteinander zu **vergleichen**.

In einem Kurvendiagramm (*line graph*) kann man gut darstellen, wie sich etwas über einen längeren Zeitraum hinweg **entwickelt** hat.

Wenn Sie ein Diagramm analysieren möchten, gehen Sie schrittweise vor.

1. Benennen, was dargestellt wird

Lesen Sie die Überschrift. Sie verrät Ihnen, was im Diagramm, der Tabelle usw. dargestellt wird. Falls es keine Überschrift gibt, verraten Ihnen die Beschriftung der Kreisstücke, die Achsen oder Diagramme und die Spalten der Tabellen, was dargestellt wird.

Sagen Sie, um welche Art von Diagramm es sich handelt (Form) und was damit dargestellt wird (Thema).

Nennen Sie die Quelle des Diagramms (z. B. Internetseite, Zeitung, Zeitschrift) und den Zeitpunkt, an dem es veröffentlicht wurde.

2. Beschreiben

Beschreiben Sie kurz, welche Informationen Sie aus dem Diagramm ablesen können.

Wenn Sie aus dem Diagramm eine Entwicklung ablesen können, beschreiben Sie diese kurz.

3. Zusammenfassen

Fassen Sie die wichtigsten Aussagen des Diagramms in 1–2 Sätzen zusammen.

Beschreiben Sie, welche Ergebnisse Sie aus dem Diagramm ziehen können.

V
It is about … / shows … / deals with … | It was published by … in …
This is a pie chart / bar chart / line graph …
This chart / graph was published in / by …
The (next) largest group of … | The majority / minority of … | Half of … | Most of … | 40 percent of …
The number of … goes up / increases by … / drops / goes down / doesn't change.
The chart / numbers / figures show(s) / suggest(s) that …
We can draw the conclusion that …

S3 Textsorten und ihre Besonderheiten Different kinds of texts

Für das Leseverstehen kann es hilfreich sein, wenn man von Anfang an weiß, welche Art von Text man lesen wird: einen erfundenen bzw. aus persönlichen Eindrücken bestehenden Text (*fictional*) oder einen Sachtext (*factual*).

Die meisten Textsorten haben ihre spezifischen Merkmale, an denen man sie erkennen kann – manchmal bereits bevor man eine Zeile gelesen hat.

Wenn Sie also einen Text lesen sollen, gehen Sie schrittweise vor:

1. Schauen Sie sich zunächst das Layout, den Aufbau, die Überschrift, evtl. die Schrift und die Bilder an. Ein Zeitungsartikel ist z. B. meist 2-spaltig abgedruckt und enthält oft Fotos. In der Überschrift steckt meist schon die Information, um was es geht.
2. Überprüfen Sie beim Lesen Ihre Vermutung. Achten Sie auf die Absicht des Autors / der Autorin: Will er/sie informieren, überzeugen, unterhalten …?

Fictional texts

Screenplay Mit einem Drehbuch lernen Schauspieler ihren Text, daher wird mündliche Sprache verwendet, also z. B. *short forms*, *question tags*, verstärkende Ausdrücke usw. In den Regieanweisungen (*stage directions*) für ein Filmskript steht nur, was man auch sehen oder darstellen kann. Hinweise auf Gedanken und Gefühle einer Person drücken z. B. Anweisungen für Gesichtsausdrücke aus.

Graphic novel In einem Comicroman wird eine Geschichte in Form eines Comics erzählt. Die einzelnen Bilder (*panel*) ergeben eine Bildsequenz, die um Bildtexte (*caption*) ergänzt werden. Die Dialoge, Gedanken und Gefühle der Charaktere werden in Sprech- oder Denkblasen (*speech/thought bubble*) dargestellt.

Story Geschichten oder Bildergeschichten sind oft fiktiv und sprachlich abwechslungsreich und meist im *past tense* geschrieben. Sie erzählen die Handlung (*plot*) aus der Ich-Perspektive oder der Er/Sie Perspektive. Sie enthalten verschieden Figuren (*characters*) und spielen in einer bestimmten Zeit an einem bestimmten Ort (*setting*). ▶ **S15** Eine Geschichte schreiben

Factual texts

Biography Eine Biografie erzählt vom Lebensweg einer besonderen Person und enthält meist auch ein Foto von ihr. Es werden Fakten genannt und keine Meinungen. Die Leser/innen erfahren etwas über die Herkunft, die Leistungen und den Einfluss der Person auf andere Menschen – oft über den Tod hinaus.

Blog(post) Ein Blog ist eine Art Online-Tagebuch, in dem regelmäßig Beiträge veröffentlicht werden. Es gibt verschiedene Arten von Blogs, z. B. Reise- oder Musikblogs. Meist sind sie in der Ich-Perspektive geschrieben und von der Meinung des Bloggers / der Bloggerin geprägt.
▶ **S8** Einen Blogpost schreiben

Email/Letter Diese Textformen enthalten immer eine Anrede für den Adressaten/die Adressatin, z. B. *Dear …* und Grußformeln am Schluss, z. B. *Best wishes/Sincerely*. Je nach Adressat ist der Text eher förmlich oder persönlich geschrieben. Bei formellen E-Mails oder Briefen verwendet man eher die Langformen, z. B. *I am* statt *I'm*. Bei Briefen ist außerdem die Empfänger- und Absenderadresse sowie das Datum angegeben. Ein Beispiel für einen formellen Brief ist das Bewerbungsschreiben.
▶ **S12** Eine E-Mail schreiben / **S20** Eine Bewerbung schreiben

Recommendation Eine Empfehlung ist eine Art Ratschlag oder Vorschlag, oft basierend auf eigenen Erfahrungen oder Meinungen. Um eine Empfehlung zu schreiben oder zu geben, ist es hilfreich, Fakten oder Argumente (z. B. Pro- und Kontra) zu nennen, aber auch von der eigenen Meinung oder Erfahrung zu berichten und diese zu begründen (z. B. mit Beispielen). ▶ **V7** Giving a recommendation

Flyer Ein Flyer ist eine kleine Broschüre, der meist für etwas wirbt. Er ist kurz und knapp gehalten und enthält nur die wichtigste Information: *Who? What? When? Where? Why?* Oft beinhaltet er auch einen ansprechenden Slogan.

S Skills

Interview Ein Interview ist ein Gespräch, in dem eine Person (*interviewer*) Informationen von einer oder mehreren anderen Personen (*interviewee*) erfragt. Jedes Mal, wenn jemand anfängt zu sprechen, wird der Name oder die Funktion (z. B. *reporter/journalist*) genannt. ▶ **S22 Ein Interview führen**

Comment/Statement Ein Kommentar behandelt ein Thema, einen Text oder ein Zitat, zu dem es verschiedene Sichtweisen gibt. Sie können entweder nur eine Sichtweise darstellen, also Ihre eigene Meinung zu einem Thema (*statement*). Oder Sie stellen mehrere Sichtweisen einander gegenüber und entscheiden sich am Schluss für eine davon (*comment*). ▶ **S6 Einen Kommentar schreiben**

News report Ein Zeitungsbericht beruht auf Tatsachen und Fakten und enthält keine persönliche Meinung. Die Sprache ist sachlich und verständlich und verwendet keine oder wenige emotionale Ausdrücke. Es wird der Verfasser/die Verfasserin und das Datum genannt und es gibt eine Schlagzeile. Diese weist direkt auf das Thema hin und weckt das Interesse des Lesers/der Leserin. In Zeitungsberichten werden häufig Passivformen verwendet. Es wird im *past tense* geschrieben und enthält oft ein Foto des Geschehens. ▶ **S14 Einen Zeitungsbericht schreiben**

Recipe Ein Rezept ist wie eine Anleitung in klare Schritte unterteilt. Meist stehen zu Beginn eine Zutatenliste mit Mengenangaben (*100 g butter, two teaspoons of* …) sowie Angaben zur Dauer und zum Zubehör. Dann werden die einzelnen Schritte erklärt.

Wiki entry Ein Wikitext gibt Informationen zu einer Person, einer Sache oder einem Ereignis. Er fasst in wenigen Sätzen zusammen, um wen oder was es geht. Die Sprache ist sachlich. Der Text ist im *present* oder *past tense* geschrieben.

S4 Eine Präsentation halten Giving a presentation

Eine Präsentation kann unterschiedliche Ziele haben: Informationen weitergeben; erklären, wie etwas funktioniert; die Zuhörer von etwas überzeugen. Der Inhalt der Präsentation kann eine Person oder eine Sache sein. Wichtig ist, dass Sie sich von Anfang an klar machen, was das Thema und das Ziel Ihrer Präsentation sind – und was Ihre Zuhörer schon darüber wissen.

1. Der Aufbau

Einleitung: Begrüßen Sie Ihre Zuhörer und stellen Sie sich vor (falls Ihre Zuhörer Sie noch nicht kennen). Nennen Sie Ihr Thema und die einzelnen Punkte der Präsentation.
Wecken Sie Interesse für Ihr Thema (z. B. mit einem passenden Zitat, einem interessanten Bild, einer Frage etc.).

Hauptteil: Präsentieren Sie Ihr Thema in 3–4 Hauptpunkten mit Hilfe von Beispielen.

Schluss: Wiederholen Sie die Hauptpunkte. Bedanken Sie sich bei Ihren Zuhörern und lassen Sie sie Fragen stellen.

> **V**
> Good morning. | Hello everyone. | My name is … My presentation is about … | I'm going to talk about … | My topic today is …
> As … once said: "…" | Have a look at this picture. It shows/says … | Have you ever …?
>
> I have chosen the category … | First/Second/Third/Now, I'd like to talk about … | The reason is … | Let me give you an example. | My next topic/point is … | Another interesting point is … | Finally, I'm going to talk about …
>
> To sum up, … | So what we have learned today is … | That's the end of my presentation. Thank you for listening/your attention. Do you have any questions?

Skills **S**

2. Die Sprache

Sprechen Sie möglichst frei.

Sprechen Sie die Zuhörer direkt an, z. B. indem Sie Fragen verwenden. Sie können auch auf Ihre Zuhörer eingehen oder sie auffordern, etwas zu tun.

Sprechen Sie in einfachen, kurzen Sätzen.

Betonen Sie wichtige Wörter.

Wiederholen Sie die wichtigsten Punkte. Das prägt sich ein.

Verwenden Sie Vergleiche. Das macht Ihre Rede anschaulich.

Erklären Sie unbekannte Wörter.

Erläutern Sie Ihre verwendeten Materialien.

V

Have you ever thought of …? | Did you know that …? | I can see that you are surprised | Let us ask ourselves … | It's up to you/us to …

… is 2,300 kilometers long. That's about the distance from London to south Italy. | … is like … | … is as … as …

… is a kind of … | It's something that … | It's a person who …

In this picture you can see … . | That's a … . | These are … .
The poster / photo / map / diagram / video shows … . As you can see in this picture / video / diagram, … .

3. Die Präsentationsform

Sie können ein Poster, Folien für den Overhead-Projektor / die Dokumentenkamera oder eine Computerpräsentation erstellen.

Tipps:
- eine Folie/Seite pro Präsentationspunkt
- nur Stichwörter aufschreiben
- Schriftgröße: mindestens 16 Punkt
- Rechtschreibung kontrollieren
- anschauliches Bildmaterial verwenden (Fotos, Karten, Diagramme, Videoclips etc.)
- Bildgröße prüfen
- Farben und Effekte sparsam verwenden

4. Hilfsmittel

Zusätzlich zu den Stichwörtern in der Präsentation können Sie weitere Stichpunkte, Zahlen, Daten, Fakten und unbekannte Wörter notieren, die Sie für Ihre Rede brauchen. Sie können sie z. B. auf Karteikarten schreiben oder in der Computerpräsentation als Notizen einfügen.

BASIC RULES
– team sport
– each team: 11 players on the field
– one game: 4 quarters
  (1 quarter = 15 minutes) plus breaks
– time is stopped during breaks
– average game = more than 3 hours long

GENERAL FACTS
– Super Bowl: most famous sporting event in the US
– first Sunday in February
– famous sporting event on TV
– unofficial national holiday
– final match of the season
– first game played in USA in 1869

S Skills

5. Weitere Tipps

- Üben Sie Ihre Präsentation mehrmals. Sie können Ihre Rede vor dem Spiegel üben, vor Ihrer Familie oder vor einem Mitschüler / einer Mitschülerin. Sie können sich dabei auch filmen lassen!
- Achten Sie auf die Zeit.
- Probieren Sie das Material und die Technik vorher aus.
- Halten Sie Blickkontakt zu Ihren Zuhörern (in den vorderen und hinteren Reihen).
- Schauen Sie freundlich.

6. Nach der Präsentation

Holen Sie sich von Ihren Zuhörern Feedback zu Ihrer Rede ein.

S5 Hörsehverstehen Viewing

Um einen Film auswerten zu können, müssen Sie – wie bei Hörtexten – vor allem verstehen, was gesprochen wird. Ein Film hat jedoch den Vorteil, dass das Gesprochene durch die Bilder unterstützt wird. Sie können das, was Sie sehen, also für das Verständnis nutzen.

1. Vor dem Ansehen

- Machen Sie sich klar, um welche Art von Film es sich handelt: Spielfilm, Dokumentarfilm, Reportage, Werbefilm usw.
  Es gibt verschiedene Hinweise darauf: Titel, abgedruckte Standbilder, Arbeitsauftrag.
- Überlegen Sie sich, was Sie von dem Film erwarten.
- Lesen Sie sich den Arbeitsauftrag genau durch.

2. Während des Ansehens

Machen Sie sich beim Ansehen Notizen zu den folgenden Punkten:

Erstes Ansehen:

• **Wo** fand die Filmaufnahme statt?	Achten Sie auf Landschaften, Gebäude und Räume.
• **Was** ist zu sehen?	Achten Sie auf Kleidung und Gegenstände im Vorder- und Hintergrund.
• **Wer** kommt vor?	Achten Sie darauf, wer spricht, wer dabei steht, wen man sieht.
• **Was** ist das Thema?	Achten Sie darauf, ob Dinge oder Personen in Nahaufnahme gezeigt werden.
• **Wann** hat etwas stattgefunden / findet etwas statt?	Achten Sie darauf, ob es um ein Ereignis in der Vergangenheit, in der Gegenwart oder der Zukunft geht.

Für das **erste Ansehen** kann es sinnvoll sein, den Film zunächst **ohne Ton** zu sehen. So können Sie Ihre Aufmerksamkeit auf die anderen Dinge lenken.

Zweites Ansehen:

• Was wird zum Thema gesagt?	
• Wie wird es gesagt?	Achten Sie auf Mimik und Gestik.
• Wie wird eine bestimmte Atmosphäre geschaffen?	Achten Sie auf Bilder, Licht, Farben, Musik und Geräusche.

Für das **zweite Ansehen** kann es – wenn möglich – sinnvoll sein, den Film ab und zu anzuhalten.

3. Nach dem Ansehen

Ergänzen Sie Ihre Notizen und bearbeiten Sie die Aufgaben.

S6 Einen Kommentar schreiben — Writing a statement / a comment

Ein Kommentar behandelt ein Thema, einen Text oder ein Zitat, zu dem es verschiedene Sichtweisen gibt. Sie können entweder nur eine Sichtweise darstellen, also Ihre **eigene Meinung** zu einem Thema (*statement*) oder Sie stellen mehrere Sichtweisen einander gegenüber und entscheiden sich am Schluss für eine davon (*comment*).
In beiden Fällen hat der Text drei Teile:

1. Einleitung

- Sagen Sie, warum das Thema wichtig ist.
- Stellen Sie nun Ihre Fragestellung bzw. Sichtweise vor.

> **V** The topic of … is of great interest to … . | It is an important topic because … . | The question is: Should … ?

2. Hauptteil

- Wenn Sie nur Ihre eigene Sichtweise darstellen wollen, beginnen Sie mit dem schwächsten und enden Sie mit dem stärksten Argument.
- Möchten Sie mehrere Sichtweisen darstellen, können Sie aus zwei Varianten wählen:

```
   Einleitung              Einleitung
       ↓                       ↓
   Pro → Kontra              Pro
       ↓                       ↓
   Pro → Kontra   oder      Kontra
       ↓                       ↓
   Pro → Kontra            Schluss
       ↓
    Schluss
```

> **V** Firstly/secondly … Moreover, … | Either …, or … . | not only … but also … . | Another way to look at this is … . | On the other hand, … .

- Unterstützen Sie Ihr Argument mit Fakten und anschaulichen Beispielen.
- Wenn möglich, präsentieren Sie Hintergrundinformationen zu dem Thema. Das macht Ihren Text überzeugend.

> **V** For example … . | A good example of this is … . | … as in the following example … . | Statistics show that …

3. Schluss

- Fassen Sie Ihre persönliche Sichtweise zusammen. An dieser Stelle können Sie noch einmal auf die wichtigsten Argumente verweisen.

> **V** My conclusion is … . | In conclusion, … . | To sum up, … . | All in all, … .

S Skills

Sehen Sie sich dieses Beispiel an:

> **'Schools don't need pens and paper any more: Students should only use tablets and laptops.' Do you agree with this statement?**

① **Einleitung (introduction)**
Beispiele, Fakten

① Today technology is used everywhere. Statistics show that almost 85 % of workers in the US use a laptop or PC at work. But in most schools students still learn with books and write on paper. So, should schools still use pens and paper today?

② **Hauptteil (main part)**
Argumente pro

② Firstly, if students use computers from a very young age, their IT skills will develop more quickly. For example, Mark Zuckerberg learned programming early and developed his social media site while he was still at college. In addition, using computers could make life easier for students who find writing difficult. They could type their answers without worrying about their handwriting.

③ **Hauptteil (main part)**
Argumente contra

③ But there are negative effects of using too much technology too. Science has shown that when you write something down by hand, you can remember it better. Also, when students use their hands, it helps them with other skills, like drawing.

④ **Schluß (conclusion)**

④ In conclusion, I think that schools should use technology because students should learn skills which they will later need in a job. But it would be a bad idea to not use pens or paper at all because young children also need to develop other skills for daily life.

S7 Ideen und Vokabular sammeln und ordnen
Collecting and structuring ideas and vocabulary

Egal, ob Sie eine Präsentation vorbereiten müssen, eine Anzeige gestalten oder eine Geschichte schreiben sollen – der erste Schritt ist es immer, Ideen zu sammeln und zu ordnen. Das klassische Brainstorming also.

1. Aufschreiben ▶ M4 Placemat

Schreiben Sie zunächst alle Ideen zu Ihrem Thema in beliebiger Reihenfolge auf – genau so, wie sie Ihnen in den Kopf kommen. Sie können auf Deutsch, Englisch oder auf beiden Sprachen schreiben. Sie können die Ideen auch gemeinsam mit anderen Leuten in der Gruppe sammeln.

Skills

2. Auswählen

- Markieren Sie die Ideen, die Ihnen wichtig erscheinen.
- Streichen Sie die Ideen durch, die Sie nicht wichtig finden.
- Klammern Sie Ideen ein, bei denen Sie sich nicht sicher sind.

3. Ordnen

- Schreiben Sie das Thema auf.
- Suchen Sie in Ihrer Ideenliste nach **Oberbegriffen** oder überlegen Sie, welche Ihrer Ideen Sie unter einem Oberbegriff zusammenfassen können. Schreiben Sie zunächst diese Oberbegriffe auf.
- Schreiben Sie zu jedem Oberbegriff **Unterbegriffe** (z. B. Einzelheiten oder Beispiele) auf.
- Prüfen Sie zum Schluss, ob Sie alle wichtigen Punkte aus Ihrer Ideenliste verwendet haben.

Es gibt verschiedene Möglichkeiten, Ihre Ideen zu ordnen: Sie können z. B. eine Mindmap, eine Wörterwolke (*word cloud*), ein *fishbone diagram* (wie im Beispiel auf dieser Seite) oder eine Tabelle schreiben. Ab jetzt sollten Sie nur noch englische Begriffe verwenden. Schlagen Sie unbekannte Wörter nach.

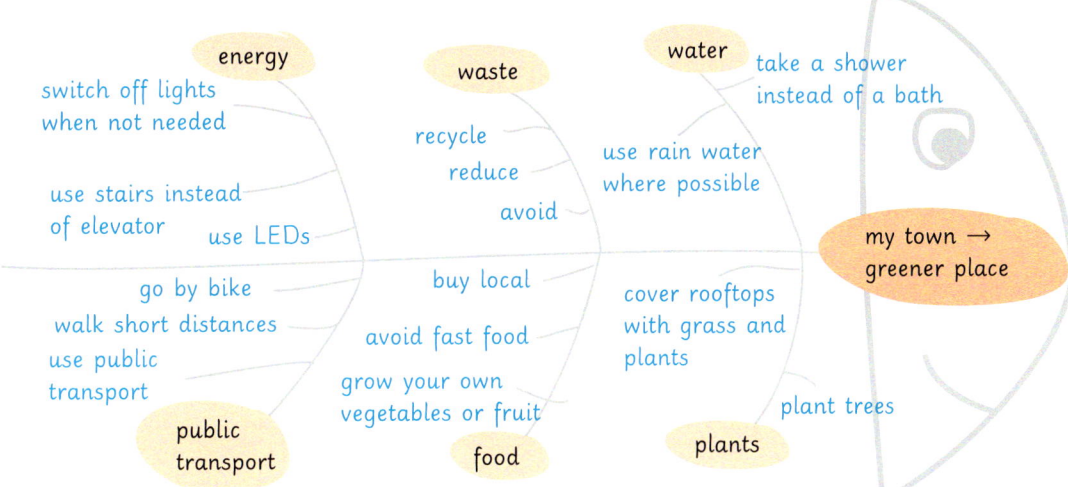

Auch Vokabeln lassen sich gut sammeln und ordnen, um sie sich besser einprägen zu können. Dazu gibt es verschiedene Methoden, die Sie alle bereits kennen.

- Klebezettel mit englischen Wörtern an die entsprechenden Gegenstände in Ihrem Zimmer kleben
- Wörter als Bildwörter oder mit passenden Bildern aufmalen
- Wörter pantomimisch darstellen und gegenseitig erraten lassen
- Wörter aussprechen, zusammen mit ihrer Übersetzung und vielleicht einem Beispielsatz aufnehmen und immer wieder anhören
- Wörter mit ähnlichen Wörtern in anderen Sprachen notieren
- Wörter, die miteinander in Beziehung stehen, zusammen notieren, z. B. verwandte Wörter, Gegensatzpaare, zusammengehörige Paare

S Skills

S8 Einen Blogpost schreiben Writing a blog post

Ein Blog ist eine Art Online-Tagebuch, in dem regelmäßig Beiträge veröffentlicht werden (*posts*). Es gibt verschiedene Arten von Blogs, z. B. Reise- oder Musikblogs. Meist sind sie in der Ich-Perspektive geschrieben und von der Meinung des Bloggers / der Bloggerin geprägt.

1. Vor dem Schreiben

Werden Sie sich zunächst klar darüber, wie genau das Thema lautet und für wen der Text bestimmt sein soll. Wählen Sie einen interessanten, kurzen Titel.

2. Das Schreiben

1. Planung
Ein guter Text besteht normalerweise aus den folgenden drei Teilen:

Einleitung (*introduction*): Hier erfährt der Leser / die Leserin, worum es im Text geht. Sie können auch eine Fragestellung einführen, die im Text erörtert werden soll.

Hauptteil (*main part*): Der Hauptteil ist in mehrere Abschnitte gegliedert und beinhaltet die Details (Fakten, Argumente, Beispiele usw.) zu Ihrem Thema.

Schluss (*conclusion*): Der Schlussteil kann eine Zusammenfassung von dem sein, was Sie im Hauptteil geschrieben haben, oder eine persönliche Äußerung.

2. Der erste Entwurf
Auf der Grundlage Ihrer Planung können Sie einen ersten Entwurf schreiben. Schreiben Sie in einem freundlichen und persönlichen Stil. Verwenden Sie die Ich-Perspektive und bringen Sie Beispiele aus Ihrer eigenen Erfahrung. Denken Sie dabei an Ihre Leser/Leserinnen: Was möchten sie erfahren? Was finden sie interessant?
Weitere Tipps finden Sie hier: ► **S16** Tipps für einen guten Schreibstil

3. Die Überarbeitung
Es ist wichtig, dass Sie (oder ein Mitschüler / eine Mitschülerin) den Text noch einmal kritisch durchlesen. Am hilfreichsten ist es, wenn Sie den Text mehrmals lesen, jedes Mal mit einem anderen Schwerpunkt (siehe Checkliste rechts). Wenn Sie Feedback von einer anderen Person bekommen haben, entscheiden Sie, was davon Sie für Ihren Text übernehmen möchten.
Wenn Sie den Text eines Mitschülers / einer Mitschülerin lesen, achten Sie darauf, bei Ihrer Kritik fair zu bleiben.

CHECKLISTE
Rechtschreibung:
- Wörter richtig geschrieben?
- Am Satzanfang groß?
- Getrennt oder zusammen?

Grammatik:
- Richtige Zeitform, Satzbau, Pluralbildung usw.?

Inhalt:
- Alle wesentlichen Punkte enthalten?
- Zusammenhänge erkennbar / logisch?

Skills **S**

S9 Leseverstehen Reading

Um die Fragen zu einem Text richtig beantworten zu können, müssen Sie zuerst den Text gut verstehen. Dabei hilft es, verschiedene Lesestrategien anzuwenden. Die bekanntesten Lesestrategien sind Skimming, Scanning und Close-reading.

1. Vor dem Lesen

Bevor Sie den Text lesen, haben Sie bestimmte Erwartungen, die sich beim späteren Lesen bestätigen lassen oder die Sie verwerfen müssen. Versuchen Sie vorherzusagen, worum es in dem Text gehen könnte.
- Klären Sie die Textsorte (Geschichte, Zeitungsartikel, Blog, Sachtext, Reisebericht …)
  ► **S3** Textsorten und ihre Besonderheiten
- Sehen Sie sich das Layout und Illustrationen (Bilder, Grafiken) an.
- Lesen Sie die Überschrift und Zwischenüberschriften.

2. Während des Lesens

Skimming = orientierendes Lesen
Beim Skimming überfliegen Sie den Text, um sich einen Gesamtüberblick zu verschaffen.
- Es ist nicht nötig, jedes Wort zu verstehen.
- Lesen Sie ungefähr drei- bis viermal schneller als gewöhnlich.
- Lesen Sie die Überschrift(en), um herauszufinden, worum es in dem Text geht.
- Versuchen Sie, sich ganze Abschnitte anzusehen, zentrale Begriffe zu erfassen (*keywords*) und nicht Wort für Wort zu lesen.
- Lesen Sie nur den ersten und den letzten Satz jedes Abschnitts.

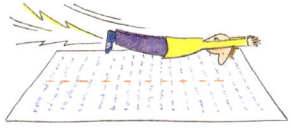

Scanning = suchendes Lesen
Die Scanning-Technik kann besonders hilfreich sein, wenn Sie Fragen zum Text beantworten sollen und gezielt nach Informationen (*details*) suchen.
- Lesen Sie die Fragen/Aufgaben zum Text sorgfältig durch.
- Lassen Sie Ihre Augen über den Text fliegen und fokussieren Sie sich dabei auf Schlüsselbegriffe. Sie zeigen an, welche Teile Sie genauer lesen sollten, um mehr zu erfahren.
- Markieren Sie Schlüsselbegriffe oder wichtige Details im Text oder notieren Sie diese.
- Versuchen Sie, anhand Ihrer Notizen die Fragen mit eigenen Worten zu beantworten.

Close-reading = intensives Lesen
Beim Close-reading entnehmen Sie dem Text alle Informationen, um wie z. B. bei einem Kochrezept oder in einer Bedienungsanleitung alle wichtigen Schritte bzw. Hinweise nachvollziehen zu können.

S Skills

S10 Hörverstehen Listening

Radiosendungen, Nachrichten, Audioguides und Durchsagen sind Beispiele, in denen Sie Informationen nur übers Hören entnehmen können.

1. Vorbereitung

• Was erfahren Sie über das Thema und über die Personen, um die es geht?	– Überschrift, Bilder und Aufgaben genau ansehen! – Bei mehreren Bildern: Worin unterscheiden sie sich?
• Worauf kommt es in der Aufgabenstellung an?	– Globalverstehen: den Hauptgedanken verstehen. – Detailverstehen: Einzelheiten verstehen (z. B. Namen, Zahlen, …)
• Was wissen Sie schon über dieses Thema?	– Welche Wörter kennen Sie zu diesem Thema? – Können Sie Fragen schon vor dem Hören beantworten? Achtung: Prüfen Sie unbedingt, ob der Text die gleiche Antwort gibt.
• Stellen Sie sich auf folgende Dinge ein:	– Die Antworten im Text sind meistens in der gleichen Reihenfolge wie in der Aufgabe. – Manchmal hören Sie andere Wörter als in der Aufgabe, die aber das Gleiche bedeuten. – Die Sprecher können mit einem mehr oder weniger ausgeprägten Akzent sprechen. – Die Art, wie etwas gesagt wird, kann Ihnen auch weiterhelfen: fröhlich, verärgert, gelangweilt, …

2. Den Text anhören

- Lass Sie sich nicht ablenken. Schauen Sie auf die Aufgaben und halten Sie einen Stift bereit.
- Schreiben Sie nur englische Stichwörter oder Wortfetzen auf.
Verwenden Sie Abkürzungen.

+	and/yes	++	good/great	=	the same as, equals, means
–	not/no	e.g.	for example	≠	not the same as, does not equal
				→	becomes, will be

- Lassen Sie eine Leerzeile zwischen den einzelnen Aufgaben, damit Sie später etwas ergänzen können.
- Bei Multiple-Choice-Aufgaben: Markieren Sie die richtige Antwort oder Antworten. Wenn Sie sich nicht sicher sind, streichen Sie die Antworten durch, von denen Sie wissen, dass sie falsch sind. Wenn Sie gar nicht weiterkommen, raten Sie. Das ist immer besser, als gar keine Antwort zu geben.

3. Fragen beantworten

Antworten Sie mithilfe Ihrer Notizen in der Sprache, in der die Aufgaben gestellt sind.

4. Den Text ein zweites Mal hören

- Konzentrieren Sie sich auf die Dinge, die Sie beim ersten Mal nicht verstanden haben.
- Überprüfen Sie Ihre Antworten bzw. Notizen.

Skills **S**

S11 Visualisierung Making visuals

Durch Visualisierung kann man abstrakte oder umfangreiche Informationen sichtbar und dadurch besser verständlich und merkbar machen. Die Formen von Visualisierung reichen von einfachen Diagrammen (z. B. für Zahlen) über Computerpräsentationen (z. B. für Projektprozesse) bis zu aufwändig produzierten Spots (z. B. für Marketingkonzepte). Wie etwas dargestellt wird, hängt von der Art der Information und dem Ziel der Sichtbarmachung ab.

1. Planung

Um die richtige Visualisierungsform zu finden, müssen Sie vorab bestimmte Fragen beantworten:
1. Was genau ist Ihr Thema: Zahlen, Text- oder Bildinformationen?
2. Welche Möglichkeiten haben Sie für eine Visualisierung: Computer, Kamera, Papier und Stift?
3. Welche Art der Visualisierung ist für Ihr Thema passend: Infografik, Diagramm, Poster, Computerpräsentation, Film, Audioguide?
4. Wo und wem soll das Endprodukt gezeigt werden: Freundeskreis, Familie, Klasse, breitere Öffentlichkeit?

2. Vorbereitung

Sammeln Sie alles zusammen, was Sie für die Visualisierung brauchen, bzw. teilen Sie die Aufgaben in Ihrer Arbeitsgruppe auf:

1. Inhalt:
- Zahlen, Daten, Fakten, Texte, Geschichten, Statistiken, Grafiken …
- Bildmaterial (digital oder auf Papier)
- Hördokumente

2. Material:
- Geräte wie Computer, Kamera, Handy, Aufnahmegerät usw. (zur Erstellung und ggf. zum Abspielen)
- Material wie Papier, Stifte, Fotos, Schere, Klebstoff, Modelle usw.

3. Erstellung

- Fügen Sie Inhalt und Form zusammen.
- Fertigen Sie ggf. vorab eine Skizze an.
- Spielen Sie mit Schriftgrößen, Farben und anderen Elementen.
- Halten Sie die Texte eher kurz (z. B. Schlüsselwörter und Notizen) und konzentrieren Sie sich auf die Hauptaussagen.
- Teilen Sie sich die zur Verfügung stehende Zeit sinnvoll ein, damit Sie nicht alles auf einmal machen müssen.
- Bedenken Sie, dass Sie in einer Gruppenarbeit auch Zeit brauchen, um die Einzelteile zusammenzusetzen.

4. Präsentation

Stellen Sie Ihr Produkt in einem angemessenen Rahmen vor. ▶ **S4** Presentation
▶ **M3** 1-minute presentation ▶ **M11** Gallery walk

S Skills

S12 Eine E-Mail schreiben — Writing an email

Mittlerweile werden kaum noch formelle Briefe geschrieben, da nahezu alles per E-Mail erledigt werden kann. Dennoch gelten für formelle E-Mails die gleichen Kommunikationsregeln wie für formelle Briefe: Nennen Sie den Betreff Ihrer E-Mail, achten Sie auf Höflichkeit und verwenden Sie eine angemessene Begrüßung und Verabschiedung.

Das Beispiel zeigt Ihnen, wie eine formelle E-Mail in der Regel aufgebaut ist. Lesen Sie Ihre E-Mail noch einmal auf Fehler durch, bevor Sie sie abschicken. ▶ **S16** Tipps für einen guten Schreibstil

① **Sender**
Ihre E-Mail-Adresse

② **Empfänger**
Die E-Mail-Adresse des Empfängers

③ **CC**
Wenn Sie eine Kopie der E-Mail an eine weitere Person versenden möchten, dann geben Sie die E-Mail-Adresse unter cc (*carbon copy* = Kopie an …) ein.

④ **Datum und Uhrzeit**
Beim Versenden der E-Mail erscheinen das Datum sowie die Uhrzeit automatisch.

⑤ **Betreff**
Betreffzeile mit Grund des Schreibens

⑥ Die **Anlagen** bei E-Mails heißen *attachments*.

⑦ **Anrede** (formaler: *Dear Mr/Mrs* …)

⑧ Text der E-Mail. Wie bei Geschäftsbriefen achten Sie auch hier auf Höflichkeit und klare Formulierungen.

⑨ **Grußformel** am Ende der Mail (*Yours sincerely/Yours faithfully*)

⑩ Angaben zu Ihren **Kontaktdetails**

---

① From: studentadvice@london-uni…uk
② To: sam_80@wellingtoninstitute…nz
③ CC: headmaster@wellingtoninstitute…nz
④ Sent: Fri, Jan 16, 2019 at 11:48 AM
⑤ Subject: Student visit
⑥ Attachments: visitorguide.pdf

⑦ Dear Sam,

⑧ …

⑨ Kind regards

Matt Smith
Training Manager

++++++++++++++++++++++++++++

⑩ London Uni Student Advice
342 Bournville Road
London L256EE
England
Tel +44(0)151-109268733 – Fax +44(0)151-109268834
www.london-uni.uk – studentadvice@london-uni…uk

V Dear Sir or Madam, | Dear (name), | Good morning/afternoon, | Hi/Hello, …
I am writing to you because … / … to inform you … | I would like to … | I herewith revoke the contract I signed on … | Could you let me know.
Please find attached … | Please confirm … |
Thank you for your help. | I look forward to hearing from you soon.
Yours sincerely/faithfully | Kind regards
All the best | Best wishes | Bye for now | Love | Lots of love

S13 Bildbeschreibung Describing pictures

Wenn Sie ein Bild (z.B. ein Foto, eine Zeichnung oder ein Gemälde) beschreiben möchten, sehen Sie es sich zuerst genau an. Die wichtigsten Inhalte sieht man meistens ganz leicht. Nehmen Sie sich aber auch Zeit, Details zu entdecken. Gehen Sie schrittweise vor:

1. Allgemeine Informationen

Wer? Was? Wo? Wann?

Überschrift / Bildunterschrift (falls vorhanden)

> **V** This photo / picture shows … | In this picture you can see … | This photo was taken in / at … The title / caption of this picture is …

2. Genaue Beschreibung

Wählen Sie eine sinnvolle Reihenfolge (z.B. Mitte – Vordergrund – Hintergrund oder von links oben nach rechts unten), um Einzelheiten zu beschreiben. Nicht alle Einzelheiten sind bei jedem Bild wichtig.

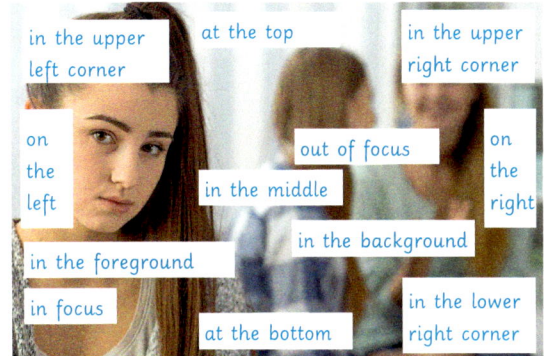

Beschreiben Sie:

- wie die Personen aussehen
- was die Personen tun (Zeitform: *present progressive* ▶ G1)
- Vermutungen: was die Personen fühlen oder denken
- Sonstiges: Gegenstände, Farben, Ortsangaben etc. (Zeitform: *simple present* ▶ G1)

> **V** He / She is young / old / about 17 / … | He / She has … hair | He / She is wearing … | He / She is smiling / crying …
> The person looks happy / sad / busy / lonely / relaxed … | Maybe he / she is thinking about … There is … | It looks / is … | black and white | colourful | next to | between | behind | in | on | under | in front of

3. Wirkung des Bildes

Wie wirkt das Bild auf Sie?
Was denken Sie über das Bild?

> **V** I think the picture is special / amazing / shocking / realistic … because … | The picture makes me feel happy / sad / worried … | I think the message of the picture is …

4. Sonderfall Cartoon

Cartoons haben oft eine Bildunterschrift und/oder Sprechblasen. Ein Cartoon stellt meistens etwas Aktuelles dar und zwar in einer übertriebenen Art und Weise. Überlegen Sie sich: Auf welches Thema möchte der Cartoonist aufmerksam machen? Was denken Sie darüber?

> **V** The caption of the cartoon says … | The person / sign says … | The cartoon is funny because … | I think the cartoonist is criticising … | I don't get the joke. | I don't understand (why) … | I agree / don't agree with the point the cartoon is making because …

S Skills

S14 Einen Zeitungsbericht schreiben — Writing a news report

In einem Zeitungsbericht geben Sie sachliche Informationen wieder. Wichtig dabei ist, dass die Informationen vollständig und verständlich sind. Im Folgenden finden Sie ein Beispiel für einen Zeitungsbericht über eine Naturkatastrophe:

1. Die Elemente eines Zeitungsberichts

① **headline** – die Schlagzeile, die die Aufmerksamkeit der Leser/Leserinnen gewinnt

② **byline** – der Name des Verfassers/der Verfasserin und das Erscheinungsdatum

③ **placeline** – die Ortsangabe gibt an, wo sich das Berichtete ereignet hat

④ **lead** – der Vorspann, in dem die wichtigsten Informationen präsentiert und die W-Fragen beantwortet werden

⑤ **body** – der Hauptteil, in dem weitere Details beschrieben werden

⑥ **quotation** – ein Zitat von Augenzeugen oder Experten

⑦ **fact** – Fakten und Informationen, die auf Korrektheit geprüft wurden

⑧ **picture** – Foto(s), um das Ereignis zu illustrieren

⑨ **caption** – eine Bildunterschrift

① **Earthquake hits city in New Zealand!**

② Reporter: Jason May   Feb 23, 2011

③ CHRISTCHURCH – On 22 February 2011 at 12:50
④ p.m. the earth started to tremble in the city of Christchurch. The earthquake lasted only one minute but the result was a disaster.

⑤ A witness named Brian was sitting in City Café with his friend Mason when the earthquake happened. Brian and his friend were able to hide under a table while everything was shaking.

⑥ Brian says that everybody seemed confused and that buildings around the café even collapsed. Then the fire brigade and the police started to evacuate the buildings. The father of the witness's friend was trapped in his house but a rescue dog found hime. The rescue team then saved the man. The witness says that they were lucky.

⑦ However, 185 people died during the earthquake, more than 6,000 were seriously injured and thousands of buildings were destroyed or damaged.

⑧

⑨ A street of Christchurch after the earthquake

2. Die Schlagzeile

Die Schlagzeile ist der wichtigste Teil eines Berichtes. Ist sie interessant, werden die Leser/innen auf Ihren Bericht aufmerksam. Wenn nicht, blättern oder klicken sie weiter. Wecken Sie mit Ihrer Schlagzeile die Neugier der Leser/innen. Je kürzer die Schlagzeile, desto besser.

3. Der Hauptteil

Der Hauptteil eines Zeitungsberichts ist oft wie eine Pyramide aufgebaut: Die wichtigste Information steht ganz am Anfang, weitere Informationen folgen und das Unwichtigste kommt zum Schluss. So müssen Leser/innen nicht alles lesen, um sich zu informieren.

1. Beantworten Sie zuerst die W-Fragen:
    - **Was** geschah?
    - **Wer** war beteiligt?
    - **Wann** ist es passiert?
    - **Wo** ist es passiert?
    - **Wie** ist es abgelaufen?
    - **Warum** geschah es?
2. Nennen Sie die Quelle der Informationen.
3. Schildern Sie Einzelheiten zum Geschehen.
4. Geben Sie Informationen zu den Hintergründen.

4. Die ABC-Regel

Accuracy (= Genauigkeit)

Stellen Sie sicher, dass alle Fakten (Personen, Orte, Gegenstände, Adressen usw.) stimmen.

Brevity (= Kürze)

Fassen Sie sich kurz und beantworten Sie gleichzeitig die wichtigsten W-Fragen (siehe oben).

Clarity (= Anschaulichkeit)

Schreiben Sie so, dass der Leser ganz klar verstehen kann, was gemeint ist.

5. Die Sprache

- In Berichten wird oft die Passivform der Verben verwendet. Das macht den Bericht sachlicher und schafft Distanz. ▶ **G4, G12** Passive voice I & II
- Verwenden Sie Beispiele und/oder Zitate.
- Wer ist der Adressat Ihres Berichtes? Passen Sie die Sprache dementsprechend an.
    ▶ **S16** Tipps für einen guten Schreibstil

S15 Eine Geschichte schreiben *Writing a story*

Wenn Sie eine Geschichte schreiben, können Sie diese völlig frei erfinden oder anhand eines vorgegebenen Themas oder mit Hilfe von Bildern verfassen. ▶ **S7** Sammeln und ordnen ▶ **V5** Story

1. Die Planung

Bevor Sie anfangen zu schreiben, müssen Sie ein paar Entscheidungen treffen.

Erzähler/-in *(narrator)*
- Der Ich-Erzähler schildert die Geschichte aus seiner oder ihrer Sicht heraus.
- Ein Er-/Sie-Erzähler erzählt die Geschichte über andere Personen oder aus der Sicht einer anderen Person.

Figuren *(characters)*
- Wählen Sie eine Hauptfigur, die ganz besondere Fähigkeiten hat (z. B. magische Kräfte besitzt).
- Für weitere Figuren lassen Sie sich von Menschen aus Ihrer Umgebung inspirieren (jemand, der immer kichert, jemand, der sehr schnell/langsam spricht usw.).

Ort *(setting)*
Wählen Sie einen Ort, an dem Ihre Geschichte spielt (ein altes Schloss, einen Zauberwald usw.).

Zeit *(time)*
- Entscheiden Sie sich für eine Zeit, in der Ihre Geschichte spielt. Das kann gestern, letztes Jahr oder im nächsten Jahrhundert sein.

S Skills

Handlung *(plot)*
- Anfang: Sie können z. B. damit beginnen, die Hauptfigur vorzustellen, oder unmittelbar in die Handlung der Geschichte einsteigen.
- Hauptteil: Überlegen Sie sich, was die Handlung Ihrer Geschichte vorantreibt. Das könnte ein Konflikt oder ein Problem sein, ein lustiger oder überraschender Vorfall, eine zufällige Begegnung, …
- Schluss: Sie können z. B. ein offenes Ende wählen oder eines, das die Geschichte auflöst.

2. Schreiben ▶ S16 Tipps für einen guten Schreibstil

- Überlegen Sie, was Ihre Figuren in den jeweiligen Situationen sagen könnten.
- Schlagen Sie Wörter und Ausdrücke nach, die Sie verwenden möchten.
- Verwenden Sie beim Erzählen die Vergangenheitsform. ▶ G5, G6, G11 Past tenses
- Benutzen Sie Adjektive und Adverbien (z. B. für Sinneswahrnehmungen wie Geräusche, Farben, Gerüche) und beschreiben Sie Details (z. B. Orts- und Personenbeschreibungen).
  ▶ G13 Adjectives and adverbs   ▶ V21 Describing sensations

Dieses Beispiel zeigt Ihnen, wie Ihre Geschichte beginnen könnte.

It was evening and there were no cars or people on the street. I ran until I came to a big, old building, which looked dark and dirty. The sign said, 'Magic bought and sold here.' I pushed the door open.
"Good evening, young lady," said the old man behind the desk. He spoke very slowly and looked at me closely. I knew he was thinking, 'What has she got for me?'
"Buying or selling?" he asked curiously.
"Er … selling… I think." My voice sounded less nervous than I was. My father would go crazy if he knew I was here, talking to a man who could take some of my magic skills, put them into a bottle and sell them to a stranger. But we needed money, and this was the only way to get some fast. I hated this place, hated this man, but he had what I needed, and I had what he wanted. "Show me what you've got for me then," he said.
Although I was really scared, I took a deep breath and showed him my hands. His eyes uddenly looked round and shocked. "I can't believe it," he said. …

---

3. Eine Geschichte fortsetzen

1. Beachten Sie die inhaltlichen und stilistischen Merkmale der Textsorten.
Wenn Sie eine Geschichte fortsetzen oder ein Ende für eine Geschichte schreiben, achten Sie darauf, Erzählperspektive und Stil beizubehalten und die Handlung so fortzusetzen, dass keine inhaltlichen Widersprüche entstehen.

2. Machen Sie sich Notizen. Fertigen Sie einen ersten Entwurf an.
Wenn Sie eine Geschichte fortsetzen möchten, machen Sie sich zunächst Notizen zu den folgenden Aspekten:
- Nennen Sie Gründe für die Ereignisse in Ihrer Geschichte. Sie können in Ihrer Fortsetzung z. B. eine überraschende Wendung oder eine Auflösung eines Konflikts beschreiben.
  Die Fortsetzung muss sich allerdings logisch an die Ausgangsgeschichte anschließen.
- Beschreiben Sie die Gedanken, Gefühle oder Ideen der Person(en).

3. Überarbeiten Sie Ihren Entwurf.
Lesen Sie zunächst die Ausgangsgeschichte und direkt im Anschluss Ihre Fortsetzung.
- Achten Sie beim Lesen darauf, ob es Brüche in der Logik oder im Fluss der Geschichte gibt.
- Ist die Erzählperspektive gleich?
- Haben Sie alle Personen aus der Geschichte in Ihrer Fortsetzung aufgegriffen?

4. Eine Geschichte zu einem Bild schreiben

Wenn Sie eine Geschichte zu einem Bild schreiben, lassen Sie sich bei der Planung Ihrer Geschichte davon inspirieren. Die folgenden Leitfragen können dabei helfen:

1. Wer ist in dem Bild zu sehen?
Entscheiden Sie, wer der Erzähler / die Erzählerin (*narrator*) sein könnte und wer die Hauptfigur (*character*) in Ihrer Geschichte ist. Denken Sie daran, die Gefühle, Gedanken und Sinneseindrücke der Figuren zu beschreiben. ▶ **V21** Describing sensations

2. Was ist in dem Bild zu sehen?
Der Ort (*setting*) und die Zeit (*time*) Ihrer Geschichte sollten zu dem Inhalt und der Stimmung des Bildes passen.

3. Was passiert in dem Bild?
Überlegen Sie sich eine Handlung (*plot*), die zum Bild passt. Machen Sie sich dabei auch Gedanken dazu, was vor der Situation im Bild passiert sein könnte und was nach der Situation im Bild passieren könnte. Das hilft Ihnen, eine interessante Handlung für Ihre Geschichte zu entwickeln.

S16 Tipps für einen guten Schreibstil   Writing good texts

Je größer dein Wortschatz wird, desto mehr Möglichkeiten eröffnen sich dir beim Schreiben deiner eignene Texte. Lies die folgenden Tipps aufmerksam durch, bevor du mit dem Schreiben beginnst:

Adjektive und Adverbien *(adjectives and adverbs)* ▶ **G13** Adjectives and adverbs
Du kannst deine Sätze interessanter gestalten, indem du z. B. Nomen durch Adjektive näher beschreibst. Verben kannst du durch Adverbien oder adverbiale Bestimmungen ergänzen. Vergleiche:

A I went to the shop.
B I went to the big pet shop with my sister last Saturday.

Achte darauf, dass du Adjektive wie *good*, *bad*, *nice* und *big* nicht zu häufig verwendest. In der Tabelle findest du Beispiele für Adjektive, die du stattdessen verwenden kannst:

good	amazing, awesome, beautiful, brilliant, exciting, fantastic, fascinating, great, interesting, spectacular, wonderful
bad	awful, boring, terrible
nice	amazing, beautiful, fascinating, interesting, lovely, pretty, wonderful
big	gigantic, great, huge, large, wide

Konjunktionen *(conjunctions)* ▶ **G20** Conjunctions and adverbial clauses
Ein Text liest sich leichter, wenn die Sätze darin miteinander verknüpft sind. Mit Hilfe von Konjunktionen werden logische Zusammenhänge hergestellt. Vergleiche die beiden folgenden Textausschnitte. Der erste wirkt durch die unverbundenen Hauptsätze abgehackt. Der zweite liest sich durch Satzgefüge aus Haupt- und Nebensätzen und durch Konjunktionen flüssiger. Außerdem geben die vielen Adjektive und Adverbien genauere Informationen und machen den Text interessanter.

S Skills

A I went to the shop. I wanted a guinea pig. We looked at all the guinea pigs. I didn't like them. We wanted to leave. A girl came in with a box. She brought back a guinea pig. It was cute!

B I went to the large pet shop with my sister last Saturday because I wanted to buy a pretty guinea pig. We looked at all the guinea pigs, but I didn't like them. Just when I wanted to leave, a girl came in with a box. She brought back a guinea pig which was really cute.

Zeitangaben (time markers)

Adverbiale Bestimmungen der Zeit können dem Leser / der Leserin helfen, sich in einem Text oder einer Geschichte zeitlich zurechtzufinden. Du kannst *time markers* unterschiedlich einsetzen:

- um die Ereignisse zeitlich einzuordnen: *two years ago, last summer, when I came home yesterday, …*
- um zu zeigen, in welcher Reihenfolge sie passieren: *at first, next, finally, …*
- um zu verdeutlichen, wie viel Zeit zwischen den Ereignissen vergeht: *for two hours, just five minutes later, …*
- um auszudrücken, wie schnell oder langsam etwas passiert: *immediately, quickly, it took hours, …*
- um zu sagen, dass mehrere Ereignisse zeitgleich passieren: *while I was waiting, during lunch, …*

S17 Mediation Sprache mitteln

Sprache mitteln (*mediation*) bedeutet, dass Sie wichtige Informationen von einer Sprache in eine andere übertragen, z. B. vom Englischen ins Deutsche oder umgekehrt. Manchmal kann es auch sein, dass Sie zwischen Gesprächspartnern mitteln. Dabei geht es nicht um eine wörtliche Übersetzung, sondern darum, nur die wichtigen Informationen weiterzugeben.
Beachten Sie dabei folgende Punkte:

Adressat

- Lesen Sie die Arbeitsanweisung aufmerksam durch und finden Sie heraus, an wen Sie die Information mitteln sollen.
- Überlegen Sie: Was weiß der Adressat, was nicht? Welche Informationen braucht er oder sie? Wozu?
- Geben Sie nur die Informationen weiter, die für den Adressaten wichtig sind.
- Mitteln Sie die Informationen so, dass der Adressat sie gut verstehen kann. Bilden Sie kurze Sätze.

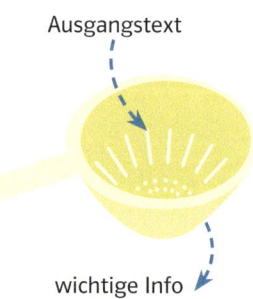

Ausgangstext

wichtige Info

Paraphrasieren

Wenn Sie die genaue Übersetzung für ein Wort nicht kennen, umschreiben Sie es mit anderen Worten.
Beispiel: Gewerkschaft → an organisation of workers

Text in eigenen Worten zusammenfassen

Übersetzen Sie den Ausgangstext nicht Wort für Wort (*translation*). Geben Sie nur die wichtigen Informationen sinngemäß und in Ihren eigenen Worten wieder (*summarising*).

Beispiel

Ihr Freund Hamza sucht nach einem Ferienjob im Ausland. Er hat nicht viel Geld, will aber Urlaub machen. Er ist gerne in der Natur und kann gut mit Menschen umgehen. Online haben Sie die Stellenanzeige auf der nächsten Seite gefunden. Beschreiben Sie ihm den Job in drei bis vier Sätzen. Sagen Sie, warum der Job zu ihm passt.

Skills **S**

ISLAND CARETAKER

Swedish Tourism is looking for Island Caretakers. Do you like to be outside a lot? Are you friendly and outgoing? Then come to Sweden! We are looking for helpers to join us on our little island this summer: you will clean the beaches and help tourists. In return, you will get free bed and board in a cosy cabin by the lake. We will also pay for your flight to the island. To apply, send an email and your CV to Ruby from Swedish Tourism: ruby@swedish_island…se

Lösung

Passen Sie den Stil der Sprache so an, dass er zu Ihrem Adressaten passt. → „**Du suchst doch** nach einem Ferienjob im Ausland, oder? Ich hab da was für dich gefunden: In Schweden werden Leute gesucht, die sich im Sommer um eine Insel in der Nähe von Stockholm kümmern. Du müsstest helfen, den Strand zu säubern und dich um Touristen kümmern. Voraussetzung ist, dass man gern draußen, freundlich und aufgeschlossen ist – das bist du! Und das Beste ist, dass du dort in einer Hütte am See **kostenlos** übernachten und essen kannst und sie für deinen Flug zahlen. Ich glaube, der Job passt perfekt zu dir."

Umschreiben Sie schwierige Wörter.

S18 Sprechen Speaking

In Kommunikationsprüfungen werden Sie oft gebeten, spontan für ein paar Minuten über ein Thema aus Ihrem Alltag zu reden. Die folgenden Redemittel können Ihnen helfen, über Ihre Vorlieben, Meinung, Erfahrungen und Zukunftspläne zu sprechen.

1. Monologisches Sprechen

- über Vorlieben sprechen

  V | In my free time, I like to …. | I enjoy …. | I love …. | One of my favourite things is …. | I'm very passionate/excited about …. | My hobby is ….

- die eigene Meinung sagen

  In my opinion …. | I think …. | I would/wouldn't …. | I'm (not) sure if …. | If you ask me ….

- über Erfahrungen sprechen

  In my experience …. | Last year/month I …. | I have made the experience that …. | Usually,/Normally, …. | A lot of times …. | I've often seen that ….

- über Zukunftspläne sprechen

  In ten years, I want to be/have …. | It's my dream to … one day. | I'm going to … next year. | I hope/I'm sure I will …. | I would like to …. | I have plans to ….

2. Dialogisches Sprechen

Ein weiterer Teil der Kommunikationsprüfung ist ein Dialog (z. B. ein Gespräch, eine Diskussion oder ein Rollenspiel) mit einem Gesprächspartner / einer Gesprächspartnerin.

1. **Vorbereitung (ca. 10 Minuten)**
- Machen Sie sich zunächst Notizen: Was wird von Ihnen inhaltlich erwartet? Notieren Sie wichtige Schlüsselwörter, Beispiele, Erklärungen und hilfreiche Redemittel.

Skills

- Achten Sie auf den Kontext des Gesprächs: in einem Vorstellungsgespräch oder im Gespräch mit Älteren sollten Sie sich formell ausdrücken; in einem Gespräch unter Gleichaltrigen, verwenden Sie hingegen Umgangssprache.

2. **Während des Gesprächs (ca. 8 Minuten)**
- Hören Sie Ihrem Partner / Ihrer Partnerin aufmerksam zu und gehen Sie auf die andere Person in Ihren Antworten ein, z. B. indem Sie zustimmen oder ein Gegenargument einbringen.
- Stellen Sie Fragen, wenn Sie etwas nicht verstanden haben.
- Bleiben Sie höflich.
- Achten Sie darauf, dass beide Gesprächspartner/Gesprächspartnerinnen zu Wort kommen.

3. **Hilfreiche Redemittel**

Ein Gespräch beginnen:

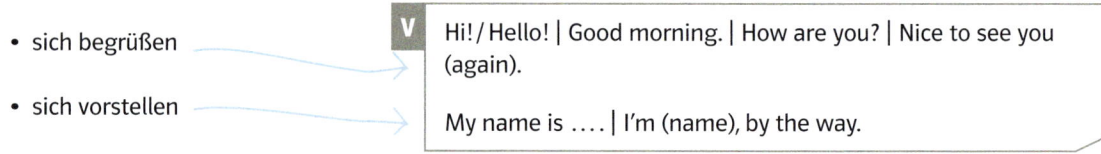

- sich begrüßen — Hi! / Hello! | Good morning. | How are you? | Nice to see you (again).
- sich vorstellen — My name is …. | I'm (name), by the way.

Ein Gespräch am Laufen halten:

- Fragen stellen — Did you know that …? | How do you like …? | What do you think about …? | Could I ask a question, please? | Could you tell me about …, please?
- Interesse zeigen — I see. | Of course. | That sounds interesting. | Could you tell me more, please? | I can imagine that. | I know what you mean.
- höflich und taktvoll sein — …, please | Thank you. | You're welcome. | Excuse me, but … | May I …? | Would you …? | I'd like …. | Yes, that's true but …. | Not exactly.
- nachfragen — Excuse me, could you say that again, please? | I'm sorry, but I didn't get that. | Could you explain that again, please? | I'm sorry, but I'm not sure what you mean.
- zustimmen — I agree. | You're right. | Absolutely. | That's a good idea/point.
- ablehnen — I'm happy that …. | I'm worried about …. | Oh no! | What a shame! | How funny! | That's nice! | Really? | That's surprising! | I wouldn't have thought that! | Gosh!
- Gefühle/Erstaunen ausdrücken — I'm sorry, but I don't think so. In my opinion …. | This is true, but …. | I see what you mean, but …. | Well, I'm not sure about that.
- unterbrechen und unterbrochen werden — Sorry for interrupting, but …. | Could I just say something here? | Just a second, please, I haven't quite finished.
- auf Zeit spielen — Well, I don't know. | Er, I'm not sure about that. | Let me think for a moment. | That's a very good question.

Ein Gespräch beenden:

- sich bedanken und verabschieden

> **V** Well, I think that's everything. | It was nice talking to you! | Thank you for your time. | Take care. | Goodbye. | Bye. | See you!

3. Gespräche zwischen mehreren Personen

1. Ein Rollenspiel durchführen

In einem Rollenspiel setzen Sie sich mit Lebenssituationen, die nicht unbedingt Ihren eigenen entsprechen, spielerisch auseinander. Indem Sie verschiedene Perspektiven einnehmen, werden Ihnen alternative Handlungsmöglichkeiten aufgezeigt, Sie können über eigene Einstellungen nachdenken und sich in andere Menschen hineinversetzen (Empathie).

Erarbeitungsphase
- Bereiten Sie Ihre Rolle vor, indem Sie sich Notizen zur Ihrer Rolle machen. Machen Sie sich dabei auch Gedanken über die beschriebene Situation und den Handlungsort.
- Überlegen Sie sich welche unterschiedlichen Stimmlagen, Gesichtsausdrücke und Körperhaltungen Ihrer Rolle und der Situation entsprechen.
- Überlegen Sie vorab, was Ihr Partner / Ihre Partnerin im Rollenspiel sagen könnte, sodass Sie angemessen darauf reagieren können.

Durchführung
- Sprechen Sie nicht zu schnell und nicht zu leise.
- Passen Sie Ihre Stimmlage, Gesichtsausdrücke und Körperhaltungen an die Situation des Rollenspiels an.
- Versuchen Sie auf Ihr Gegenüber angemessen zu reagieren und einzugehen. So wird das Rollenspiel lebendiger und interessanter.

2. Eine Diskussion/Debatte führen ▶ V8 Discussion

Im Mittelpunkt einer Diskussion steht ein Streitthema.

- Machen Sie sich zunächst Notizen zum eigenen Standpunkt (Argumente und Beispiele).
- Strukturieren Sie Ihre Argumente und Beispiele, z. B. vom schwächstem zu stärkstem Argument.
- Überlegen Sie vorab, welche Gegenargumente in der Diskussion aufkommen könnten und wie Sie darauf reagieren können.
- Wenn die Diskussion mit mehr als zwei Gesprächspartnern/Gesprächspartnerinnen stattfinden soll, bestimmen Sie eine Diskussionsleitung: Sie eröffnet und beendet die Diskussion. Sie achtet darauf, dass die Regeln eingehalten werden und dass alle zu Wort kommen.
- Wählen Sie gegebenenfalls eine Sitzordnung, bei der sich alle Gesprächspartner/Gesprächspartnerinnen gegenseitig anschauen können.
- Versuchen Sie während der Diskussion, die andere Seite mit Argumenten zu überzeugen.
- Gehen Sie auf die andere Seite ein und widerlegen Sie deren Argumente.
- Beachten Sie die Diskussionsregeln: andere ausreden lassen; höflich und sachlich sein; beim Thema bleiben.

S Skills

S19 Wortarten erkennen und bilden
Recognising and forming parts of speech

Um in Prüfungsaufgaben Lücken in Texten korrekt zu ergänzen, müssen Sie in der Lage sein, Wortarten (*parts of speech*) zu erkennen und zu bilden (z. B. *noun* → *verb*). Dazu ist es hilfreich, Wörter in ihren Wortfamilien (*word families*) zu lernen und grundlegende Regeln zur Wortstellung in Sätzen zu kennen.

1. Wortarten erkennen

Wortarten sind die „Bausteine" einer Sprache, um Sätze zu bilden. Die wichtigsten Wortarten sind:

noun	Hauptwort/Nomen	book, Sam, girl, parents
verb	Tunwort/Verb	go, eat, feel, think
adjective	Wie-Wort/Adjektiv	small, intelligent, blue
adverb	Umstandswort/Adverb	slowly, yesterday, always
preposition	Verhältniswort/Präposition	next to, on, over , in, until
pronoun	Fürwort/Pronomen	he, them, yourselves, ones
article, determiner	Artikel, Begleiter	the, a, an, this, those
conjunction	Konjunktion	and, but, when, although
quantifier	Mengenbezeichnung	some, any, a couple of

1. Nomen
Die Endung der Nomen zeigt an, ob das Nomen im Singular (z. B. *house*) oder im Plural (z. B. *houses*) steht. Wiederholen Sie die Regeln der Pluralbildung (▶ **G22** Plural).
Zudem ist es wichtig zu wissen, wann Nomen mit oder ohne Artikel verwendet werden und ob ein bestimmter oder unbestimmter Artikel verwendet wird. (▶ **G17** Articles).

2. Verben
Die Form des Verbes ist abhängig von der Singular- oder Pluralform des Nomens. Sie sollten die verschiedenen Zeitformen, sowie die Modalverben und das Passiv wiederholen und üben:
▶ **G1, G5, G6, G11** Tenses; **G2** Modals; **G4, G12** Passive voice I & II

3. Adjektive und Adverbien
Adjektive beschreiben, wie etwas ist und beziehen sich auf Nomen (z. B. *an **interesting** job*). Adverbien beschreiben, wie etwas getan wird und beziehen sich auf Verben (z. B. *She **quickly** ran home.*).
Wiederholen Sie die Steigerungsformen von Adjektiven (▶ **G8** Comparison of adjectives), die Unterschiede zwischen Adjektiven und Adverbien (▶ **G13** Adjectives and adverbs) und die Reihenfolge von Adverbien im Satz (▶ **G19** Adverbs and sequence of adverbs).

4. Präpositionen
Präpositionen drücken das Verhältnis zwischen Personen und Dingen aus (z. B. *He sat **on** the chair.*). Achten Sie darauf, dass manche Verben fest mit einer Präposition verbunden sind (*phrasal verbs*). Diese sollten Sie beim Vokabellernen auswendig lernen (z. B. *look up / look at*).
▶ **G15** Prepositions

Skills **S**

5. Pronomen
Pronomen ersetzen oder beziehen sich auf Nomen. Lernen Sie die unterschiedlichen Pronomen und ihre Funktionen im Satz. ▶ **G14** Pronouns

6. Artikel
Artikel stehen vor Nomen und Adjektiven. In manchen Fällen werden Artikel im Englischen anders als im Deutschen verwendet. Machen Sie sich mit den Regeln und Ausnahmen zur Verwendung von Artikeln vertraut. ▶ **G17** Articles

7. Konjunktionen
Konjunktionen leiten einzelne Sätze in Satzverbindungen ein. Wiederholen Sie, welche Konjunktionen Haupt- oder Nebensätze einleiten. ▶ **G20** Conjunctions and adverbial phrases

8. Mengenbezeichnungen
Um über Mengen zu sprechen, können Sie Zahlwörter oder Ausdrücke wie z. B. *some*, *much/many*, *a couple of* verwenden. Eine Übersicht finden Sie hier: ▶ **G22** Quantifiers

2. Wortstellung

Achten Sie beim Einsetzen verschiedener Wortarten in einen Lückentext auf die Position und die umgebenden Wörter:
- Vor einem Nomen steht meist ein Artikel oder ein Adjektiv.
- Ein Adjektiv bezieht sich immer auf ein Nomen oder Pronomen.
- Jeder Satz verfügt über ein Verb.
- Die allgemeine Regel der Wortstellung ist **S-V-O**: *subject – verb – object*. ▶ **G18** Word order
- Kommen mehrere Adverbien im Satz vor, stehen diese oft in folgender Reihenfolge: *manner – place – time*. ▶ **G19** Adverbs and sequence of adverbs

3. Wortbildung

In manchen Aufgaben müssen Sie die Wortart verändern, indem Sie z. B. aus dem Verb (*to sing*) ein Nomen (*singer*) bilden. Um aus vorhandenen Wörtern neue Wörter zu bilden, hängen Sie oft Vor- oder Nachsilben an ein Wort an.

1. Vorsilben
Vorsilben können vor Verben, Nomen und Adjektive gesetzt werden, um deren Bedeutung zu verändern.

Vorsible	Bedeutung	Beispiel	Übersetzung
dis- in- /im- ir-	nicht, Gegenteil von nicht, nicht, Gegenteil von Gegenteil von	disagree impatient irresponsible	nicht übereinstimmen ungeduldig unverantwortlich
mis-	falsch	misinterpretation	Fehlinterpretation
pre-	vor	prehistoric	vorgeschichtlich
re-	nochmals, zurück	reuse	nochmal benutzen
un-	nicht, Gegenteil von, rückgängig machen	unbelievable unlock	unglaublich aufschließen

Skills

2. Nachsilben

Nachsilben können an Verben, Nomen und Adjektive angehängt werden, um deren Bedeutung zu verändern. Hierbei verändert sich die Wortart.

Nachsilbe	Veränderung der Wortart	Beispiel
-er -or -ing -ment -ion -ation	Verb → Nomen	sing → singer act → actor end → ending employ → employment express → expression organize → organization
-ing -ed -ive -able -y	Verb → Adjektiv	care → caring educate → educated create → creative recommend → recommendable rain → rainy
-ness -(i)ty -ence	Adjektiv → Nomen	happy → happiness certain → certainty different → difference
-ous -al -ful	Nomen → Adjektiv	glory → glorious fiction → fictional beauty → beautiful
-en -ize -ify	Adjektiv → Verb	short → shorten special → specialize simple → simplify
-ly -ally	Adjektiv → Aderb	quick → quickly democratic → democratically

4. Wortfamilien

Es kann hilfreich sein, beim Vokabellernen Wortfamilien (*word families*) anzulegen. Erstellen Sie dazu eine Tabelle mit den unterschiedlichen Wortarten. Nutzen Sie auch ein Wörterbuch, um weitere Wörter in der Wortfamilie zu finden. ▶ **S7** Sammeln und ordnen

noun	verb	adjective	adverb
beauty	to beautify	beautiful	beautifully
agreement	to agree ↔ to disagree	agreeable	/
knowledge	to know	knowing	knowingly
possibility	/	possible ↔ impossible	possibly

S20 Eine Bewerbung schreiben — Writing a letter of application

Für ein Bewerbungsschreiben gelten die Regeln, die man von formellen Briefen kennt (z. B. Briefkopf, Betreffzeile) – aber natürlich kommen noch ein paar Besonderheiten dazu.

▶ V14 Writing an application

① Briefkopf
Eigene Adresse
Adresse des Empfängers
Datum

② Betreffzeile

③ Anrede

④ Erster Abschnitt:
- Sagen Sie, auf welche Stelle Sie sich bewerben.
- Erwähnen Sie, wie/wo Sie von dieser Stelle erfahren haben.

⑤ Zweiter Abschnitt:
- Zählen Sie Qualifikationen und Ihre Erfahrungen auf, die für diese Stelle relevant sind.
- Nennen Sie Ihre persönlichen Stärken.
- Sagen Sie, dass Sie in der Lage sind, die neuen Aufgaben gut zu erfüllen.
- Sagen Sie, warum Sie die richtige Person für die Stelle sind.
- Erklären Sie, warum Sie an der Stelle interessiert sind.

⑥ Schluss:
- Sagen Sie, dass Sie sich auf eine Antwort und die Einladung zu einem Vorstellungsgespräch freuen.

⑦ Grußformel

⑧ Verweis auf Anhang

---

① Hanna Fischer
Kartöfflestr. 123
50162 Köln
Germany

① Ms Juliane Reed
Train Travels UK
15 Handforth Road
London
SE34 7GH

① 6th April 2021

② Re: Your job advertisement of March 2021

③ Dear Ms Reed,

④ Please find attached my application for the job as a trainee team assistant with Train Travels UK as advertised in Rail Magazine in March 2021.

⑤ I am 18 years old and I am doing a business course at a vocational college in Cologne. I will finish in June this year.
As you can see from my CV I have work experience as a sales assistant in a wine shop. I have worked there at weekends since last summer. I can deal with customers politely and efficiently.
The shop is busy and the hours are very long so I have learned to work well under pressure. I am good at English and German.
The job that you are offering would give me the chance to get more work experience in a lively and international working environment

⑥ I can attend a job interview at any time. Thank you for taking the time to consider this application. I look forward to hearing from you.

⑦ Yours sincerely,
Hanna Fischer
Hanna Fischer

⑧ Encl.: CV

V Dear Sir or Madam | To whom it may concern | I would like to apply for the job as … | I am very interested in your position as … | I read your advertisement for … in / on … | I refer to your advertisement in / on …
I qualify well for the position because … | My skills and experience qualify me well for the job …
I have a part-time job as … | I have work experience as … | Although I have no previous experience, …
I am very interested in this job because … | I would like to work for you because …
Please find my CV attached.

S Skills

S21 Einen Lebenslauf schreiben Writing a CV

Hier finden Sie ein Beispiel für einen Lebenslauf, wie er in Großbritannien geschrieben wird. Es gibt Unterschiede zwischen deutschen, britischen und amerikanischen Lebensläufen.

▶ V13 Writing a CV

① Persönliche Daten
- Name, Adresse, Telefonnummer, E-Mail
- Sie können Ihr Geburtsdatum angeben, müssen aber nicht.

② Persönliches Statement
- Beschreiben Sie sich kurz.
- Was ist Ihre Motivation?

③ Schulbildung
- Grundschule
- Weiterführende Schule (bei beiden: Name und Ort + Angabe der Jahreszahlen von – bis

④ Prüfungen/Abschlüsse
- Name und Jahr der Prüfung und/oder des Abschlusses

⑤ Kenntnisse
- Ihre Stärken und Fähigkeiten, z. B. computer, language usw …

⑥ Berufliche Erfahrungen
- Praktika und Jobs, die Sie gemacht haben: Was? Wo? Wann?

⑦ Interessen
- Hobbys, Sport, Ehrenamt usw. …

⑧ Referenzen
- Arbeitszeugnisse oder Empfehlungen

---

① Name: Hanna Fischer
Address: Kartöfflestraße 123, 50162 Köln, Germany
Phone: + 49 123 456 7890
Email: fischer_h@online.de
Date of birth: 12th August 2002

② A positive team player who is interested in travelling and being there for people.

③ Education:
2019 – now:	Berufsfachschule für Informatik (vocational college, IT course), Cologne
2013 – 2019:	Schloss-Realschule (comprehensive school), Cologne
2009 – 2013:	Fuchsweg-Schule (primary school), Cologne

④ Qualifications:
2019: Mittlerer Schulabschluss (secondary school leaving certificate), with special interest in English and geography

⑤ Skills:
Very good communication skills and excellent team worker.
Fluent English.

⑥ Experience:
2020 – now: Sales assistant in a wine shop, Cologne
April 2019: Volunteer at a soup kitchen, London (UK)

⑦ Interests:
Travelling and learning about other cultures - trips to the UK, North Africa and Thailand

⑧ References:
Available upon request.

S22 Ein Interview führen — Doing an interview

Um ein Interview zu führen, müssen Sie sich gut vorbereiten und Informationen über die Person bzw. das Thema recherchieren. So können Sie leichter Fragen stellen, das Gespräch steuern und ein interessantes Interview gestalten.

1. Recherche

Finden Sie Informationen zu dem Thema oder der Person, die Sie interviewen. Wenn Sie ein Interview über das Leben / die Erfahrungen einer Person führen, sollten Sie vorab Informationen zu den folgenden Aspekten recherchieren:

- Alter
- Familiärer Hintergrund / Familie
- Ausbildung und Karriere
- Besondere Ereignisse im Leben der Person
- Interessante Hobbies oder Interessen
- Engagement (Politik, Umwelt, etc.)

▶ **S1** Informationen beschaffen

2. Vorbereitung

- Notieren Sie sich vorab Fragen, die Sie stellen möchten. Stellen Sie möglichst keine Entscheidungsfragen (Ja/Nein-Fragen), sondern offene Fragen, sodass Ihr Interviewpartner / Ihre Interviewpartnerin ausführlich antworten kann.
- In welcher Reihenfolge möchten Sie Ihre Fragen stellen (z. B. chronologisch nach Lebensabschnitten oder nach Themen)? Ihr Interview sollte idealerweise so gestaltet sein, dass sich ein natürliches Gespräch entwickelt.
- Welche Aspekte sind besonders interessant für Zuhörer/Zuhörerinnen oder Leser/Leserinnen?
- Wie reagieren Sie, wenn Ihr Gesprächspartner nicht auf eine Frage antworten möchte? Notieren Sie sich hilfreiche Redemittel, um schnell reagieren zu können.

> **V** Who do you …? | What have you …? | Where/When did you …? | Why …? | How …? | Can you tell me …? | Can you remember? | Have you ever …? | Is it true that …? | Please, tell us about … | Would you explain why/how …? | What is your opinion on …? | Do you think people should …?

3. Durchführung

- Begrüßen Sie Ihren Interviewpartner / Ihre Interviewpartnerin und bedanken Sie sich für die Gelegenheit, ein Gespräch zu führen.
- Wenn Sie das Gespräch aufnehmen möchten, fragen Sie Ihren Interviewpartner / Ihre Interviewpartnerin um Erlaubnis.
- Seien Sie höflich, wenn Sie Ihre Fragen stellen. Sprechen Sie klar und deutlich. Halten Sie Blickkontakt.
- Hören Sie aufmerksam zu, wenn Ihr Interviewpartner / Ihre Interviewpartnerin antwortet. Gehen Sie auf die Antworten ein und stellen Sie vertiefende Fragen oder wiederholen Sie das Gesagte in ihren eigenen Worten, um sicherzustellen, dass Sie es richtig verstanden haben.
- Bedanken Sie sich zum Abschluss des Gesprächs und sagen Sie, was Ihnen an dem Gespräch gut gefallen hat, was Sie gelernt haben oder was für Sie besonders interessant war.

> **V** Good morning / afternoon. | My name is …. | Thank you for doing this interview with me today. | I'm excited to do this interview with you today.

> **V** Do you mind if I record our conversation? | It's easier to record your answers than to take notes while we are talking.

> **V** Thank you very much …. | That was very interesting. | I enjoyed learning about …. | I was surprised to hear that …. | Thank you for your time.

G Grammar

G1 Simple present / Present progressive

Die einfache Form der Gegenwart / Die Verlaufsform der Gegenwart

GV1
GV2

1 Das *simple present* verwenden Sie:

→ um zu sagen, was jemand immer oder regelmäßig macht / nicht macht.
→ um Tatsachen auszudrücken.
→ um in Fotos oder Szenen Gegenstände zu beschreiben und Ortsangaben zu machen.

Many people **spend** their free time online.	Viele Menschen **verbringen** ihre Freizeit online.
A casino owner usually **makes** a lot of money.	Ein Casinobesitzer **verdient** gewöhnlich viel Geld.
You **don't see** the dangers of gambling.	Du **siehst** die Gefahren vom Glücksspiel **nicht**.
She **doesn't understand** the problem.	Sie **versteht** das Problem **nicht**.
Gambling **is** dangerous.	Glücksspiel **ist** gefährlich.

Signalwörter:
always immer | **usually** gewöhnlich | **often** oft | **sometimes** manchmal | **never** nie | **on Mondays** montags | **every day** jeden Tag

2 So können Sie Fragen im *simple present* stellen:

Do they always **need** help?	**Brauchen** sie immer Hilfe?
Does the casino **open** at 8 p.m.?	**Macht** das Casino abends um acht **auf**?
Where **does** all the money **come** from?	Wo **kommt** all das Geld her?
When **do** most people **play** online games?	Wann **spielen** die meisten Menschen Onlinespiele?
Can we start the meeting at 9 a.m.?	**Können** wir mit dem Treffen um 9 Uhr beginnen?

Fragewörter:
what was | **when** wann | **where** wo | **who** wer | **why** warum | **how** wie

3 So stellen Sie Fragen mit dem Verb *to be*:

Are the tickets expensive?	**Sind** die Eintrittskarten teuer?
Is he the boss?	**Ist** er der Chef?

Grammar G

4 Das *present progressive* verwenden Sie:

→ um zu sagen, was jetzt gerade passiert bzw. nicht passiert.
→ um Handlungen und Ereignisse in Fotos oder Szenen zu beschreiben.

At the moment we're gambling at the poker table.	Im Moment spielen wir am Pokertisch.
I'm doing this now, not later.	Ich mache das jetzt, nicht später.
The guests aren't listening.	Die Gäste hören (jetzt gerade) nicht zu.

Signalwörter:
right now jetzt/nun | just gerade | at the moment im Moment

5 So können Sie Fragen im *present progressive* stellen:

Are you taking the money to the bank now?	Bringst du das Geld jetzt zur Bank?
Is Jay asking for the way to the casino now?	Fragt Jay jetzt nach dem Weg zum Casino?
What is he looking for?	Was sucht er (gerade)?

6 Complete the exercises. Check your answers on page 190.

a) Complete the sentences with the simple present.
  1. The chart ■ (show) the number of people who gamble regularly.
  2. The numbers ■ (not tell) how many people are addicted.
  3. It ■ (be) dangerous to think that it's easy to quit.
  4. ■ she never ■ (read) the newspaper?
  5. What ■ you ■ (do) when you're in trouble?

b) Make sentences with the present progressive.
  1. checking | now | more | the website | for | information | He's
  2. programmes | a lot of | today | They're | offering
  3. to go | she | online | isn't | At the moment | trying
  4. new game | playing | I'm | this | just
  5. the doctors | What | in this interview | are | now? | saying

c) Complete the sentences with the simple present or the present progressive.
  1. Right now all casinos ■ (close) but they ■ (be) usually open seven days a week.
  2. They always ■ (play) tricks on people but at the moment they ■ (not work).
  3. The managers never ■ (tell) their secrets but today one of them ■ (tell) the truth.
  4. I ■ (not watch) the news now. I often ■ (feel) bad afterwards.
  5. At the moment the family ■ (leave) the house. But where ■ they ■ (go) every day?
  6. ■ he really ■ (call) the police now? He always ■ (make) trouble.

G   Grammar

G2   Modals   Modalverben

1 So drücken Sie aus, was jemand machen kann (*can*) / nicht machen kann (*can't*):

Can you check the website again?	**Kannst** du die Webseite noch einmal prüfen?
He **can't** just hang around.	Er **kann nicht** einfach nur rumhängen.
Could you please wear a hat in the sun?	**Könntest** du bitte einen Hut in der Sonne tragen?

> 🏁 In englischsprachigen Ländern ist Höflichkeit sehr wichtig.
> Verwenden Sie immer die höflichere Form „could":
> *Could you help me, please?*
> *Könntest du mir bitte helfen?*

Denken Sie daran:
Can und **can't** können im Gegensatz zu den anderen Modalverben auch im *simple past* benutzt werden:
can → could; can't → couldn't

2 So drücken Sie aus, was jemand tun muss (*must* / *have to*) / nicht tun muss (*don't have to*):

She **must** decide quickly.	Sie **muss** sich schnell entscheiden.
You **don't have to** do it.	Ihr **müsst** das **nicht** machen.

Denken Sie daran:
mustn't = nicht dürfen
Statt **must** können Sie auch **have to / has to** verwenden. So können Sie auch ausdrücken, was jemand in der Vergangenheit tun / nicht tun musste: **had to / didn't have to**.

3 So drücken Sie aus, dass etwas nicht notwendig ist (*needn't*):

You **needn't** buy any more plastic water bottles. We have a reusable bottle now.	Du **brauchst nicht** noch mehr Wasser in Plastikflaschen zu kaufen. Wir haben jetzt eine wiederverwendbare Flasche.
They **needn't** travel far. It's fun at home too.	Sie **müssen nicht** weit reisen. Zu Hause macht es auch Spaß.

4 So drücken Sie aus, was jemand tun sollte (*should*) / nicht tun sollte (*shouldn't*):

I **should** buy more green products.	Ich **sollte** mehr umweltfreundliche Produkte kaufen.
They **shouldn't** drive everywhere by car.	Sie **sollten nicht** überall mit dem Auto hinfahren.

5 So bieten Sie jemandem etwas an, erfragen Wünsche oder machen Vorschläge (*shall*):

Shall we go by car or by bus?	**Sollen** wir mit dem Auto oder mit dem Bus fahren?
Shall I answer the comment?	**Soll** ich den Kommentar beantworten?

Grammar G

6 Complete the exercises. Check your answers on page 190.

a) Match the sentences.

1 It's better to get there early.
2 We used to travel a lot.
3 It's cold in here with all the windows open.
4 They needn't pay more money this year.
5 You mustn't post all your pictures online.
6 I think it's a good idea.

A It is still the same price.
B Shall we go then?
C But this year we had to stay at home.
D What if your boss sees them?
E So we shouldn't be late.
F Could you shut them, please?

b) Complete the sentences with the correct modal.

1. We **can / shouldn't** book this place. It's too expensive.
2. I **had to / could** check the hotel's website tomorrow.
3. It **shall / doesn't have to** be a hotel. What about a hostel?
4. You **needn't / mustn't** bring your own towels. They're included.
5. What **shall / must** I say? I don't think it's OK.

c) Translate the sentences into English.

1. Wir sollten mehr Energie sparen.
2. Du kannst helfen, die Natur zu schützen.
3. Soll er euch ein Hotel empfehlen?
4. Ihr dürft das Zimmer jetzt nicht betreten.
5. Könnten bitte alle leise sein?

G3 Relative clauses Relativsätze

1 So können Sie eine Person oder eine Sache näher beschreiben:

Tina is the one **who/that** writes a blog about her home town.	Tina ist diejenige, **die** einen Blog über ihre Heimatstadt schreibt.
Jamaica is the country **which/that** produces cocoa, sugar and coffee.	Jamaika ist das Land, **das** Kakao, Zucker und Kaffee produziert.

→ Folgt nach **who**, **which** oder **that** ein Personalpronomen (**I, you, he/she/it, we, they**) oder eine **Person**, können Sie das Relativpronomen weglassen. Diesen Satz nennt man **contact clause**.

The recipe **(which)** you sent me was easy.	Das Rezept, **das du** mir geschickt hast, war einfach.
The man **(who)** we met in the shop was friendly.	Der Mann, **den wir** im Laden getroffen haben, war freundlich.

Denken Sie daran:
I saw a postcard **which (that)** had a picture of a beach on it.
→ Dieser Relativsatz ist notwendig (*defining*). Der Hauptsatz ergibt ohne ihn keinen Sinn.
  Also: Keine Kommas! Hier können Sie **which** (oder **who**) durch **that** ersetzen.

The singer, **who** was very good, played a lot of songs.
→ Dieser Relativsatz ist nicht für das Verständnis notwendig (*non-defining*). Er enthält zusätzliche Informationen. Deshalb stehen Kommas. **Who** (oder **which**) kann **nicht** durch **that** ersetzt werden.

G Grammar

2 So können Sie Besitz und Zugehörigkeit ausdrücken:

Tina is a blogger **whose** blog is successful.	Tina ist eine Bloggerin, **deren** Blog erfolgreich ist.
That's Marlow **whose** parents are from Jamaica too.	Das ist Marlow, **dessen** Eltern auch aus Jamaika kommen.

3 Complete the exercises. Check your answers on page 190.

a) Complete the sentences with *who* or *which*.

1. A blogger is a person ■ writes about interesting things online.
2. Tina wrote a blog entry about her favourite places, ■ many people liked.
3. The women ■ sell fruit at the market like to chat with their customers.
4. Most tourists ■ come to Jamaica enjoy the great food.
5. The recipe ■ I was looking for wasn't online any more.

b) Complete the relative clauses. Use *who* or *whose*.

1. A Rastafarian is someone ■ often has a special hairstyle called dreadlocks.
2. Jamaicans, ■ country is beautiful, are very proud people.
3. There are many people ■ work in tourism.
4. Most tourists ■ want to go to Jamaica on holiday go from December to April.
5. Usain Bolt, ■ name every Jamaican knows, won eight Olympic medals.

c) Make one sentence from two. Use *who*, *which* or *whose*.

1. Tina likes her home. It's not far away from her parents'.
2. She often visits her parents. Their house is only five minutes away.
3. Their dog Tabby is a Golden Retriever. She likes to play in the garden.
4. The family enjoys BBQs. They all love them.
5. Her home town is very important to Tina. She couldn't imagine living anywhere else.

G4 Passive voice I (simple present) Das Passiv I (einfache Gegenwart)

GV20

1 Das Passiv verwenden Sie:

→ um zu betonen, *was* gemacht wird und nicht, *wer* etwas tut.

History **is written** by many people.	Die Geschichte **wird** von vielen Menschen **geschrieben**.
Many goods **are imported**.	Viele Waren **werden importiert**.

Die Passivform eines Verbs bildet man mit dem Hilfsverb **to be** und dem **Partizip Perfekt** (3. Form des Verbs).

Denken Sie daran:
Die handelnden Personen oder Verursacher müssen in einem Passivsatz nicht immer genannt werden. Oft sind die Personen oder Verursacher unwichtig oder unbekannt. Wenn sie doch genannt werden sollen, dann werden sie mit **by** angehängt.

Grammar G

2 Complete the exercises. Check your answers on page 190.

a) Complete the sentences with *is* or *are*.

1. English and Patois ■ spoken in Jamaica.
2. Jamaica ■ seen as the perfect place for holidays by many people.
3. Kingston ■ visited by most tourists between December and April.
4. A lot of things ■ produced in Jamaica.
5. Not all places ■ shown to tourists because many people are poor.

b) Complete the sentences.

1. Jamaica's independence day ■ (celebrate) on 6 August.
2. Big parties ■ (organise) on that day.
3. Music ■ (play) everywhere.
4. Food and drinks ■ (sell) in bars and restaurants.
5. Flags ■ (raise) all over the country.

c) Change these sentences from passive to active.

1. Songs are practised by the people in church.
2. Music is made by young and old people.
3. Money is given to charity projects by many people.
4. Religious symbols are worn by a priest.
5. A person is protected by a spell in voodoo religion.

G5 Simple past / Present perfect

GV3
GV4

Die einfache Form der Vergangenheit / Die vollendete Gegenwart (Perfekt)

1 Das *simple past* verwenden Sie:

→ um Ereignisse zu beschreiben, die in der Vergangenheit passiert sind und bereits vorbei sind.

| The singer **sang** live on stage yesterday. | Der Sänger **hat** gestern live auf der Bühne **gesungen**. |
| The people **wanted** to listen to more songs last night. | Die Leute **wollten** gestern Abend mehr Lieder hören. |

Um zu sagen, was in der Vergangenheit **nicht** passiert ist, setzt man **didn't** (= **did not**) vor das Verb.

| She **didn't earn** much money last month. | Sie **hat** letzten Monat **nicht** viel Geld **verdient**. |
| The band **didn't win** the prize. | Die Band **hat** den Preis **nicht gewonnen**. |

Die Vergangenheit von *to be* bildet man mit **was/were** bzw. **wasn't/weren't** (= **was not / were not**).

| I **wasn't** at home last night, I **was** at a concert. | Ich **war** gestern Abend **nicht** zu Hause, ich **war** auf einem Konzert. |
| The bands **weren't** bad, they **were** OK. | Die Bands **waren nicht** schlecht, sie **waren** OK. |

G Grammar

2 So können Sie Fragen stellen:

Did you **know** that he has 2 million followers?	**Wusstest** du, dass er 2 Millionen Follower hat?
Did the albums **sell** well?	**Haben** sich die Alben gut **verkauft?**
When **did** she **become** famous?	Wann **wurde** sie berühmt?

Bei manchen Verben ist die Vergangenheitsform ganz anders. Diese Formen sollten Sie am besten auswendig lernen. Eine Liste finden Sie auf Seite 186.

Signalwörter:
(a week, a month, a year) ago vor (einer Woche, einem Monat, einem Jahr) | **yesterday** gestern | **last (week, month, year)** letzte/n/s (Woche, Monat, Jahr)

3 Das *present perfect* verwenden Sie:

→ um auszudrücken, dass etwas in der Vergangenheit stattfand und das Ergebnis noch in der Gegenwart spürbar oder sichtbar ist.
→ um über Handlungen zu sprechen, die gerade erst abgeschlossen wurden.

Claire **has** never **organised** an event before.	Claire **hat** noch nie zuvor ein Event **organisiert**.
I **haven't heard** this song yet.	Ich **habe** das Lied noch nicht **gehört**.
He **has had** an accident on stage but he's OK.	Er **hat** einen Unfall auf der Bühne **gehabt**, aber er ist OK.

Denken Sie daran:
Einige Verben haben unregelmäßige 3. Formen: z. B. **be → been; write → written**
Eine Liste finden Sie auf Seite 186.

Signalwörter:
already schon | **just** gerade | **ever** jemals | **never** nie | **not ... yet** noch nicht
Die Signalwörter stehen mit einer Ausnahme immer zwischen *have* und dem Partizip Perfekt.
Die Ausnahme ist **not ... yet**.

4 So können Sie Fragen stellen:

Have you already **read** her latest post?	**Hast** du schon ihren letzten Post **gelesen**?
Has he **prepared** everything for the meeting?	**Hat** er alles für das Treffen **vorbereitet**?
Why **haven't** they **sent** the confirmation yet?	Warum **haben** sie die Bestätigung noch **nicht geschickt**?

5 Complete the exercises. Check your answers on page 190.

a) Complete the sentences with the simple past.

1. Mark ■ (have) his first interview with a pop star yesterday. He ■ (prepared) all week for it.
2. He ■ (not seem) nervous but his questions ■ (not be) very clear.
3. The pop star ■ (be) friendly. She ■ (not make) fun of Mark.
4. After the interview Mark ■ (go) home happily. He ■ (want) to tell his friends all about it.
5. His company ■ (offer) him to do more interviews but he ■ (not feel) ready for more.
6. He ■ (decide) to take some classes first and ■ (tell) his boss about his plans.

b) Complete the sentences with the present perfect.

1. My friend ■ already ■ (see) the show three times but I ■ never ■ (be) there before.
2. The bands ■ (not start) yet. They ■ (not find) their instruments yet.
3. They ■ just ■ (finish) their preparations and the singer ■ just ■ (walk) on stage.
4. ■ the singer ever ■ (write) songs herself? – Yes, she ■ (be) interested in it for a long time.
5. Who ■ (do) this before? I ■ just ■ (try) it but it didn't work.

c) Complete the sentences with the simple past and the present perfect.

1. ■ you already ■ (see) the concert? – Yes, I ■ (watch) it on TV yesterday.
2. She ■ just ■ (release) a new song. Her last album ■ (come) out last year.
3. The actor ■ never ■ (do) this stunt before. He ■ (train) with an instructor yesterday.
4. ■ you ■ (change) the title last week? – No, I ■ (not find) a good title yet.
5. Years ago nobody ■ (think) this was possible. It ■ (be) a great experience so far.
6. I ■ (walk) past the new concert hall last week. It's the most beautiful building I ■ ever ■ (see).

G6 Past perfect Die vollendete Vergangenheit

GV5

1 Das *past perfect* verwenden Sie:

→ um über Ereignisse zu sprechen, die noch **vor** einem vergangenen Ereignis stattfanden.

After Henry Ford **had introduced** the assembly line, the workers produced cars faster.	Nachdem Henry Ford das Fließband **eingeführt hatte**, stellten die Arbeiter die Autos schneller her.
Before Henry Ford invented the assembly line, it **had taken** up to 12 hours to build just one car.	Bevor Henry Ford das Fließband erfunden hat, **hatte** es bis zu 12 Stunden **gedauert**, um ein einziges Auto zu bauen.

Denken Sie daran:
Einige Verben haben unregelmäßige 3. Formen: z. B. **be → been; write → written**
Eine Liste finden Sie auf Seite 186.

Signalwörter:
after nachdem | **before** bevor, ehe

2 So können Sie Fragen stellen:

Had his company ever **made** enough money?	**Hatte** seine Firma je genug Geld **gemacht**?
What **had** he **done** before the accident happened?	Was **hatte** er **getan**, bevor der Unfall passierte?

3 Complete the exercises. Check your answers on page 190.

a) Complete the sentences with the past perfect.

1. After she ■ (finish) college, she went to New York.
2. After the company ■ (not make) enough money, it had to close.
3. After the boss ■ (speak) to his workers, they were very angry.
4. Before they became famous, they ■ (work) in restaurants.
5. Before the new cars were allowed on the streets, test drivers ■ (test) them.
6. Before Detroit was famous for its car industry, it ■ just ■ (be) like any other American city.

G Grammar

b) Complete the sentences. Use the simple past and the past perfect.

1. After Detroit ■ (grow), many immigrants ■ (go) there to find a better life.
2. Before Detroit's industry ■ (stop) growing, it ■ (be) a rich city.
3. After many people from Europe ■ (move) to Detroit, many African Americans ■ (come) there too.
4. Before they ■ (get) a job, they ■ (not have) a chance of a good life.
5. After the numbers of sales ■ (fall), many companies ■ (not make) it and closed.
6. Before most of Detroit's companies ■ (go) bankrupt, many programmes ■ (try) to help.

G7 Will-future / Going to-future Will-Futur / Going to-Futur

GV6

1 Das *will-future* verwenden Sie:

→ für Vermutungen über die Zukunft.
→ für spontane Entscheidungen.
→ für Wünsche, Hoffnungen und Vorhersagen (nach *I hope, I think, I'm sure, probably, maybe,* etc.).

I'**ll call** an ambulance.	Ich **rufe** einen Krankenwagen. (spontan)
I hope the stadium **will open** soon.	Ich hoffe, das Stadion **öffnet** bald. (Hoffnung)
Will you **be** back from Glasgow soon?	**Bist** du bald wieder aus Glasgow zurück? (Wunsch)
It **won't rain** tomorrow.	Es **wird** morgen **nicht regnen**. (Vorhersage)

Denken Sie daran:
Gesprochen werden meist die Kurzformen: **I'll** watch the game. **They'll** visit us.

2 Das *going to-future* verwenden Sie:

→ für Absichten und Pläne.
→ um auszudrücken, dass etwas sicher eintreten wird, weil es schon Anzeichen dafür gibt.

I'**m going to talk** to the supervisor tomorrow.	Ich **habe vor**, morgen mit dem Chef **zu sprechen**. (Absicht, Plan)
Are you **going to visit** Brighton? No, we **aren't going to travel** to England this year.	**Habt** ihr **vor**, Brighton **zu besuchen**? (Plan) Nein, wir **werden** dieses Jahr **nicht** nach England **reisen**. (Plan)
Look at those black clouds. It'**s going to rain** in a few minutes.	Schau dir diese schwarzen Wolken an. Es **wird** in ein paar Minuten **regnen**. (Anzeichen)

3 Complete the exercises. Check your answers on page 191.

a) Complete the sentences. Use the will-future.

1. I hope the game ■ (be) exciting.
2. Wait a moment. Joel ■ (help) you to get the tickets for the show.
3. I hope it ■ (not rain) tomorrow.
4. Maybe Susan and Jane ■ (find) a place to stay in Glasgow soon.
5. When ■ the sun ■ (come) out again?
6. ■ the players ■ (say) hi to the fans?

Grammar G

b) Complete the sentences. Use the going to-future.

1. My friends ■ (visit) Edinburgh in July.
2. They ■ (stay) in a cute hotel in the city centre.
3. My app shows that it ■ (rain) in two hours.
4. Mark ■ (look) for a new job. He doesn't like his boss.
5. I ■ (have) a birthday party next week.

c) Translate the sentences into English. Use the will-future or the going to-future.

1. Vielleicht scheint morgen die Sonne.
2. Ich werde morgen meine Bewerbung abschicken.
3. Wirst du dich auf diese Stellenanzeige bewerben?
4. Sie hoffen, dass das neue Jahr besser wird.
5. Gib mir zwei Minuten, dann helfe ich dir.
6. Sina wird morgen um 14 Uhr mit ihrem Chef sprechen.

G8 Comparison of adjectives Vergleichen und Steigern von Adjektiven

GV14

1 So vergleichen Sie Personen und Gegenstände:

The girls yelled **louder** than the boys.	Die Mädchen brüllten **lauter** als die Jungen.
It was the **hardest** game this season.	Es war das **schwierigste** Spiel der Saison.
This team is **more successful**.	Dieses Team ist **erfolgreicher**.
Steve is the **most expensive** player.	Steve ist der **teuerste** Spieler.
This football game is **as exciting as** the last one.	Dieses Fußballspiel ist **so spannend wie** das letzte.
These products are **not as good as** the other ones.	Diese Produkte sind **nicht so gut wie** die anderen.

2 So steigern Sie Adjektive:

Grundform ●	Komparativ ●●	Superlativ ●●●
cheap	cheaper (than …)	cheapest
easy	easier (than …)	easiest
expensive	more expensive (than …)	most expensive
good	better (than …)	best
bad	worse (than …)	worst

Denken Sie daran:
Bei allen **einsilbigen** und bei **zweisilbigen** Adjektiven, die auf -le, -er, -ow oder -y enden, hängt man ein **-er** und **-est** an: l<u>ou</u>d – loud**er** – loud**est** | clever – c<u>leve</u>r**er** – clever**est**
Diese Steigerung ist so ähnlich wie im Deutschen: laut – lauter – am lautesten.
Alle anderen **mehrsilbigen** Adjektive werden mit **more** und **most** gesteigert:
<u>expensive</u> – **more** expensive – **most** expensive

! Endet das Adjektiv auf **-t** oder **-g**, wird der Buchstabe verdoppelt: fi**t** – fi**tt**er | bi**g** – bi**gg**er.
Endet das Adjektiv auf **-y**, wird das **-y** zu **-ier**: eas**y** – eas**ier**.

G Grammar

3 Complete the exercises. Check your answers on page 191.

a) Make a table with three grids: ● / ●● / ●●●. Complete it with all three forms of each adjective in the list.

more popular ✓ | best | fast | harder | exciting | longest | funnier | worst | more professional | happy | most serious | nice

Example:

●	●●	●●●
popular	more popular	most popular

b) Claire and Mary play in the same team. Complete their dialogue.

1. Claire: The ■ (●●● exciting) part of our job is playing together in a team. I have great teammates!
2. Mary: Yes, I agree. I have played in different teams in the past. I think this team is ■ (= friendly / as … as) the last one I played for, but it is ■ (●● professional). And the girls and coaches are ■ (● reliable). Everybody really cares about each other.
3. Claire: Yes, that's true. In some teams, the coaches just want their players to play ■ (● hard) and give their all. They think that's the ■ (●●● efficient) way to win.
4. Mary: Exactly! But that's not true. The ■ (●●● good) way is to play by the rules and to be ■ (●● fast) than the other team.
5. Claire: We just have to be ■ (●● fit) than the others. And hope that the other team is ■ (= not fit / as … as) we are.

G9 Reported speech I (simple present) Indirekte Rede I (Gegenwart)

1 So berichten Sie, was jemand gerade sagt, fragt oder worum jemand bittet:

GV21
GV22

Direkte Rede	Indirekte Rede
Brian: "**It's** so scary."	Brian says (that) **it's** so scary.
Brian: „**Es ist** so unheimlich."	Brian sagt, dass **es** unheimlich **sei**/**ist**.
Mason: "**We've** never **felt** so lucky."	Mason says (that) **they've** never **felt** so lucky.
Mason: „**Wir haben uns** noch nie so glücklich **gefühlt**."	Mason sagt, dass **sie sich** noch nie so glücklich **gefühlt hätten**.
A police officer: "Please, **stay** at home."	A police officer asks them **to stay** at home.
Ein Polizist: „Bitte **bleiben** Sie zu Hause."	Ein Polizist bittet sie, zu Hause **zu bleiben**.
A woman: "**Where are my** children?"	A woman asks **where her** children **are**.
Eine Frau: „**Wo sind meine** Kinder?"	Eine Frau fragt, **wo ihre** Kinder **seien**/**sind**.
A man: "**Is it** safe now?"	A man wants to know **if it's** safe now.
Ein Mann: „**Ist es** jetzt sicher?"	Ein Mann möchte wissen, **ob es** jetzt sicher **sei**/**ist**.

Denken Sie daran:
Achten Sie auf die Änderung der Pronomen und Begleiter.

! In der indirekte Rede ändern sich auch die Zeitangaben:
today → that day | this morning → that morning | yesterday → the day before | last week → the week before | a year ago → a year before | tomorrow → the next/following day | next Monday → the following Monday

Grammar G

2 Complete the exercises. Check your answers on page 191.

a) Read what the reporter says. Is it a statement, a question or an order? Then report what he says.

1. "I've never seen anything like that before."
   Example: The reporter says that he has never seen anything like that before.
2. "There are lots of people."
3. "A woman is taking care of a person who is bleeding."
4. "An ambulance arrived five minutes ago."
5. "Where does the noise come from?"
6. "Don't get any closer!"

b) What do John and Alice say?

1. Alice: "We were so excited."
2. John: "It was our first trip to New Zealand."
3. Alice: "My boyfriend has planned my birthday party in Adelaide."
4. John: "Were you happy about my surprise present, Alice?"
5. Alice: "I couldn't believe you organised everything in secret."
6. John: "Your birthday was a success until the earth began to shake under our feet."

G10 Reported speech II (backshift) — Indirekte Rede II (Zeitverschiebung)

1 So berichten Sie, was jemand vor einiger Zeit gesagt hat:
GV23

Direkte Rede	Indirekte Rede
Tim: "**I enjoy** the tour very much." Tim: „**Ich genieße** die Tour sehr."	Tim said (that) **he enjoyed** the tour very much. Tim sagte, dass **er** die Tour **genieße**/**genießt**.
simple present	simple past
"**She is having** a great time." „**Sie hat** eine tolle Zeit."	I heard (that) **she was having** a great time. Ich hörte, dass **sie** eine tolle Zeit **habe**/**hat**.
present progressive	past progressive
"**We have been** to New Zealand once." „**Wir sind** einmal in Neuseeland **gewesen**."	They said (that) **they had been** to New Zealand once. Sie sagten, dass **sie** einmal in Neuseeland **gewesen seien**/**sind**.
present perfect	past perfect
"The view **was** fantastic." „Die Aussicht **war** fantastisch."	He said (that) the view **had been** fantastic. Er sagte, dass die Aussicht fantastisch **gewesen sei**/**ist**.
simple past	past perfect
Ayda: "The weather **will be** fine." Ayda: „Das Wetter **wird** gut."	Ayda added (that) the weather **would be** fine. Ayda ergänzte, dass das Wetter gut **wird**.
will-future	would + Grundform

Denken Sie daran:
Achten Sie auf die Änderung der Pronomen und Begleiter.

G Grammar

> In der indirekte Rede ändern sich auch die Zeitangaben:
> today → that day | this morning → that morning | yesterday → the day before | last week → the week before | a year ago → a year before | tomorrow → the next/following day | next Monday → the following Monday

2 So berichten Sie, was jemand vor einiger Zeit gefragt hat:

Direkte Rede	Indirekte Rede
Alan: "**Do you need** more information?" Alan: „**Brauchen Sie** mehr Informationen?"	Alan asked me **if I needed** more information. Alan fragte mich, **ob ich** mehr Informationen **brauche**.
"**Where did** the tourists **stay**?" „**Wo übernachteten** die Touristen?"	He asked **where** the tourists **had stayed**. Er fagte, **wo** die Touristen **übernachtet haben**.

Denken Sie daran:
Es gelten dieselben Regeln zur Zeitverschiebung.

3 So berichten Sie, worum jemand vor einiger Zeit gebeten/aufgefordert hat:

Direkte Rede	Indirekte Rede
Alan said, "**Be patient**, Amy!" Alan sagte: „**Hab Geduld**, Amy!"	Alan told Amy **to be patient**. Alan sagte Amy, dass sie **Geduld haben soll**.
Amy said, "**Don't forget your** passport, Alan!" Amy sagte: „**Vergiss deinen** Pass **nicht**, Alan!"	Amy told Alan **not to forget his** passport. Amy sagte Alan, dass **er seinen** Pass **nicht vergessen soll**.

4 Complete the exercises. Check your answers on page 191.

a) Report what Matt and Tanya said.

1. Tanya: "I've found a new job. The company called me."
   → Tanya told Matt that she **has found** / **had found** a new job. She explained that the company had called **me** / **her**.
2. Matt: "Great! You'll have lots of money."
   → Matt said that she **will have** / **would have** lots of money.
3. Tanya: "Don't get too excited! My job will be at a travel agent's in Wellington."
   → Tanya told him **not to get** / **to get** too excited. She said that her job **will be** / **would be** at a travel agent's in Wellington.
4. Matt: "You have already had a job in tourism? Why did you leave it? Stay with a good company when you've found one!"
   → Matt wanted to know if she **already had** / **had already had** a job in tourism. He asked why she **had left** / **left** it. He told her **to stay** / **stay** with a good company when she **had** / **has** found one.
5. Tanya: "But remember how boring my work was. I had to check numbers all day. In my new job I'll get lots of information about special offers."
   → Tanya told him **remember** / **to remember** how boring her work **was** / **had been**. She said she **had had** / **had** to check numbers all day. In her new job she **will** / **would** get lots of information about special offers.
6. Matt: "Well, don't forget me if there's an offer of a cheap trip to Australia."
   → Matt asked her **to forget** / **not to forget** him if there **was** / **is** an offer of a cheap trip to Australia.

Grammar   G

b) What did Kate say?

1. Kate said that she had just bought her plane ticket to New Zealand, but she hadn't found a job there yet.
   Example: "I've just bought my plane ticket to New Zealand, but I haven't found a job here yet."
2. She said that her parents had taken her to New Zealand for the first time in 2015.
3. She explained that she didn't remember much about the trip, but she had loved the landscape.
4. She said she was sure that she would have a wonderful time in New Zealand.

G11 Past progressive Die Verlaufsform der Vergangenheit

GV13

1 So sagen Sie, dass zwei Handlungen in der Vergangenheit zur gleichen Zeit und gleich lange abliefen:

While he **was talking** to his mother, his father **was working** in the garden.	**Während** er mit seiner Mutter **redete**, **arbeitete** sein Vater im Garten.
While they were listening to music, they **were preparing** the table.	**Während** sie Musik **hörten, deckten** sie den Tisch.

2 So sagen Sie, dass etwas in der Vergangenheit noch andauerte und noch nicht beendet war, als (plötzlich) ein zweites Ereignis eintrat:

Ahmed and Delia **were sitting** in a restaurant **when** Delia's ex-boyfriend **showed up**.	Ahmed und Delia **saßen** gerade im Restaurant, **als** Delias Ex-Freund **auftauchte**.
While he **was yelling** at her, another guest **called** the police.	**Während** er sie **anschrie**, **rief** ein Gast die Polizei.

Denken Sie daran:
Für das neue Ereignis wird das *simple past* benutzt.

Signalwörter:
when als | **while** während

3 So können Sie Fragen stellen:

What **were** you **doing** when your ex-boyfriend showed up?	Was **hast** du gerade **gemacht**, als dein Ex-Freund **auftauchte**?
Who **were** you **talking to** while you were **waiting**?	Mit wem **hast** du **geredet**, während du **gewartet hast**?

4 Complete the exercises. Check your answers on page 191.

a) Complete the sentences. Use the past progressive.

1. While Mary ■ (run) home, she got a phone call from her sister.
2. Mary ■ (listen) to her sister's news when someone said, "Hi, Mary!"
3. When she looked up, a tall boy ■ (wave) at her. It was Jimmy.
4. Jimmy asked Mary on a date while they ■ (walk) together.
5. Mary ■ (think) about her answer when Jimmy asked, "How about tomorrow at six p.m.?"
6. While they ■ (talk) about their date, Mary suddenly remembered something. "Sorry. I can't because ..."

G Grammar

b) Read the sentences. Do they describe two things that were happening at the same time? Or do they describe an ongoing and an interrupting action in the past? Which is the ongoing action, which is the interrupting action? Complete the sentences with the past progressive and/or the simple past.

1. Two girls ■ (walk) down the street when a group of boys ■ (shout) at them.
2. While the boys ■ (laugh), the girls ■ (start) to run.
3. While a shop owner ■ (look) outside, the girls ■ (run) from the boys. The shop owner waved at them.
4. While the girls ■ (rush) into his shop, he ■ still ■ (yell) at the boys.
5. While the boys ■ (make) fun of the girls, a group of older women ■ (arrive).
6. One woman ■ (ask) for their names while the others ■ (tell) them off.

G12 Passive voice II (simple past) Das Passiv II (einfache Vergangenheit)

GV20

1 So verwenden Sie das Passiv im *simple past*:

The document **was signed** by everyone last month.	Das Dokument **wurde** letzten Monat von allen **unterzeichnet**.
Many articles **were written** about Gandhi last year.	Viele Artikel **wurden** letztes Jahr über Gandhi **geschrieben**.
Was the meeting **cancelled** yesterday?	**Wurde** das Treffen gestern **abgesagt**?

Denken Sie daran:
Die Form des Hilfsverbs **be** hängt vom zeitlichen Zusammenhang ab (Vergangenheit, Zukunft usw.).
Passivsätze können auch in anderen Zeitformen verwendet werden:
Present perfect: **Have** you ever **been influenced** by someone famous?
Will-future: The prize **will be given** to this hotel.
Simple present: A review **is written** by the hotel tester.

Signalwörter *simple past*:
(a week, a month, a year) ago vor (einer Woche, einem Monat, einem Jahr) | **yesterday** gestern |
last (week, month, year) letzte/n/s (Woche, Monat, Jahr)

2 Complete the exercises. Check your answers on page 191.

a) Complete the sentences. Use the simple past.

1. A lot of articles ■ (write) about a girl named Malala.
2. She ■ (inspired) by her father to speak up.
3. Schools for girls ■ (close) under the Taliban regime.
4. She ■ (attack) when she was just 15 years old.
5. Many projects ■ (found) by Malala to help women in need.
6. Malala and Kailash Satyarthi ■ (give) the Nobel Peace Prize in 2014.

b) Complete the sentences. Use the present perfect.

1. Stories and traditions ■ (pass) on from generation to generation.
2. People ■ (ask) about their role models for a study.
3. The results ■ (not present) online yet.
4. The presentation ■ (not read) by many people.
5. ■ influencers ■ (see) as role models too?
6. Who ■ (elect) "Most influential person of the year"?

Grammar G

G13 Adjectives and adverbs — Adjektive und Adverbien

1 Sie verwenden *adjectives*:

→ um zu beschreiben, wie etwas oder jemand ist.
→ direkt vor einem Nomen oder nach dem Verb *to be*.
→ nach Zustandsverben: *to feel, to look, to sound, to stay, to taste*

This is **beautiful**!	Das ist **wunderschön**!
How are you? – I'm **fine**.	Wie geht es dir? – Mir geht's **gut**.
Shannon looks **tired**.	Shannon sieht **müde** aus.
This coffee tastes **delicious**.	Dieser Kaffee schmeckt **köstlich**.

2 Sie verwenden *adverbs*:

→ um zu beschreiben, auf welche Weise jemand etwas tut oder etwas geschieht.

Adverb = Adjektiv + **-ly**	nice → **nicely**	nett
Adjektiv auf **-le** → **-ly**	terrible → **terribly**	schrecklich
Adjektiv auf **-y** → **-ily**	happy → **happily**	glücklich
Adjektiv auf **-ic** → **-ically**	automatic → **automatically**	automatisch
Adjektiv und Adverb sind gleich	**fast, high, low, long, far, hard, early, daily**	schnell, hoch, niedrig, lang, weit, hart, früh, täglich
unregelmäßig	good → **well**	gut

Ken walked **slowly**.	Ken lief **langsam**.
My parents go to bed **early**.	Meine Eltern gehen **früh** ins Bett.
He **quickly** shut the door.	Er machte **schnell** die Tür zu.
Well done!	Gut gemacht!

G14 Pronouns — Pronomen

1 Personalpronomen verwenden Sie:

→ für Personen, Tiere oder Gegenstände.
→ als Subjekt oder als Objekt eines Satzes.

Personalpronomen als Subjekt	Personalpronomen als Objekt
I, you, he, she, it, we, they	**me, you, him, her, it, us, you, them**
You are a great friend!	Can you help **me**, please?
She is in my class.	Mark doesn't like **them**.

G Grammar

2 So können Sie ausdrücken, wem etwas gehört:

→ Possessivbegleiter: stehen immer zusammen mit einem Nomen
→ Possessivpronomen: stehen alleine, anstelle eines Nomens

Possessivbegleiter	Possessivpronomen
my, your, his, her, its, our, your, their	mine, yours, his, hers, ours, yours, theirs
I like your car.	Is this yours?
This is our dog.	Jay is a friend of mine.

3 So können Sie ausdrücken, dass jemand etwas selbst oder für sich selbst tut:

Reflexivpronomen

myself, yourself, himself, herself, itself, ourselves, yourselves, themselves

He was looking at himself in the mirror.

We introduced ourselves to the new neighbour.

Denken Sie daran:
Die Reflexivpronomen drücken aus, dass die Person oder die Gruppe etwas für sich selbst tut.
Wenn die Handlung auf Gegenseitigkeit beruht, verwendet man **each other**:
The girls looked at themselves in the mirror.   Die Mädchen sahen **sich** im Spiegel an.
The girls looked at each other.   Sie sahen sich **gegenseitig** an.

G15 Prepositions Präpositionen

1 So können Sie das Verhältnis oder eine Beziehung zwischen Personen oder Dingen auszudrücken:

Präpositionen der Zeit: Zeitpunkt	**at** noon **at** Christmas **on** Friday / **on** Fridays	mittag**s** **an** Weihnachten **am** Freitag, freitag**s**
Präpositionen der Zeit: Zeiträume Auch: **between**, **... ago**, **since**, **for**, **from ... to**, **until**	**in** the morning **after** midnight **before** dinner	**am** Morgen, morgen**s** **nach** Mitternacht **vor** dem Abendessen
Präpositionen des Ortes Auch: **near**, **at**, **in**, **on**, **above**, **below**, **behind**, **opposite**, **over**, **next to**	**by** the lake **under** the bridge **in front of** the house	**am** See **unter** der Brücke **vor** dem Haus
Präpositionen der Richtung Auch: **to**, **into**, **out of**, **past**, **along**, **across**, **down**, **round**, **off**	**from** the table **towards** the house **up** the hill	**vom** Tisch **in Richtung** Haus den Hügel **hinauf**

2 Präpositionen in *phrasal verbs*:

→ *Phrasal verbs* sind Verben, die fest mit einer Präposition oder einem Adverb verbunden sind. Die Bedeutung des Verbs ändert sich je nach Verbindung und muss gelernt werden.

break down	zusammenbrechen	pass away	sterben
break in/into	einbrechen	pass by	vorbeigehen
break up	eine Beziehung beenden	pick out	aussuchen; heraussuchen
get in/on	einsteigen	pick up	aufheben; sich aneignen
get off/out	aussteigen	put down	abstellen; hinlegen
get over	über etwas hinwegkommen	put in	einsetzen
get up	aufstehen	put on	anziehen; aufsetzen
give away	verschenken; weggeben	put up	aufstellen; anbringen
give in	nachgeben	run away	wegrennen
give up	aufgeben	run into	unerwartet treffen
look at	ansehen	run out of	ausgehen; nicht mehr haben
look after	sich kümmern um	run over	überfahren
look away	wegsehen	take along	mitnehmen
look for	suchen	take on	übernehmen; auf sich nehmen
look forward	sich freuen auf	take off	starten; ausziehen; entfernen; frei nehmen
look up	nachsehen		

G16 Conditional clauses Bedingungssätze

1 So verwenden Sie *conditional clauses*:
GV18

→ Bedingungssätze bestehen aus zwei Teilen: dem *if*-Satz (Nebensatz) und dem Hauptsatz.
→ Der *if*-Satz drückt eine Bedingung aus.
→ Im Hauptsatz sagt man, was passiert, wenn diese Bedingung erfüllt wird (Folge).
→ Es gibt drei Typen Bedingungssätze, je nachdem, wie wahrscheinlich die Erfüllung der Bedingung ist.
→ Der *if*-Satz kann vor oder nach dem Hauptsatz stehen.

If I get this job, I will be happy.

I will be very happy **if I get this job.**

Denken Sie daran:
Steht der *if*-Satz am Anfang, dann braucht man ein Komma vor dem Hauptsatz.
Achtung: **if** = wenn, falls ≠ **when** = wenn (zeitlich)

G Grammar

2 *Conditional clauses type 1* verwenden Sie:

→ um zu zeigen, dass es um eine wahrscheinliche Situation geht.
→ um auszudrücken, dass die Bedingung, die im *if*-Satz formuliert wird, erfüllbar ist.

If you work well, you will get a bonus.	**Wenn du gut arbeitest**, bekommst du einen Bonus.
You won't get the job **if you are late for the interview.**	Du wirst den Job nicht bekommen, **wenn du zu spät zu dem Vorstellungsgespräch kommst.**
You must be on time **if you want to make a good impression.**	Du musst pünktlich sein, **wenn du einen guten Eindruck machen willst.**

Denken Sie daran:
Im Hauptsatz können statt des *will-future* auch die modalen Hilfsverben *can*, *may* oder *must* stehen.

3 *Conditional clauses type 2* verwenden Sie:

→ um zu zeigen, dass es um eine theoretisch mögliche, aber relativ unwahrscheinliche Situation geht.
→ um auszudrücken, dass die Bedingung, die im *if*-Satz formuliert wird, nur theoretisch erfüllbar ist.

Susan would take the job **if the company paid more money.**	Susan würde den Job annehmen, **wenn das Unternehmen mehr Geld zahlen würde.**
Would you visit me **if I moved to another country?**	Würdest du mich besuchen kommen, **wenn ich in ein anderes Land ziehen würde?**
If I had a million pounds, I could quit my job.	**Wenn ich eine Million Pfund hätte,** könnte ich meinen Job kündigen.
How much would you miss me **if I lived far away?**	Wie sehr würdest du mich vermissen, **wenn ich weit weg leben würde?**

Denken Sie daran:
Im Hauptsatz kann *would* auch durch *could* oder *might* ersetzt werden.
Bei Fragen wandert *would* oder das **Fragewort** + *would* an den Satzanfang.

4 *Conditional clauses type 3* verwenden Sie:

→ um zu zeigen, dass es um eine Situation geht, die in der Vergangenheit liegt und nicht mehr eintreten kann.
→ um auszudrücken, dass die Bedingung, die im *if*-Satz formuliert wird, nicht erfüllbar ist.

You wouldn't be unemployed **if you had finished your internship.**	Du wärst nicht arbeitslos, **wenn du dein Praktikum beendet hättest.**
If Bryce had prepared more, he would have done better during interview.	**Wenn Bryce sich mehr vorbereitet hätte,** wäre er bei dem Vorstellungsgespräch besser gewesen.

Grammar G

5 Complete the exercises. Check your answers on page 192.

a) Complete the conditional clauses type I.

1. If you (need) me, I (help) you.
2. Mike (be) sad if you (not phone) him.
3. If she (not come) on time, she (lose) her job.
4. Matt (not find) a job if he (not look) on the Internet.
5. I (talk) to Meghan if I (meet) her.
6. You (not sleep) well if you always (watch) scary movies.

b) Complete the conditional clauses type II.

1. Kate (buy) new clothes if she (have) more money.
2. If I (lose) my job, I (be) in trouble.
3. If the manager (shout) at him, Ben (not work) at the store.
4. Jennifer (not worry) about the interview if she (feel) more confident.
5. Sally (become) a manager if she (try) harder.
6. If the customers (be) friendlier, Claudia (enjoy) her work more.

c) Complete the conditional clauses type III.

1. I (call) you if I (know) your phone number.
2. If Michael (not prepare) for the interview, he (not get) the job.
3. If she (wear) a helmet, she (not hurt) her head.
4. If Tony (buy) a new car, he (not have) an accident.
5. Nicole (not miss) the bus if she (wake up) earlier.

G17 Articles Bestimmte und unbestimmte Artikel

GV9

1 Den bestimmten Artikel *the* verwenden Sie:

→ vor Nomen, die sich auf bestimmte Personen oder Dinge beziehen und wenn klar ist, wer/was gemeint ist.
→ vor Namen von Flüssen, Meeren, Gebirgsketten
→ vor Ländernamen im Plural
→ vor Musikinstrumenten

I like **the** book.	Ich mag **das** Buch.
Mary enjoyed **the** delicious meal.	Mary genoss **die** leckere Mahlzeit.
John was swimming in **the** Pacific Ocean.	John schwamm **im** Pazifik.
We spent two weeks in **the** United States.	Wir haben zwei Wochen in **den** Vereinigten Staaten verbracht.
Her friend plays **the** guitar and **the** piano.	Ihr Freund spielt Gitarre und Klavier.

Denken Sie daran:
Es gibt zwei Aussprachevarianten des bestimmten Artikels *the*. Dabei kommt es darauf an, wie der erste Laut des folgenden Wortes ausgesprochen wird, nicht wie er geschrieben wird:
vor Konsonanten: **the** man, **the** United States → [ðə]
vor Vokalen: **the** airport, **the** hour → [ði]

G Grammar

2 Den bestimmten Artikel *the* verwenden Sie nicht:

→ vor abstrakten Nomen
→ vor Namen von Bergen, Seen, Städten, Straßen und Ländernamen
→ vor *most* im Sinne von „fast alle"

Money is important.	Geld ist wichtig.
Life is beautiful.	Das Leben ist schön.
John was swimming in Lake Ontario.	John schwamm im Lake Ontario.
We spent two weeks in Germany.	Wir haben zwei Wochen in Deutschland verbracht.
Most people like ice cream.	Die meisten Menschen mögen Eis.
I like most people.	Ich mag die meisten Menschen.

3 Den unbestimmten Artikel *a/an* verwenden Sie:

→ vor Nomen, die sich auf einen nicht näher bestimmten Vertreter einer Gruppe beziehen
→ vor Jobs
→ vor Maßeinheiten, Zeitangaben, den Zahlen 100 und 1000
→ nach *half*, *quite*, *kind of* und *such*
→ in bestimmten Ausdrücken (z. B. *to be in a hurry*, *to have a headache*, *to wait for a long time*)

I gave my book to **a** friend.	Ich habe mein Buch **einem** Freund gegeben.
Mrs Wilson works as **a** police officer.	Frau Wilson arbeitet als Polizistin.
Can I borrow **a** hundred euros?	Kann ich mir hundert Euro ausleihen?
Let's meet in half **an** hour.	Lass uns uns in **einer** halben Stunde treffen.
Carley was in **a** hurry.	Carley war in Eile.
Zack has **a** headache.	Zack hat Kopfschmerzen.

Denken Sie daran:
Der unbestimmte Artikel hat zwei Formen: **a/an**. Auch hier kommt es darauf an, wie der erste Laut des folgenden Wortes ausgesprochen wird, nicht wie er geschrieben wird.
a [ə] vor Konsonanten: **a b**anana, **a u**seful tip
an [ən] Vokalen und stummem „h": **an a**pple, **an h**our

Grammar G

G18 Word order Wortstellung

1 Die Wortstellung im Aussagesatz und im verneinten Satz:

→ ist immer gleich: 1. **Subjekt**, 2. **Verb**, 3. **Objekt** (wenn vorhanden)

Eve is waiting.	Eve wartet.
Eve is waiting patiently.	Eve wartet geduldig.
Harsin buys a book.	Harsin kauft ein Buch.
After school Harsin buys a book at the store.	Nach der Schule kauft Harsin ein Buch im Geschäft.
While Eve is patiently waiting for the bus, Harsin is buying a book.	Während Eve geduldig auf den Bus wartet, kauft Harsin ein Buch.
Eve is waiting for the bus because she doesn't have a car.	Eve wartet auf den Bus, weil sie kein Auto hat.

Denken Sie daran:
→ Die S-V-O-Regel gilt auch, wenn Adjektive, Adverbien, Orts- oder Zeitangaben ergänzt werden.
→ Die S-V-O-Regel gilt auch für Haupt- und Nebensätze.

2 Die Wortstellung im Fragesatz:

→ Bei Fragen mit einem **Hilfsverb** steht dieses vor dem Subjekt.
  Danach bleibt die Reihenfolge 1. **Subjekt**, 2. **Verb**, 3. **Objekt**
→ Auch bei Fragen mit einem Fragewort (z. B. *when*/*why*) kommt das **Hilfsverb** vor dem **Subjekt**
→ Wenn das Fragewort selbst das **Subjekt** ist (*who*/*which*) gilt wieder die Reihenfolge 1. **Subjekt**, 2. **Verb**, 3. **Objekt**

Can you help me?	Kannst du / Können Sie mir helfen?
Is Sam doing his homework at the moment?	Macht Sam gerade seine Hausaufgaben?
When did you buy a car?	Wann hast du ein Auto gekauft?
Who is waiting at the bus stop?	Wer wartet an der Bushaltestelle?

G19 Adverbs and sequence of adverbs Adverbien und ihre Reihenfolge

1 So können Sie ausdrücken, auf welche Weise jemand etwas tut, und wann, wo oder auf welche Art etwas geschieht.

→ **Adverbs of manner** (how something is done) → **G13** Adjectives and adverbs

Wyatt is singing his favourite song **happily**.	Wyatt singt **fröhlich** sein Lieblingslied.
Wyatt is **happily** singing in the car.	Wyatt singt **fröhlich** im Auto.
The team is working **hard**.	Das Team arbeitet **hart**.
Kathy and Mike are shouting **angrily**.	Kathy und Mike schreien **wütend**.

G Grammar

→ **Adverbs of place** (where something is done)

Let's sit **here**.	Lass / Lasst uns **hier** sitzen.
Their house is **at the end of the street**.	Ihr Haus ist am **Ende der Straße.**
I have lived **in South Africa**.	Ich habe **in Südafrika** gelebt.

→ **Adverbs of time** (when something is done)

Can we meet **tomorrow**?	Können wir uns **morgen** treffen?
I go to the gym **every day**.	Ich gehe **jeden Tag** ins Fitnessstudio.
Yesterday Luke was in London.	**Gestern** war Luke in London.

2 In einem Satz stellen Sie:

→ **adverbs of manner** ans Ende des Satzes. **Adverbs of manner**, die auf **-ly** enden, können auch vor dem Verb platziert werden, wenn sie nicht betont werden sollen.
→ **adverbs of place** ans Ende des Satzes.
→ **adverbs of time** ans Ende des Satzes oder an den Anfang des Satzes, wenn sie betont werden sollen.
→ mehrere Adverbien in die folgende Reihenfolge: **manner – place – time**.

I **quietly** walked **outside**.	Ich ging **leise nach draußen**.
Steve **happily** goes **to the gym every morning**.	Steve geht **gerne jeden Morgen ins Fitnessstudio**.
Yesterday Claire **quickly** ran **to the bus stop**. / Claire **quickly** ran **to the bus stop yesterday**.	**Gestern** rannte Claire **schnell zur Bushaltestelle**.

3 Complete the exercise. Check your answers on page 192.

Add the adverbs to the sentences.

1. Jake goes to school. (at 7 o'clock)
2. Luke is working at the gym. (hard)
3. Kate is going to visit her friends. (next weekend, in Edinburgh)
4. Brian eats his breakfast. (quickly, in the mornings)
5. But Brian doesn't drive. (fast, to work)
6. Lucy waited. (nervously, after the interview)

G20 Conjunctions and adverbial clauses

Konjunktionen und adverbiale Bestimmungen

1 So können Sie zwei Hauptsätze durch *conjunctions* verbinden:

Julie had a problem **and** she was sad.	Julie hatte ein Problem **und** sie war traurig.
She wanted to talk to Brittany **but** Brittany didn't answer her phone.	Sie wollte mit Brittany sprechen, **aber** Brittany ging nicht ans Telefon.
Maybe Brittany was walking her dog **or** she was at the gym.	Vielleicht war Brittany mit ihrem Hund spazieren **oder** sie war im Fitnessstudio.

Grammar G

Denken Sie daran:
Die Satzstellung ist im Englischen immer gleich: 1. *Subjekt*, 2. *Verb*, 3. *Objekt* (S-V-O-Regel).
→ **G 18** Word order

2 So können Sie einen Hauptsatz und einen Nebensatz durch *conjunctions* verbinden:

Time (Zeit)	after	**After** she came home from school, she phoned her friend.
	while	We met Leo **while** we were waiting for the bus.
	as soon as	She'll send him a text **as soon as** she has time.
	before	I'll clean the kitchen **before** you come back.
	until	I'll wait for her **until** she finishes work.
	when	**When** they arrive, we can go to the cinema.
Reason / Result (Grund)	because	The Leonards can't come tonight **because** they already have plans.
Purpose (Zweck)	so that	Please come here **so that** we can start.
Concession (Einräumung)	although	Nadine likes her hobby **although** it's dangerous.
	though	**Though** she was tired, she went to the party.
Condition (Bedingung)	as long as	You will be successful **as long as** you practise.
	if	**if** I had the time, I would help her.

Denken Sie daran:
Nebensätze sind allein unvollständig und müssen mit Hauptsätzen verbunden sein.
Nebensätze werden von Konjunktionen oder Relativpronomen (→ **G 3** Relative clauses) eingeleitet.
Es gelten folgende Kommaregeln:
1. Hauptsatz – Nebensatz (ohne Komma): We met Leo *while* we were waiting.
2. Nebensatz – Komma – Hauptsatz: *While* we were waiting, we met Leo.

3 Complete the exercises. Check your answers on page 192.

a) Complete the sentences with a conjunction.

1. ■ Zoey went to school, she had breakfast.
2. Sarah was angry ■ her friend hadn't called her back.
3. Ben climbed up the tree ■ he was afraid of heights.
4. Caleb opened the windows ■ fresh air could come in.
5. Jess relaxed ■ the interview was over.
6. There was a lot of damage ■ the earthqake had happened.

b) Translate the sentences into English.

1. Paul hörte Musik, während er joggte.
2. Möchtest du ins Kino gehen oder ein Eis essen?
3. Brooke war sehr glücklich, als sie den Job bekam.
4. Michael wartet oft, bis seine Freundin fertig ist.

G Grammar

G21 Quantifiers Mengenangaben

GV11
GV12

1 Die Mengenangaben *some* und *any* verwenden Sie:

→ wenn Sie keine genauen Mengenangaben machen können.
→ vor zählbaren Nomen im Plural (z.B. *books*, *pencils*) und vor nicht zählbaren Nomen (z.B. *money*, *clothes*).
→ in bejahten Aussagen (**some**) und in Fragen und verneinten Aussagen (**any**).

I need **some** new clothes.	Ich brauche neue Kleidung.
Do you have **any** questions?	Haben Sie / Hast du Fragen?
No, I don't have **any** questions.	Nein, ich habe **keine** Fragen.

2 Die Mengenangaben *much*, *many* und *a lot of* / *lots of* verwenden Sie:

→ um in bejahten Aussagen zu sagen, dass viel von etwas vorhanden ist (**a lot of** / **lots of**).
→ in Fragen und verneinten Aussagen vor nicht zählbaren Nomen im Singular (**much**) und vor zählbaren Nomen im Plural (**many**).

Let's buy **a lot of** chocolate.	Lass uns **viel** Schokolade kaufen.
How **many** sunglasses do you have?	Wie **viele** Sonnenbrillen hast du?
I don't have **many** sunglasses?	Ich habe nicht **viele** Sonnenbrillen.

3 Die Mengenangaben *a few*, *a little* and *a couple of* verwenden Sie:

→ um auszudrücken, dass einige, ein bisschen oder ein paar von etwas vorhanden ist/sind.

Can I have **a few** sandwiches?	Kann ich **einige** Sandwiches haben?
How many books did you bring? – Just **a few**.	Wie viele Bücher hast du mitgebracht? – Nur **ein paar**.
There are **a couple of** boxes in the garage.	In der Garage sind **ein paar** Kisten.
Sean is meeting **a couple of** friends.	Sean trifft sich mit **zwei** Freunden.
They only have **a little** money.	Sie haben nur **ein bisschen** Geld.
How much time do you have? – **A little**.	Wie viel Zeit hast du? – **Ein bisschen**.

Denken Sie daran:
Je nach Kontext kann *a couple of* entweder „ein paar" oder „zwei" bedeuten.
Im Deutschen wird *a few* entweder mit „ein paar" oder „einige" übersetzt.

G22 Plural Pluralformen

1 So können Sie regelmäßige und unregelmäßige Pluralformen bilden:

Die meisten Nomen: → regelmäßiger Plural mit **-s**	one friend one boy	two friend**s** two boy**s**
Nomen, die auf *-ch, -s, -sh, -x, -z* enden: → regelmäßiger Plural mit **-es**	one box one sandwich	two box**es** two sandwich**es**
Nomen, die auf *-o* enden: → regelmäßiger Plural mit **-es**	one hero one tomato	two hero**es** two tomato**es**
Nomen, die auf Konsant und *-y* enden: → **-y** wird zu **-ies**	one country one family	two countr**ies** two famil**ies**
Nomen, die auf *-f* oder *-fe* enden: → Aus **-f** oder **-fe** wird meist **-ves**. (Ausnahme: *one roof, two roofs*)	one life one thief	two li**ves** two thie**ves**
Die unregelmäßigen Pluralformen muss man lernen.	one man one woman one child one foot one fish one sheep	two m**e**n two wom**e**n two child**ren** two f**ee**t two **fish** two **sheep**

2 Diese Nomen verwenden Sie nur im Singular:

Do you like **fruit**?	Magst du **Obst**?
We have lots of **homework** to do.	Wir haben viele **Hausaufgaben** auf.
This **information** isn't useful.	Diese **Information** ist nicht nützlich. / Diese **Informationen** sind nicht nützlich.
This **furniture** is expensive.	Diese **Möbel** sind teuer.
That is helpful **advice**, thank you.	Das ist hilfreicher **Rat**, danke. / Das sind hilfreiche **Ratschläge**, danke.
Maths isn't easy.	**Mathe** ist nicht einfach.
Now **news** is good news.	Keine **Nachrichten** sind gute **Nachrichten**.

3 Diese Nomen verwenden Sie nur im Plural:

I never wear these **trousers**.	Ich trage diese **Hose** nie.
Where are my **glasses**?	Wo ist meine **Brille**?
Do you have some **scissors**?	Hast du eine **Schere**?
The **stairs** are very dirty.	Die **Treppe** ist sehr schmutzig.

G Grammar

G23 Genitive Der Genitiv

1 So können Sie ausdrücken, dass etwas einer Person oder einem Tier gehört oder zugeordnet ist:

I'm going to my friend**'s** house.	Ich gehe zum Haus meines **Freundes** / **meiner Freundin**.
The children**'s** tablets are in the classroom.	Die Tablets **der Kinder** sind im Klassenzimmer.
Whose phone is this? – It's my brother**'s**.	Wessen Handy ist das? – Das **meines Bruders**.
I'm going to my friend**s'** house.	Ich gehe zum Haus **meiner Freunde**.
This is my parent**s'** car.	Das ist das Auto **meiner Eltern**.
Have you seen the Johnson**s'** cat?	Hast du die Katze **der Johnsons** gesehen?

2 So können Sie die Zugehörigkeit zu Dingen ausdrücken oder Zeit- und Ortsangaben machen:

I damaged the door **of** the car.	Ich habe die Tür **des Autos** beschädigt.
Chris called in the middle **of** the night.	Chris rief **mitten in der Nacht** an.

G24 Gerund Das Gerundium

So können Sie über Tätigkeiten und Aktivitäten sprechen:

Working full-time can be exhausting.	Vollzeit **zu arbeiten** kann anstrengend sein.
Being employed gives me a lot of security.	Angestellt **zu sein**, gibt mir viel Sicherheit.
Ben likes **meeting** his friends after work.	Ben **trifft sich** nach der Arbeit gerne mit Freunden.
I don't like **answering** emails at work.	Ich **beantworte** nicht gerne E-Mails auf der Arbeit.
Sheila looks forward to **getting** a bonus this year.	Sheila freut sich darauf, dieses Jahr einen Bonus **zu bekommen**.

→ Man benutzt das *Gerund*, wenn man Verben als Nomen gebrauchen will.
→ Das *Gerund* kann Subjekt oder Objekt eines Satzes sein.
→ Das *Gerund* wird oft nach bestimmten Verben (*like, enjoy, love, prefer, hate, not like*) oder nach bestimmten Ausdrücken (z. B. *be good at …, think about …, worry about …, look forward to …, What about …?*) verwendet.

Denken Sie daran:
Das Gerundium darf man nicht mit dem *present progressive* verwechseln:

I am working overtime.	Ich mache gerade Überstunden.
I love **working** overtime.	Ich liebe es, Überstunden **zu machen**.

G25 Infinitive and participle constructions
Infinitiv- und Partizipkonstruktionen

1 *Participle constructions* verwenden Sie:

→ anstatt eines Nebensatzes mit *when*.
→ um Ihren Schreibstil abwechslungsreicher zu gestalten.

Coming home, I felt tired. (statt: When I came home, I felt tired.)	Als ich nach Hause kam, fühlte ich mich müde.
Running out of the house, I forgot my phone. (statt: When I ran out of the house, I forgot my phone.)	Als ich aus dem Haus rannte, vergaß ich mein Handy.

Denken Sie daran:
Die Form des Partizips wird genauso gebildet wie die *-ing*-Form des *present progressive* (→ **G1** Present progressive): run – running; come – coming

2 *Infinitive constructions* verwenden Sie:

→ nach **the first**, **the last**, **the only one** und nach Superlativen wie **the worst** anstatt eines Relativsatzes (→ **G3** Relative clauses).
→ um Ihren Schreibstil abwechslungsreicher zu gestalten.

I'm usually **the first** one **to get up** in the morning. (statt: I'm usually the first one who gets up in the morning.)	Ich bin normalerweise die Erste / der Erste, die/der morgens aufsteht.
She was **the only** one **to arrive** late. (statt: She was the only one who arrived late.)	Sie war die Einzige, die zu spät kam.
They were **the last** two students **to leave** the school building. (statt: They were the last two students who left the building.)	Sie waren die letzten beiden Schüler, die das Schulgebäude verließen.
That's **the worst** thing **to do**. (statt: That's the worst thing that you can do.)	Das ist das Schlimmste, was du tun kannst.

3 Complete the exercises. Check your answers on page 192.

1. ■ the house, Claire realised that it was very cold outside. (leave)
2. On Saturdays, Luke is often the last one ■ ■. (wake up)
3. ■ home late at night, Mark felt tired. (drive)
4. ■ her watch, Susan remembered that she had a meeting in five minutes. (check)
5. But Susan was the first ■ ■ for the meeting. (show up)
6. John's boss was the only one ■ ■ about his birthday. (forget)

G Grammar

List of irregular verbs

●●●
bet, bet, bet *wetten*
shut, shut, shut *schließen*

others
bet, bet, bet *wetten*
cost, cost, cost *kosten*
hit, hit, hit *schlagen*
fit, fit, fit *passen*
quit, quit, quit *kündigen, aufhören*
hurt, hurt, hurt *(sich) wehtun*
let, let, let *lassen*
put, put, put *legen, stellen*
spread, spread, spread *verbreiten*

●●●
feel, felt, felt *fühlen*
hold, held, held *halten*
keep, kept, kept *aufbewahren*
lend, lent, lent *(ver)leihen*
lead, led, led *führen*
leave, left, left *(ver)lassen*
meet, met, met *treffen*
read, read, read *lesen*
say, said, said *sagen*
lay, laid, laid *legen, verlegen*
sleep, slept, slept *schlafen*

have, had, had *haben*
sit, sat, sat *sitzen*

mean, meant, meant *meinen, bedeuten*
send, sent, sent *senden*
spend, spent, spent *ausgeben*

bring, brought, brought *(mit)bringen*
buy, bought, bought *kaufen*
catch, caught, caught *fangen*
fight, fought, fought *(be)kämpfen*
teach, taught, taught *unterrichten*
think, thought, thought *denken*
get, got, got *bekommen*
lose, lost, lost *verlieren*
shoot, shot, shot *(er)schießen*

stand, stood, stood *stehen*
understand, understood, understood *verstehen*

sell, sold, sold *verkaufen*
tell, told, told *sagen, erzählen*

others
build, built, built *bauen*
find, found, found *finden*
hang, hung, hung *hängen*
hear, heard, heard *hören*
pay, paid, paid *bezahlen*
make, made, made *machen*
win, won, won *gewinnen*

●●●
become, became, become *werden*
come, came, come *kommen*
overcome, overcame, overcame *überwinden*

●●●
begin, began, begun *beginnen*
drink, drank, drunk *trinken*
ring, rang, rung *klingeln*
run, ran, run *laufen*
swim, swam, swum *schwimmen*
sing, sang, sung *singen*
sink, sank, sunk *sinken*

drive, drove, driven *fahren*
ride, rode, ridden *reiten, fahren*
rise, rose, risen *steigen*
write, wrote, written *schreiben*

bite, bit, bitten *beißen*
hide, hid, hidden *(sich) verstecken*
forbid, forbade, forbidden *verbieten*
give, gave, given *geben*
forgive, forgave, forgiven *vergeben*
swear, swore, sworn *beschimpfen; schwören*
wear, wore, worn *tragen*

fly, flew, flown *fliegen*
blow, blew, blown *pfeifen*
grow, grew, grown *wachsen*
know, knew, known *wissen*
throw, threw, thrown *werfen*

break, broke, broken *(zer)brechen*
choose, chose, chosen *wählen*
freeze, froze, frozen *frieren*
speak, spoke, spoken *sprechen*
steal, stole, stolen *stehlen*
wake, woke, woken *aufwachen*

others
be, was/were, been *sein*
beat, beat, beaten *schlagen*
draw, drew, drawn *zeichnen*
do, did, done *tun, machen*
eat, ate, eaten *essen*
fall, fell, fallen *fallen*
forget, forgot, forgotten *vergessen*
go, went, gone *gehen, fahren*
lie, lay, lain *liegen*
see, saw, seen *sehen*
sew, sewed, sewn *nähen*
show, showed, shown *zeigen*
take, took, taken *nehmen*

●●
can, could – *können*

Methods M

M1 Milling around Marktplatz

1. Bearbeiten Sie die Aufgabe zunächst allein. Auf ein Signal der Lehrkraft stehen Sie auf und gehen durch den Raum. Nehmen Sie die Aufgabe und einen Stift mit.
2. Wenn erneut ein Signal ertönt, bleiben Sie stehen. Besprechen Sie die Aufgabe mit der Person, die Ihnen am nächsten steht.
3. Beim nächsten Signal trennen Sie sich und gehen weiter durch den Raum. Wiederholen Sie Schritt 2.

M2 Think-pair-share Nachdenken-austauschen-teilen

1. **Think:** Schreiben Sie Ihre Ideen, Gedanken oder Lösungen zur Aufgabe alleine auf.
2. **Pair:** Tauschen Sie Ihre Notizen mit einem Partner / einer Partnerin aus und besprechen Sie diese.
3. **Share:** Präsentieren Sie Ihre Ergebnisse anderen Paaren oder der gesamten Klasse.

M3 1-minute presentation Kurzpräsentation

1. Nehmen Sie sich ein DIN A4-Blatt. Falten Sie es so, dass das untere Drittel nach hinten wegknickt.
2. Schreiben Sie den Text Ihrer Präsentation auf die oberen zwei Drittel.
3. Notieren Sie nun die wichtigsten Stichpunkte noch einmal auf dem unteren Drittel. Dies ist Ihr Spickzettel.
4. In Ihrer Präsentation verwenden Sie nur den Spickzettel. Wenn Sie nicht mehr weiter wissen, dürfen Sie kurz auf den Text oben schauen.

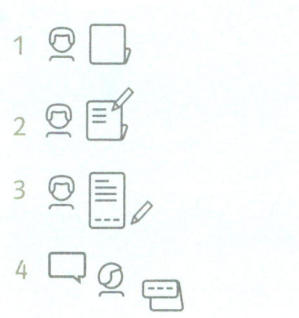

M4 Placemat Platzdeckchen

1. Bilden Sie Vierergruppen.
2. Teilen Sie ein großes Blatt Papier in fünf Bereiche ein.
3. Setzen Sie sich so hin, dass jeder in eine Ecke des Blattes schreiben kann.
4. Jedes Gruppenmitglied denkt allein über das Thema nach und schreibt Ideen auf seinen / ihren Teil des Blattes.
5. Tauschen Sie sich über die Ideen aus. Einigen Sie sich auf die besten Ideen und schreiben Sie diese in die Mitte des Blattes.

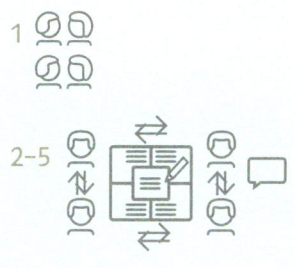

M Methods

M5 Round robin Blitzlicht

1. Überlegen Sie sich einen Satz zu der Aufgabe / der Frage / dem Thema.
2. Wenn alle bereit sind, tauschen Sie sich in der Klasse / in Gruppen aus, indem Sie nacheinander Ihren Satz sagen.
3. Alle anderen hören aufmerksam zu, kommentieren aber nicht.

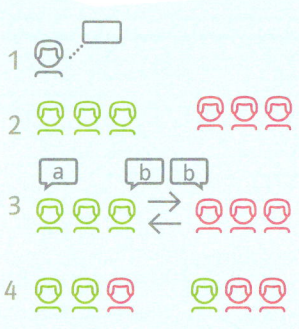

M6 Opinion line Meinungslinie

1. Überlegen Sie, welche Meinung Sie zum genannten Thema haben. Sind Sie dafür oder dagegen? Warum?
2. Stellen Sie sich auf einer gedachten Linie im Klassenzimmer auf. Auf der linken Seite stehen die Schüler/-innen, die DAFÜR sind. Auf der rechten Seite stehen die Schüler/-innen, die DAGEGEN sind.
3. Tauschen Sie sich zunächst innerhalb Ihrer Gruppe (a) und danach mit der anderen Gruppe (b) aus. Nennen Sie Ihre Argumente und Gründe.
4. Am Schluss positionieren Sie sich erneut. Haben Sie Ihre Meinung geändert?

M7 Peer correction Partnerkontrolle

1. Bearbeiten Sie die Aufgabe zunächst selbstständig.
2. Tauschen Sie Ihre Lösungen mit einem Partner / einer Partnerin. Kontrollieren Sie seine oder ihre Lösungen.
3. Tauschen Sie sich danach zu der Aufgabe aus und korrigieren Sie den Text.

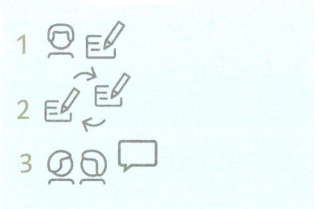

M8 Writers' conference Schreibwerkstatt

1. Bilden Sie Vierergruppen.
2. Lesen Sie sich Ihre Sätze / Texte gegenseitig vor.
3. Die anderen sagen, was ihnen gefallen hat, und machen Verbesserungsvorschläge.
4. Wählen Sie als Gruppe den besten Text aus und lesen Sie ihn der Klasse vor.

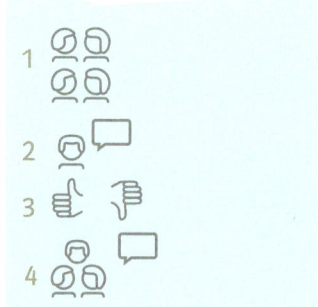

Methods M

M9 Read and look up — Lesen und Aufschauen

1. Lesen Sie die erste Zeile / den ersten Satz ganz genau. Schauen Sie hoch und sprechen Sie Ihre Zeile / Ihren Satz lautlos oder leise vor sich hin. Nehmen Sie sich dann die nächste Zeile oder den nächsten Satz vor.
2. Üben Sie nun mit einem Partner / einer Partnerin. Sprechen Sie Ihren Text Zeile für Zeile oder Satz für Satz so frei wie möglich. Dazwischen schauen Sie immer wieder nach unten auf Ihren Text.
3. Wiederholen Sie alles, bis Sie den Text auswendig können.

M10 Tip-top — Feedback

1. Sagen Sie zunächst, was Ihnen gut gefallen hat – also „top" war.
2. Sagen Sie nun, was noch nicht so gut war. Geben Sie einen Tipp, was man verbessern könnte.

M11 Gallery walk — Galerierundgang

1. Hängen Sie nach Ihrer Gruppenarbeit Ihr Produkt gut sichtbar im Klassenzimmer auf.
2. Einer von Ihnen, der „Experte", bleibt bei Ihrem Projekt stehen und erklärt es den anderen. Die anderen gehen herum. Nach jedem Durchgang wechselt der Experte.
3. Sehen Sie sich die Produkte der anderen an und geben Sie Feedback.
4. Werten Sie im Anschluss Ihre Ergebnisse in der Klasse aus.

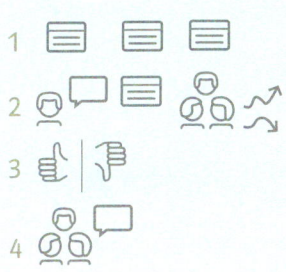

M12 Double circle — Kugellager

1. Bilden Sie zwei Kreise: einen Innen- und einen Außenkreis.
2. Setzen / Stellen Sie sich paarweise gegenüber und tauschen Sie sich zu dem Thema / der Frage aus.
3. Auf ein Signal der Lehrkraft „wandern" die Personen im inneren Kreis zwei Plätze nach links, um ein neues Paar zu bilden.
4. Tauschen Sie sich mit Ihrem neuen Partner / Ihrer neuen Partnerin aus.

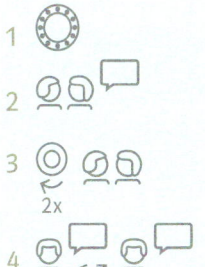

333
Solutions

Grammar

G1

6a)
1. shows; 2. don't tell; 3. is; 4. Does … read; 5. do … do

6b)
1. He's checking the website for more information now.
2. They're offering a lot of programmes today.
3. At the moment she isn't trying to go online.
4. I'm just playing this new game.
5. What are the doctors saying in this interview now?

6c)
1. are closing, are
2. play, are not/aren't working
3. tell, is telling
4. 'm/am not watching, feel
5. is leaving, do … go
6. Is … calling, makes

G2

6a)
1 E; 2 C; 3 F; 4 A; 5 D; 6 B

6b)
1. shouldn't; 2. could; 3. doesn't have to; 4. needn't; 5. shall

6c)
1. We should save more energy.
2. You can help to protect nature.
3. Shall he recommend you a hotel?
4. You mustn't enter the room now.
5. Could everyone be quiet, please?

G3

3a)
1. who; 2. which; 3. who; 4. who; 5. which

3b)
1. who; 2. whose; 3. who; 4. who; 5. whose

3c)
1. Tina likes her home, which is not far away from her parents'.
2. She often visits her parents, whose house is only five minutes away.
3. Their dog Tabby is a Golden Retriever, who likes to play in the garden.
4. The family enjoys BBQs, which they all love.
5. Her home town is very important to Tina, who couldn't imagine living anywhere else.

G4

2a)
1. are; 2. is; 3. is; 4. are; 5. are

2b)
1. is celebrated; 2. are organised; 3. is played; 4. are sold; 5. are raised

2c)
1. The people in church practise songs.
2. Young and old people make music.
3. Many people give money to charity projects.
4. A priest wears religious symbols.
5. In voodoo religion a spell protects a person.

G5

5a)
1. had, prepared
2. didn't seem, weren't
3. was, didn't make
4. went, wanted
5. offered, didn't feel
6. decided, told

5b)
1. has … seen, have … been
2. haven't started, haven't found
3. have … finished, has … walked
4. Has … written, has been
5. has done, have … tried

5c)
1. Have … seen, watched
2. has … released, came
3. has … done, trained
4. Did … change, haven't found
5. thought, has been
6. walked, have … seen

G6

3a)
1. had finished; 2. hadn't made; 3. had spoken; 4. had worked; 5. had tested; 6. had … been

3b)
1. had grown, went
2. stopped, had been
3. had moved, came
4. got, hadn't had
5. had fallen, didn't make
6. went, had tried

Solutions

G7
3a)
1. will be; 2. will help; 3. won't rain; 4. will find; 5. will … come; 6. Will … say

3b)
1. are going to visit; 2. are going to stay; 3. is going to rain; 4. is going to look; 5. am going to have

3c)
1. Maybe the sun will shine tomorrow.
2. I'm going to send off my application tomorrow.
3. Are you going to apply for this job advert?
4. They hope (that) the new year will be better.
5. Give me two minutes, I'll / I will help you then.
6. Sina is going to talk to her boss at 2 o'clock tomorrow.

G8
3a)
1. popular – more popular – most popular
2. good – better – best
3. fast – faster – fastest
4. hard – harder – hardest
5. exciting – more exciting – most exciting
6. long – longer – longest
7. funny – funnier – funniest
8. bad – worse – worst
9. professional – more professional – most professional
10. happy – happier – happiest
11. serious – more serious – most serious
12. nice – nicer – nicest

3b)
1. most exciting
2. as friendly as, more professional, reliable
3. hard, most efficient
4. best, faster
5. fitter, not as fit as

G9
2a)
1. The reporter says that he has never seen anything like that before.
2. … there are lots of people.
3. … a woman is taking care of a person who is bleeding.
4. … an ambulance arrived five minutes ago.
5. The reporter wants to know where the noise comes from.
6. The reporter says not to get any closer.

2b)
1. Alice says that they were so excited.
2. John says it was their first trip to New Zealand.
3. Alice says that her boyfriend has planned her birthday party in Adelaide.
4. John asks if Alice was happy about his surprise present.
5. Alice says she couldn't believe that he organised everything in secret.
6. John says that her birthday was a success until the earth began to shake under their feet.

G10
4a)
1. had found, her
2. would have
3. not to get, would be
4. had already had, had left, to stay, had
5. to remember, had been, had had, would
6. not to forget, was

4b)
1. "I've just bought my plane ticket to New Zealand, but I haven't found a job there yet."
2. "My parents took me to New Zealand for the first time in 2015."
3. "I don't remember much about the trip, but I loved the landscape."
4. "I'm sure that I'll have a wonderful time in New Zealand."

G11
4a)
1. was running; 2. was listening; 3. was waving; 4. were walking; 5. was thinking; 6. were talking

4b)
1. were walking, shouted
2. were laughing, started
3. was looking, were running
4. were rushing, was still yelling
5. were making, arrived
6. was asking, were telling

G12
2a)
1. were written; 2. was inspired; 3. were closed; 4. was attacked; 5. were founded; 6. were given

2b)
1. have been passed; 2. have been asked; 3. haven't been presented; 4. hasn't been read; 5. Have … been seen; 6. has been elected

Solutions

G16

5a)
1. need, 'll/will help; 2. 'll/will be, don't phone; 3. doesn't come, she 'll/will lose; 4. won't find, doesn't look; 5. 'll/will talk, meet; 6. won't sleep, watch

5b)
1. would buy, had; 2. lost, would be; 3. shouted, wouldn't work; 4. wouldn't worry, felt; 5. would become, tried; 6. were, would enjoy

5c)
1. would have called – had known; 2. hadn't prepared – wouldn't have got; 3. had worn – wouldn't have hurt; 4. had bought – wouldn't have had; 5. wouldn't have missed – had woken up

G19

3)
1. At 7 o'clock Jake goes to school./Jake goes to school at 7 o'clock.
2. Luke is working hard at the gym.
3. Next weekend Kate is going to visit her friends in Edinburgh./Kate is going to visit her friends in Edinburgh next weekend.
4. In the mornings Brian eats his breakfast quickly./Brian eats his breakfast quickly in the mornings./Brian quickly eats his breakfast in the mornings.
5. But he doesn't drive fast to work.
6. After the interview Lucy nervously waited./Lucy nervously waited after the interview./Lucy waited nervously after the interview.

G20

3a)
1. Before; 2. because; 3. although/though; 4. so that; 5. as soon as; 6. after

3b)
1. Paul was listening to music while he was jogging.
2. Would you like to go to the cinema or would you like to eat some ice cream?
3. Brooke was very happy when she got the job.
4. Michael often waits until his girlfriend is ready.

G25

3)
1. Leaving; 2. to wake up; 3. Driving; 4. Checking; 5. to show up; 6. to forget

Quiz

Unit 1

Workshop, p. 16–17
7 What are your special skills?

Mostly As
Well, you can work on your own and you love routines. OK, you don't have the best communication skills – but you're well organised and punctual. Also, you enjoy organising things in general. People know that you're reliable.
▶ Maybe office assistant or accountant is the right job for you?

Mostly Bs
You're a fast worker and very practical. You enjoy working with your hands and you love technology. You're a motivated and hard-working person. You like challenges and solving problems. Are you the person people call when their computer stops working – their emergency hotline?
▶ Think about applying for a mechanic or IT specialist placement!

Mostly Cs
You are creative and flexible. People are important to you, and you love to take care of others. You're a real team player because you listen well, you're helpful and you like to talk and hang out with others. But if you must, you can also work on your own.
▶ Can you imagine working as a nursery assistant or hairdresser?

Unit 3

Reading workshop, p. 54
1 Ready for a marathon in South Africa?

Mostly As
You're a couch potatoe. Fitness isn't important to you at all.

Mostly Bs
You move at least a little bit. Go on – you can do more!

Mostly Cs
You try to keep yourself fit, but fitness isn't the most important thing to you.

Mostly Ds
You're a fitness star! A day without sport is OK too.

Vocabulary

Word banks

Die *Word bank*-Seiten helfen Ihnen, die *Your turn*-Aufgaben in den *Units* zu bearbeiten. Sie finden dort nützlichen individuellen Wortschatz zum Thema der Unit.

Die **fett** gedruckten Wörter kommen in der *Unit* vor. Diese Wörter müssen Sie lernen. Die in *kursiv* gedruckten Wörter können Sie lernen, müssen Sie aber nicht. Die grün gedruckten Wörter sollten Sie bereits kennen.

Unit 1: Australia: Endless options?!

dp78ec → Vokabellernlisten

V1 Giving a presentation

My presentation is about …
I'm going to talk about …
I have chosen the category/theme/subject …
First, I'd like to talk about …
First/Second/Third …
Another interesting point is …
Finally … | To sum up …
Thank you for listening / your attention!

V2 Life goals

- **to be fulfilled**
- to be popular/ rich/independent/ kind/healthy/brave/fair
- challenge
- to dream of
- *passion*
- to meet (a famous person)
- to save up for sth
- to buy / own a house/car/pet
- *happiness*, happy
- *creativity*, *creative*
- freedom
- to make a difference
- sustainability

values & goals

family & friends

- friendship
- to be there for sb
- *to become/be a stay-at-home mum/dad*
- family life
- to get/be married
- to have children
- community

Life goals

career

educaction

travel

- to move to / live / go backpacking in another country/city
- to enjoy adventures
- to explore/ discover different culture(s)

- to learn from/about
- to go to university
- to get a degree (in)
- job training programme
- to read/watch/ write about
- to become fluent in
- to improve

- to work hard
- **to succeed**
- to be successful ↔ to fail
- success ↔ failure
- (to have) **responsibility**, responsible
- to be skilled ↔ **unskilled**
- to own a company/business
- to have a big career
- job/financial security
- *to become a millionaire*
- to be your own boss

V Vocabulary

V3 Workplaces, jobs and tasks

workplace	jobs	tasks
office	accountant manager/boss *secretary* office/personal assistant call centre agent *programmer/IT specialist*	to answer the phone/emails to make phone calls to talk to customers *to write an invoice* to organise a meeting to programme software
hospital/*doctor's surgery*/*old people's home*	nurse doctor paramedic receptionist	to help patients (to get dressed) to give **medicine**/medical **advice** *to take temperature/vitals* to feed/wash sb
nursery, kindergarten	nursery assistant	**to take care of sb** to play/sing/dance to look after
salon	hairdresser make-up artist	**to cut hair** *to colour hair* to recommend a style
plane	flight attendant pilot *mechanic*	to welcome passengers on board to serve drinks/food *to give safety instructions* to fly the plane
restaurant	waiter/waitress chef kitchen helper *barkeeper*	**to clear a table** to cook/prepare meals to serve/recommend drinks/food *to take orders*
hotel	receptionist *cleaner* *gardener* *fitness instructor*	to take reservations to answer the phone/emails to clean a room **to make the bed** *to plant flowers* *to give (fitness) instructions/courses*
factory	factory worker machine operator *logistics coordinator*	to work on the assembly line *to work in shifts* to do quality checks
garage	*mechanic*	to work with/use **tools** to repair/*fix* a car to order parts to change tyres
construction site	construction worker	to build *to dig* *to drill*
shop	shop/*sales* assistant store manager *fishmonger*	to sell to recommend/give advice to talk to customers
at customer's house/business	plumber electrician	*to install pipes/lights* to repair/*fix the toilet*/shower/plumbing **to lay a cable**

Vocabulary

V4 Talking about texts

This is a … blog post | email | report | article | diary entry | story
… because it has (a/an) …
headline | subheading | date | name of the author | introduction paragraph | address
It is a fictional/factual text.
The author gives his/her personal opinion | just the facts | different arguments …

V5 Writing a story

on a sunny/cloudy/rainy day | the next day/morning
in this situation
at first/first of all
a few minutes/hours/days later | after that/next/then | afterwards/later
as soon as/when | but then
all of a sudden/suddenly | surprisingly/unexpectedly
because of that / for this reason / that's why
however/but
although
moreover | however / in addition | not only … but also
while/as | during
finally / at last / in the end

V6 Talking about preferences

Would you rather … or …? | What do you think about …? | Why do/don't you like …?
I'd rather … | I prefer … to … | I (really / quite / don't) like/love/enjoy | I don't mind …
… is as important as …
I don't have a preference. | I like both.
I don't like/enjoy either option.
I'd choose/pick/go with … | If I could choose I would … | … would be my preference.

Vocabulary

Unit 2: Working in Ireland

sq6bi9 → Vokabellernlisten

V7 Giving a recommendation

I think you need to / have to / should …
I (strongly) recommend to … | My (personal) recommendation is / would be … | In this situation I always/usually recommend … | My advice is (to) …
It's (always/usually) a good idea to …
Make sure you (don't) …
The sooner you … the better.
You have no choice but to …
Why don't you …? | You could (try) … | If I were you, I'd …
In my experience … is really great/interesting/helpful/…
One thing you could / should / have to do is …

V8 Having a discussion

In my opinion …
I (don't) think/believe that …
Some/Most people say …
I agree/disagree with …
You make a good point, but …
What do you think about/of …?
On the one hand, … On the other hand, …

Many people think that …
It could be argued that …
An argument for / against …
A big (dis-)advantage is …
Another problem/aspect/point is …
The reasons why … is that …
Considering the pros and cons I think that …

because (of) | for example | but | however | In addition

V9 Writing a comment

The topic of … is of great interest to … | It is an important topic because … |
The question is: Should …?
Firstly/secondly …
Moreover, … | Either …, or … | not only … but also … |
Another way to look at this is …. | On the other hand, …
In my opinion … | If you ask me, …
I agree/disagree with/that …
Why don't they …?
I think/believe they should …
It would be a good idea to … because …
My conclusion is … | In conclusion, … |
To sum up, … | All in all, …

Vocabulary V

V10 Analysing job adverts

position

- permanent job
- summer job
- traineeship, trainee, to train
- apprenticeship / *on-the-job training*
- internship, intern

contract
- permanent ↔ fixed-term
- *full-time* ↔ *part-time*

requirements
- skills
- interests
- to have experience / knowledge
- driving licence
- minimum age
- to be required
- passion
- know-how
- qualification, to qualify

Analysing job adverts

contact

- to apply online / **via email** / **phone** / **in person**
- to send a letter of application / CV
- to have a job interview

salary

- per hour / day
- paid ↔ *unpaid*
- fair ↔ *unfair*
- transparent
- *inequality / pay gap*

benefits

- cafeteria
- *leave*
- *parental leave*
- career opportunities
- workshop
- course / *advanced training*
- retirement plan
- insurance plan

working hours

- schedule
- to work long hours
- regular ↔ *irregular*
- *flexible*
- an eight-hour day
- a forty-hour week
- to work **shifts**
- to work from home

V11 Describing pictures

The photo/picture shows … | In this picture you can see …
This photo was taken in/at …
The title/caption of this picture is …
On the right/left …
At the top/bottom …
In the middle/foreground/background …
He/She is … (old/young) | He/She has … (hair/eyes).
They are … (old/young) | They have … (hair/eyes).
He/She is wearing … | He/She is smiling/crying …
The person looks happy/sad/busy/lonely/relaxed …
There is/are … | It looks/is …
I think …

black and white | colourful | next to | between | behind | in | on | under | in front of

one hundred and ninety-seven **197**

V Vocabulary

V12 Analysing cartoons

The cartoon shows a person who is … / … people who are …
The person is sitting/writing/… | They are …
The person/sign says …
The speech/thought bubble/caption says …
The cartoon shows/presents/criticises …
The cartoon illustrates the topic/the problem of/that …
The cartoon is making fun of …
The cartoonist is criticising …
I (don't) like the cartoon because …
I (don't) think the cartoon is funny/interesting because …
I agree/disagree with the message because … | I (don't) agree with the point the cartoon is making because … | I don't get the joke. | I don't understand (why) …

V13 Writing a CV

Vocabulary

V14 Writing a letter of application

Dear Mr/Ms …, | To whom it may concern, …
I would like to apply for the job as … | I am interested in your position as …
I read your advertisement for … in/on … | I refer to your advertisement in/on …
I qualify well for the position because … | My skills are …
I have a part-time job as … | I have work experience
as … | Although I have no previous experience, …
I am very interested in this job because … | I would
like to work for you because … |
I would welcome the opportunity to train / work in
your company (because …)
Please find my CV attached.
I look forward to hearing from you.
Yours sincerely, …

V15 Giving your opinion

In my opinion … | I believe/think … | I would/wouldn't
I'm not sure if … | I can/can't imagine that …
Firstly/Secondly … | In addition …
On the one hand, … On the other hand, …
In my experience … | From my point of view …
I (dis-)agree with … because … | I reject/accept the idea that …
It seems that …
An example for this argument would be … | For example … | A good example of this is …
To sum up, …

however | even though | while | …

V Vocabulary

V16 Doing a job interview

At the beginning of the interview
Good morning./ Good afternoon./ Hello Mr/ Ms …
How are you today?
It's so nice to meet you.
Thank you for taking the time to meet with me today.

During the interview
I graduated from … in …
I have worked for … years as a …
I was responsible for … / I worked with …
I'm good at languages / taking care of … / multi-tasking / being a team player / communicating well / working in an international environment / working under pressure / …
I'm good with numbers/computers.
I'm flexible/polite/hard-working/punctual/strong/patient/well-organised / a fast learner / motivated to learn about … / interested in …
I have good manners / know-how in … / an eye for detail
I consider working with children / being creative / solving problems quickly … to be one of my strengths/passions.
Sometimes it is hard for me to …
I'm a good fit for this job because …
I believe my qualifications make me an excellent fit for this role because …
I don't mind …
I'm willing to …

At the end of the interview
I've done some research about the company and I really love … about you.
Can you tell me more about …?
I would love to work here because …
Thanks again for taking the time to meet with me today.

Vocabulary V

Unit 3: Multicultural South Africa
🌐 v877f8 → Vokabellernlisten

V17 Multiculturalism

culture **Multiculturalism** *chances*

challenges

- *identity*, *to identify*
- *national* ↔ *international*
- *citizenship*, *citizen*
- *immigration, immigrant*
- *minority* ↔ *majority*
- *difference, different*
- *communication, to communicate*
- **(native) language**: *Afrikaans, Xhosa, Zulu, Turkish, …*
- art/music/architecture
- traditions/festivals/lifestyle
- religion/belief/value
- food
- ethnicity/origin/race: black, white, coloured, Asian, mixed

- history: **apartheid**, segregation, colonialism, slavery
- discrimination, *to discriminate against*
- racism, racist
- inequality ↔ equality
- to be narrow-minded ↔ open-minded
- to feel better than
- conflict
- to feel angry about
- to fear
- culture shock
- prejudice
- to expect sb to be bad/criminal

- rainbow nation
- **to get along with sb**
- *diversity*, **diverse**
- **to overcome**
- **equality**, equal ↔ inequality, unequal
- tolerance, tolerant
- acceptance, to accept
- unity, to unite
- peace, peaceful
- friendship
- inclusion, to include
- community
- connection, to connect with sb
- to learn from each other
- to understand sb/sth better
- to be open-minded
- respect, to respect, respectful

V Vocabulary

V18 Doing an interview

Questions
When/What/Who/Where/Why/How …?
family | origin | languages | education | phases of life | career | experience | special moments | hobbies | volunteer work | achievements

Answers
I really enjoy … | It's amazing to see …
I think that … is/isn't the most important thing.
I would describe it as …
I wish I had learned/listened to/stopped …
… taught me everything I know. | … inspired me.
… shows respect / understands me …
I'm most thankful for … | I never could have done it without …

V19 Animals

pets
- cat
- dog
- rabbit
- bird: *parrot*, …
- turtle
- hamster

farm
- horse
- cow
- goat
- chicken
- pig
- sheep (plural: sheep)

land
- lion
- elephant
- buffalo
- leopard
- *rhinoceros*
- *zebra*
- *antelope*
- giraffe
- monkey
- (polar) bear
- koala
- kangaroo
- snake
- spider
- deer
- mouse
- fox

water
- fish (plural: fish): shark, …
- dolphin
- whale
- penguin
- crocodile

air
- bird: *eagle*
- bee
- *fly*

Vocabulary

V20 Describing sensations

- **admiration**, to admire
- **dissatisfaction**, dissatisfied
- *intimidation*, **intimidated**
- *motivation*, motivated
- *exhaustion*, exhausted
- *nervosness*, nervous
- *excitement*, excited
- *happiness*, happy
- *sadness*, sad
- *anger*, angry

feelings

taste & scent

Sensations

sounds

sights

- sweet ↔ *sour*
- salty
- delicious/tasty ↔ *disgusting*
- good ↔ bad
- amazing ↔ terrible/ *horrific*

- noise, noisy
- **suspenseful**
- to chirp, chirping
- loud ↔ quiet
- *soft*/*hushed*
- bang, banging
- music, musical
- explosion, *explosive*

- impressive
- picturesque
- iconic
- dramatic
- unique
- emerald
- lush
- drab ↔ colourful
- glum ↔ happy
- familiar ↔ *unfamiliar*/ *foreign*
- *natural* ↔ *unnatural*/ *strange*
- beautiful ↔ ugly
- tall/high ↔ short/low
- wonderful

V21 Free time

I like meeting my friends / playing video games / relaxing / staying over at friends' / going to the gym / …
I love football / talking to my friends / shopping / …
I'm crazy about films / series / mountainbiking / …
I enjoy playing the piano / reading comics / going out / dancing / …
I have to help with the household / clean the bathroom / tidy up my room / …
I spend every day / hour / some time with …
In my free time I always/often/usually/sometimes/never …
I don't have a lot of free time because …

V Vocabulary

V22 Sightseeing

Sightseeing

nature
- (to explore a) **nature reserve**
- (national) park
- lake
- ocean: beach, coastline, cliff
- river
- forest/jungle
- volcano
- mountain

sights & attractions
- (to go to / visit a) theme park
- (to go on a) safari
- museum
- *selfie spot*, to take a selfie
- historic sight: castle, *monument*, famous building
- skyline
- tourist attraction
- harbour
- view

entertainment & shopping
- shoppping centre (BE), shopping mall (AE)
- *(farmer's)* market
- restaurant (BE), *diner (AE)*
- bar/pub
- cinema
- theatre/*musical*/*(magic)* show

V23 Making suggestions and finding a compromise

> Let's … / I suggest … | We could / should …
> What about …? / Would you be OK with …?
> How about…? | Why don't you …?
> If I were you, I would …
> Don't you think it's a good idea to …?
> Do you mind (if) …?
> Yes, I'd like/love to. / That's a great idea.
> Well, I'd rather … / I like your idea, but could we …?
> I don't think … will work. / I don't feel like …
> Sounds great. | Good point. | Brilliant!

V24 Talking about locations

> … is situated close to / between / next to the sea / mountains / a river / the city of …
> … is located in the north/south/west/east/middle/north-east of the country.
> … is near/not far from … | … is an hour drive from here …
> … is on the other side of town. | … is in the same neighbourhood/region/area as …
> It takes about … minute(s)/hour(s) to get there. | It's a … hour train ride/flight/drive.

Vocabulary   V

Unit 4: Digital Hong Kong   🌐 h87gg2 → Vokabellernlisten

V25 Media

Media
- type of media
- activities
- devices

- TV: film, series, documentary, ...
- radio (show)
- book/newspaper/magazine
- video game
- Internet: blog, wiki entry, social media site, *vlog*, *app*, message, chat

- TV: *remote control*, **screen**
- computer: **screen**, *keyboard*, *mouse*
- laptop
- tablet
- smartphone/mobile phone
- **VR goggle**
- game console
- *headphones*
- *camera*

- **to switch on/off**
- **to delete**
- **to track**
- to watch
- to chat
- to listen to sth
- to share
- to (re-)search/to check
- to surf
- to comment/post
- to follow ↔ to unfollow
- to connect
- *to download* ↔ *to upload*

V26 Talking about media habits

 I spend ... hours on media every day.
I spend most time reading/watching videos/looking at .../scrolling through ...
I use my phone/tablet/device for ...
I didn't realise I spent so much time doing ...
I could/couldn't live without it.
I think I spend too much/a normal amount of time on my phone/computer/game console.
I wouldn't be able to stay in touch with my friends/keep up with trends/read the news/find information/... without media.

V Vocabulary

V27 Analysing charts

Types of charts
pie chart ⊗ | bar chart ||| | line graph ⟿

Description
This chart / graph is about / shows / deals with …
It was published by … in …
The chart / numbers / show(s) / suggest(s) that …
The majority / minority of … / 40 percent of …
More than a half / a third / …
The number of … goes up / increases by … / drops / goes down / doesn't change.

Conclusion
I/We can draw the conclusion that …

V28 Feelings

V29 Writing an email

Dear Sir or Madam, | Dear (name), | Good morning/afternoon, | Hi/Hello, …
I am writing to you because … / … to inform you … | I would like to … | I herewith revoke the contract I signed on … | Could you let me know …
Please find attached … | Please confirm … |
Thank you for your help. | I look forward to hearing from you soon.
Yours sincerely/faithfully | Kind regards
All the best | Best wishes | Bye for now | Love | Lots of love

Vocabulary V

V30 Asking for help and clarifying your ideas

> I'm sorry, I don't understand … | I'm not sure that I understand …
> Can you repeat that, please?
> What do you mean by …?
> Could you explain …?
> Can you give me an example?
> If I understand you correctly, you're saying that …
> Let me explain it in another way …
> In other words … | Another/A different way to say it …
> Now I understand. | Now I get it. | Yes, now it's clear. | Thanks a lot.

Unit 5: Versatile California

🌐 g9kc3c → Vokabellernlisten

V31 Food

- bread
- pasta
- cereals
- **fruit**: apple, banana, lime, tomato
- **vegetables**: carrot, **cauliflower**, onion, (black-)bean, …
- **meat**: beef, chicken, pork
- fish
- milk
- cheese
- eggs
- spices: salt, pepper
- oil
- vinegar
- juice
- coffee

types of food

consumption

Food

activities

- **to harvest**
- **to garden**
- to cook
- to prepare
- to buy
- to clean
- to cut (into pieces)
- to serve
- to grow

- **consumer**
- **food bank**
- **profitability**
- **leftovers**
- beauty standards
- *cosmetically (im)perfect*
- *(im)perfect produce*
- **environmental** *impact*
- *affordable*/cheap ↔ expensive
- food sharing
- *(water) resources*
- healthy ↔ *unhealthy*
- fast food
- *to be on a diet*
- *vegetarian*
- *vegan*
- *low-carb*
- local/*regional* ↔ exotic
- seasonal
- organic ↔ conventional
- mass production

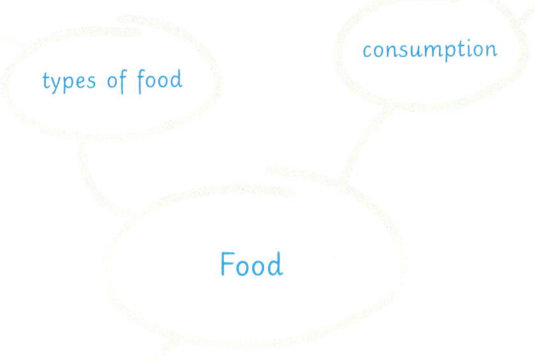

V Vocabulary

V32 Packaging and material

Packaging and material

- single-use
- reusable
- activities

- plastic: bag, **straw**, **disposables**, **cutlery**, plate, *take-out container*, *(yoghurt)* cup
- paper: bag, *wrapping*
- cardboard: box

- glass/metal: bottle, *container*, *tin*, *jar*, …
- **fabric**/wool: bag, *tote*, …
- **wood**/bamboo: box, **cutlery**, …

- to pack ↔ to unpack
- to be made of
- *to wrap*
- **to waste**
- **to tie**
- **to dump**
- to throw away
- to (re-)use

V33 School

- **chalk**
- **blackboard**
- digital devices
- desks

equipment

people

- *headmaster (BE)/* principal (AE)
- student/classmate
- teacher
- *tutor*
- *social worker*
- *secretary*

types of schools

School

activities

subjects

- primary school (BE), elementary school (AE)
- secondary school: *vocational school*, *grammar school*, *comprehensive school*, high school (AE)
- *Waldorf school*
- *Montessori school*
- university

- maths
- languages
- history
- art
- music
- science: *biology, chemistry, physics*
- physical education (PE)
- free study time
- clubs: drama, choir, …

- to focus, **focus**
- **to question**
- **to solve**
- to learn
- to practise
- to sing
- to read
- to write
- to count
- to colour
- to take a (*standardised*) test
- to prepare
- to discover
- to listen
- to improve

Vocabulary

V34 At a restaurant

The waiter/waitress
Welcome to …
Can/May I help you?
Do you have a reservation?
Let me take you to your table. | There will be a table available in a few minutes.
Can I get you some drinks? | What would you like to drink?
I can recommend our house lemonade. | I really like … | You should try …
Here is the menu.
Can I take your orders? | Are you ready to order?
Our special today is … | The … is one of our most popular items on the menu.
Is everything alright? Do you need anything else?
I'm sorry that you didn't like it. | I apologize that your food is cold/not done. I will get you a new dish.
The drinks are on the house. | Can I offer you a free dessert?
How would you like to pay, cash or card? | That will be €35, please. | Here's your receipt.
Thank you for your visit. | Have a nice day!

The guest
Hi, I have a reservation for (last name) for … people for … o'clock.
Hi, I don't have a reservation. Can I get a table for … people?
Can we get the menu, please?
Just water, please. | Can/Could I have a …? | I'd like a glass/bottle of …
What can you recommend? | Are there any specials today?
I'll have the … | I'd like to order the … | I'll have the same. | We're not ready yet.
Everything is fine, thanks. | I didn't order this. | My food is cold/not done.
Can/Could I have the bill, please | Can I pay by card?
Here you are. | The rest is for you.

V Vocabulary

Dictionary

Im *Dictionary* sind alle wichtigen Wörter aus Ihrem Buch enthalten. Die Wörter stehen in alphabetischer Reihenfolge. Die Hinweise zu Band, Unit und Seite zeigen, wo das Wort zum ersten Mal im Buch vorkommt. Die Vokabeln aus Band 1 sind nur mit der Bandnummer I gekennzeichnet.

englisches Wort	Lautschrift	deutsches Wort	Band bzw. Band, Unit, Seite
amount	[əˈmaʊnt]	Betrag	I
ancient	[ˈeɪnʃnt]	alt	II Unit 4, 73

Die mit einem Sternchen (*) versehenen Verben sind unregelmäßige Verben. Manche Wörter haben verschiedene Bedeutungen. Am besten lesen Sie alle, bevor Sie sich für eine entscheiden.

A

abandoned [əˈbændənd] aufgegeben; zurückgelassen I
Aboriginal [ˌæbəˈrɪdʒnl] von australischen Ureinwohnern abstammend; Aborigine- II Unit 1, 13
abroad [əˈbrɔːd] im Ausland; ins Ausland I
accessories (pl) [əkˈsesriz] Accessoires; Zubehör I
according to [əˈkɔːdɪŋ tə] laut; gemäß II Unit 4, 67
accountant [əˈkaʊntənt] Buchhalter/-in II Unit 1, 16
to **achieve** [əˈtʃiːv] erreichen; leisten I
acre [ˈeɪkə] Morgen (Flächenmaß von ca. 4047 m²) II Unit 5, 85
actress [ˈæktrəs] Schauspielerin I
actually [ˈæktʃuəli] eigentlich; tatsächlich; wirklich I
to **adapt** [əˈdæpt] (sich) anpassen; umstellen II Unit 4, 74
*to be **addicted** (to sth) [bi əˈdɪktɪd] süchtig sein (nach etw); abhängig sein (von etw) I
addiction [əˈdɪkʃn] Sucht; Abhängigkeit I
admiration [ˌædmɪˈreɪʃn] Bewunderung II Unit 3, 55
to **admire** [ədˈmaɪə] bewundern I
to **adopt** [əˈdɒpt] annehmen; übernehmen II Unit 3, 47

to **adore** [əˈdɔː] anhimmeln; verehren, sehr gern mögen II Unit 5, 83
advantage [ədˈvɑːntɪdʒ] Vorteil I
to **advertise** sth [ˈædvətaɪz] für etw Werbung machen I
display of **affection** [dɪˌspleɪ əv əˈfekʃn] *hier:* Austausch von Zärtlichkeiten I
affordable [əˈfɔːdəbl] bezahlbar I
I'm **afraid** … [ˌaɪm əˈfreɪd] Leider … II Unit 5, 90
afterwards [ˈɑːftəwədz] danach; hinterher II Unit 3, 56
job **agency** [ˈdʒɒb ˌeɪdʒnsi] Arbeitsagentur; Stellenbörse II Unit 2, 31
travel **agency** [ˈtrævl ˌeɪdʒnsi] Reisebüro I
agreement [əˈɡriːmənt] Vereinbarung II Unit 1, 10
agriculture [ˈæɡrɪkʌltʃə] Landwirtschaft II Unit 5, 82
air conditioning [ˌeəkənˈdɪʃnɪŋ] Klimaanlage I
alarm clock [əˈlɑːm ˌklɒk] Wecker II Unit 3, 54
alarming [əˈlɑːmɪŋ] besorgniserregend; alarmierend II Unit 4, 67
alias [ˈeɪliəs] Pseudonym; Alias II Unit 4, 75
*to be **alive** [bi əˈlaɪv] lebendig sein; leben I
alternative [ɔːlˈtɜːnətɪv] alternativ; abwechselnd; andere II Unit 4, 77

ambassador [æmˈbæsədə] Botschafter/-in II Unit 4, 73
ambitious [æmˈbɪʃəs] ehrgeizig I
among [əˈmʌŋ] unter; inmitten II Unit 4, 67
amount [əˈmaʊnt] Betrag I
ancient [ˈeɪnʃnt] alt II Unit 4, 73
to **announce** [əˈnaʊns] ankündigen; bekannt geben II Unit 4, 69
anxiety [æŋˈzaɪəti] Angst; Unruhe II Unit 4, 67
apart [əˈpɑːt] getrennt; auseinander II Unit 3, 47
apartheid (no pl) [əˈpɑːtaɪt] Apartheid (Rassentrennung per Gesetz) II Unit 3, 47
to **appreciate** [əˈpriːʃieɪt] wertschätzen; würdigen I
apprenticeship [əˈprentɪʃɪp] Ausbildung; Lehre II Unit 2, 30
apron [ˈeɪprən] Schürze II Unit 2, 37
arranged marriage [əˌreɪndʒd ˈmærɪdʒ] arrangierte Ehe I
ash [æʃ] Asche I
aspect [ˈæspekt] Aspekt; Seite I
asphalt [ˈæsfælt] Asphalt II Unit 2, 36
assembly line [əˈsembli ˌlaɪn] Fließband I
nursery **assistant** [ˈnɜːsri əˌsɪstnt] Kindergartenhelfer/-in II Unit 2, 32
at least [ət ˈliːst] mindestens; wenigstens II Unit 2, 30
athlete [ˈæθliːt] Leichtathlet/-in I

Vocabulary

flight **attendant** [ˈflaɪt əˌtendnt] Flugbegleiter/-in II Unit 1, 17
attention span [əˈtenʃn spæn] Aufmerksamkeitsspanne II Unit 5, 91
attraction [əˈtrækʃn] Sehenswürdigkeit; Attraktion I
audience [ˈɔːdiəns] Publikum I
Aussie *(coll)* [ˈɒzi] Australier/-in II Unit 1, 11
available [əˈveɪləbl] verfügbar II Unit 2, 31
to **avoid** [əˈvɔɪd] vermeiden I
award [əˈwɔːd] Auszeichnung; Preis II Unit 2, 33
to slip **away** [ˌslɪp əˈweɪ] wegrutschen; entgleiten II Unit 3, 49

B

backpacking [ˈbækpækɪŋ] Wandern; Rucksackreisen I
bamboo [bæmˈbuː] Bambus II Unit 4, 73
to **ban** [bæn] verbieten; ausschließen I
food **bank** [ˈfuːd bæŋk] Tafel (karitatative Essensausgabe) II Unit 5, 85
to **bark** [bɑːk] bellen I
military **base** [ˌmɪlɪtri ˈbeɪs] Militärbasis, -stützpunkt II Unit 3, 48
based on [ˈbeɪst ɒn] basierend auf; anhand von II Unit 2, 30
basic [ˈbeɪsɪk] Grund-; grundlegend I
public **bathroom** [ˌpʌblɪk ˈbɑːθruːm] öffentliche Toilette I
*to **be** addicted (to sth) [bi əˈdɪktɪd] süchtig sein (nach etw); abhängig sein (von etw) I
*to **be** alive [bi əˈlaɪv] lebendig sein; leben I
*to **be** born [bi ˈbɔːn] geboren werden I
*to **be** capable of doing sth [bi ˌkeɪpəbl əv ˈduːɪŋ ˌsʌmθɪŋ] in der Lage sein, etw zu tun I
*to **be** damaged [bi ˈdæmɪdʒd] beschädigt sein I
*to **be** dependent on [bi dɪˈpendənt ɒn] abhängig sein von II Unit 4, 68

*to **be** destroyed [bi dɪˈstrɔɪd] zerstört sein I
*to **be** divorced [bi dɪˈvɔːst] geschieden sein I
*to **be** fulfilled [bi fʊlˈfɪld] erfüllt werden II Unit 1, 11
*to **be** inhabited [bi ɪnˈhæbɪtɪd] bewohnt sein I
*to **be** inspired by sb/sth [bi ɪnˈspaɪəd baɪ] inspiriert werden von jdm/etw I
*to **be** located [bi ləʊˈkeɪtɪd] sich befinden; liegen I
*to **be** lost [bi ˈlɒst] sich verirrt haben II Unit 4, 68
*to **be** made up of [bi ˌmeɪd ˈʌp əv] bestehen aus II Unit 3, 46
*to **be** required to [bi rɪˈkwaɪəd tə] müssen; verpflichtet sein II Unit 1, 11
*to **be** set (in) [bi ˈset ɪn] spielen (in); seinen Schauplatz haben (in) I
*to **be** situated [bi ˈsɪtʃueɪtɪd] gelegen sein II Unit 3, 59
*to **be** trapped [bi ˈtræpt] eingeschlossen sein; in der Falle sitzen I
*to **be** true to oneself [bi ˈtruː tə wʌnˌself] sich selbst treu bleiben I
*to **be** unemployed [ˌʌnɪmˈplɔɪd] arbeitslos sein I
*to **be** willing to do sth [bi ˌwɪlɪŋ tə ˈduː ˌsʌmθɪŋ] bereit sein etw zu tun II Unit 1, 19
bean [biːn] Bohne I
beat [biːt] Takt; Rhythmus II Unit 3, 47
to **beg** [beg] betteln I
*to get left **behind** [get ˌleft bɪˈhaɪnd] liegen bleiben; zurückgelassen werden II Unit 5, 85
beneath [bɪˈniːθ] unter; unterhalb I
benefits *(pl)* [ˈbenɪfɪts] *hier:* Arbeitgeberleistungen; Sozialleistungen II Unit 1, 13
to **benefit** from [ˈbenəfɪt frəm] profitieren; nützen I
beside [bɪˈsaɪd] neben II Unit 2, 36
bet [bet] Wette I

*to **bet** (on) [bet] wetten (auf) I
bicycle [ˈbaɪsɪkl] Fahrrad I
bill [bɪl] Rechnung II Unit 5, 94
billboard [ˈbɪlbɔːd] Plakatwand; Reklamefläche II Unit 4, 64
billion [ˈbɪliən] Milliarde I
biography [baɪˈɒɡrəfi] Biografie I
*to **bite** [baɪt] beißen II Unit 2, 37
blackboard [ˈblækbɔːd] Tafel II Unit 5, 91
to **blame** [bleɪm] verantwortlich machen; beschuldigen I
to **blend** [blend] mischen; vermischen I
to **block** [blɒk] abblocken; blockieren I
*to **blow** [bləʊ] wehen; pusten; blasen II Unit 3, 54
boiling [ˈbɔɪlɪŋ] kochend I
*to be **born** [bi ˈbɔːn] geboren werden I
bottom [ˈbɒtəm] *hier:* untere Körperhälfte; unterer Teil I
from the **bottom** up [frəm ðə ˌbɒtəm ˈʌp] von Grund auf; von unten nach oben I
boulder [ˈbəʊldə] Felsblock; Felsbrocken II Unit 5, 95
to **boycott** [ˈbɔɪkɒt] boykottieren I
bracelet [ˈbreɪslət] Armband I
brand [brænd] Marke I
*to **break** down [ˌbreɪk ˈdaʊn] abbauen; zerstören I
*to **break** down [ˌbreɪk ˈdaʊn] eine Panne haben II Unit 1, 16
*to **break** up [ˌbreɪk ˈʌp] Schluss machen; sich trennen I
*to take a deep **breath** [ˌteɪk ə ˌdiːp ˈbreθ] tief einatmen; tief Luft holen II Unit 3, 54
to **breathe** [briːð] atmen I
fire **brigade** [ˈfaɪə brɪˌɡeɪd] Feuerwehr I
British Empire [ˌbrɪtɪʃ ˈempaɪə] britisches Weltreich I
brush [brʌʃ] Pinsel II Unit 1, 12
thought **bubble** [ˈθɔːt ˌbʌbl] Denkblase; Gedankenblase II Unit 1, 19
bucket [ˈbʌkɪt] Eimer I
burglar [ˈbɜːɡlə] Einbrecher/-in I

V Vocabulary

business [ˈbɪznɪs] Geschäft; Branche I
to **buzz** [bʌz] klingeln; summen II Unit 4, 71
by **chance** [baɪ ˈtʃɑːns] zufällig II Unit 2, 38

C

*to lay a **cable** [leɪ ə ˈkeɪbl] ein Kabel verlegen II Unit 1, 23
cactus *(sg)*, **cacti** *(pl)* [ˈkæktəs] Kaktus II Unit 5, 95
calm [kɑːm] ruhig; friedlich I
campaign [kæmˈpeɪn] Kampagne; Aktion II Unit 4, 74
to **cancel** [ˈkænsl] stornieren I
candidate [ˈkændɪdət] Bewerber/-in; Kandidat/-in II Unit 2, 30
*to be **capable** of doing sth [bi ˌkeɪpəbl ˌəv ˈduːɪŋ ˌsʌmθɪŋ] in der Lage sein, etw zu tun I
caption [ˈkæpʃn] Bildunterschrift II Unit 1, 19
carbon emission [ˈkɑːbn ɪˌmɪʃn] Kohlenstoffemission; Kohlenstoffausstoß I
carbon footprint [ˌkɑːbn ˈfʊtprɪnt] Kohlendioxid-Bilanz I
*to take **care** of sb [ˌteɪk ˈkeər əv] sich um jdn kümmern; für jdn sorgen II Unit 1, 13
carefree [ˈkeəfriː] sorglos I
(horse) **carriage** [(hɔːs) ˈkærɪdʒ] (Pferde) Wagen II Unit 2, 36
in **case** (of) [ɪn ˈkeɪs] im Falle (von); falls I
casual [ˈkæʒuəl] lässig; informell I
*to **catch** [kætʃ] fangen I
cauliflower [ˈkɒlɪˌflaʊə] Blumenkohl II Unit 5, 84
celebrity [səˈlebrəti] Prominente/-r; berühmte Person II Unit 5, 83
certain [ˈsɜːtn] bestimmte I
chain [tʃeɪn] Kette I
chalk [tʃɔːk] Kreide II Unit 5, 91
challenge [ˈtʃælɪndʒ] Herausforderung I
challenging [ˈtʃælɪndʒɪŋ] herausfordernd; schwierig II Unit 1, 16
by **chance** [baɪ ˈtʃɑːns] zufällig II Unit 2, 38

to **cheer** on [ˌtʃɪər ˈɒn] anfeuern; zujubeln I
cheerful [ˈtʃɪəfəl] fröhlich; heiter I
childhood [ˈtʃaɪldhʊd] Kindheit I
to **chirp** [tʃɜːp] zwitschern; piepsen II Unit 3, 54
to **chop** [tʃɒp] hacken; klein schneiden I
to **clarify** [ˈklærɪfaɪ] verdeutlichen; darlegen II Unit 4, 77
to **clear** the table [ˌklɪə ðə ˈteɪbl] den Tisch abräumen II Unit 1, 23
cliff [klɪf] Klippe; Kliff II Unit 2, 28
alarm **clock** [əˈlɑːm ˌklɒk] Wecker II Unit 3, 54
close [kləʊs] nahe; eng II Unit 1, 17
clove of garlic [ˌkləʊv əv ˈgɑːlɪk] Knoblauchzehe I
golf **club** [ˈgɒlf ˌklʌb] Golfschläger I
coastline [ˈkəʊstlaɪn] Küste II Unit 2, 28
cobblestone [ˈkɒblstəʊn] (Kopfstein) Pflaster II Unit 2, 36
collapsed [kəˈlæpst] eingestürzt; zusammengebrochen I
to **collide** [kəˈlaɪd] kollidieren; zusammenstoßen I
colonisation [ˌkɒlənaɪˈzeɪʃn] Kolonialisierung; Kolonialismus II Unit 1, 21
colony [ˈkɒləni] Kolonie I
to **colour** [ˈkʌlə] färben II Unit 1, 23
to **combine** [kəmˈbaɪn] kombinieren; verbinden II Unit 3, 47
*to **come** true [ˌkʌm ˈtruː] wahr werden; in Erfüllung gehen I
command [kəˈmɑːnd] Befehl; Anweisung I
commercial [kəˈmɜːʃl] gewerblich; kommerziell I
to **commit** a crime [kəˌmɪt ə ˈkraɪm] ein Verbrechen begehen; eine Straftat begehen I
committee [kəˈmɪti] Komitee; Ausschuss II Unit 3, 51
common [ˈkɒmən] üblich; (weit) verbreitet II Unit 3, 46
*to have in **common** [ˌhæv ɪn ˈkɒmən] gemeinsam haben I
compartment [kəmˈpɑːtmənt] Fach; Einsatz I

to **compete** (with/against) [kəmˈpiːt] an einem Wettkampf teilnehmen; antreten (gegen) I
competitive [kəmˈpetɪtɪv] leistungsorientiert; konkurrierend II Unit 5, 85
competitor [kəmˈpetɪtə] Mitbewerber/-in; Konkurrent/-in; Teilnehmer/-in I
to **complain** [kəmˈpleɪn] sich beschweren; sich beklagen I
compulsive [kəmˈpʌlsɪv] zwanghaft I
concept [ˈkɒnsept] Vorstellung; Idee; Konzept II Unit 5, 91
concrete [ˈkɒŋkriːt] Beton I
conflict [ˈkɒnflɪkt] Konflikt; Auseinandersetzung I
connection [kəˈnekʃn] Verbindung I
to **conquer** [ˈkɒŋkə] erobern I
to **consider** [kənˈsɪdə] berücksichtigen; betrachten II Unit 4, 68
consistent [kənˈsɪstnt] gleich bleibend; stetig; konsistent I
construction site [kənˈstrʌkʃn ˌsaɪt] Baustelle II Unit 1, 20
consumer [kənˈsjuːmə] Konsum-; Verbraucher/-in II Unit 5, 85
to **contain** [kənˈteɪn] enthalten II Unit 4, 64
contest [ˈkɒntest] Wettbewerb II Unit 2, 28
contract [ˈkɒntrækt] Vertrag II Unit 1, 10
in **contrast** to [ɪn ˈkɒntrɑːst tə] im Gegensatz zu II Unit 3, 53
conventional [kənˈvenʃnl] herkömmlich; konventionell II Unit 4, 74
to **convince** sb [kənˈvɪns] jdn überzeugen I
logistics **coordinator** [ləˈdʒɪstɪks kəʊˈɔːdɪneɪtə] Logistikkoordinator/-in II Unit 2, 29
corruption [kəˈrʌpʃn] Korruption; Bestechung II Unit 3, 48
couple [ˈkʌpl] Paar I
course [kɔːs] Kurs II Unit 2, 33
(golf) **course** [ˈgɒlf ˌkɔːs] Golfplatz I

Vocabulary

court [kɔːt] Gericht I
crane [kreɪn] Kran I
to commit a crime [kəˌmɪt ə ˈkraɪm] ein Verbrechen begehen; eine Straftat begehen I
crisis [ˈkraɪsɪs] Krise I
to criticise [ˈkrɪtɪsaɪz] kritisieren II Unit 2, 33
criticism [ˈkrɪtɪsɪzm] Kritik II Unit 4, 73
cruise ship [ˈkruːz ˌʃɪp] Kreuzfahrtschiff II Unit 1, 23
cry [kraɪ] Schrei; Weinen II Unit 3, 49
curious [ˈkjʊəriəs] neugierig I
cut [kʌt] Schnittverletzung I
cutlery [ˈkʌtlri] Besteck II Unit 5, 89
to cycle [ˈsaɪkl] Fahrrad fahren I

D

to damage [ˈdæmɪdʒ] schaden; beschädigen II Unit 5, 91
*to be damaged [bi ˈdæmɪdʒd] beschädigt sein I
personal data [ˌpɜːsnl ˈdeɪtə] persönliche Daten; persönliche Angaben II Unit 2, 34
daughter-in-law [ˈdɔːtərɪnlɔː] Schwiegertochter I
day off [ˌdeɪ ˈɒf] freier Tag I
deal [diːl] Abmachung; Geschäft II Unit 4, 76
debate [dɪˈbeɪt] Diskussion; Debatte II Unit 5, 82
debt [det] Schulden; Schuld I
decline [dɪˈklaɪn] Niedergang I
to decline [dɪˈklaɪn] zurückgehen; fallen I
to decorate [ˈdekreɪt] schmücken I
to decrease [dɪˈkriːs] zurückgehen; sinken II Unit 4, 72
to dedicate to [ˈdedɪkeɪt tə] widmen II Unit 3, 49
*to take a deep breath [ˌteɪk ə ˌdiːp ˈbreθ] tief einatmen; tief Luft holen II Unit 3, 54
to defeat [dɪˈfiːt] besiegen II Unit 3, 48
to delete [dɪˈliːt] löschen II Unit 4, 66
to deliver [dɪˈlɪvə] liefern I

delivery [dɪˈlɪvri] Lieferung; Zustellung I
to demand [dɪˈmɑːnd] fordern II Unit 1, 11
to deny [dɪˈnaɪ] leugnen II Unit 2, 38
departure [dɪˈpɑːtʃə] Abflug; Abreise I
*to be dependent on [bi dɪˈpendənt ˌɒn] abhängig sein von II Unit 4, 68
desperate [ˈdesprət] verzweifelt; hoffnungslos I
despite [dɪˈspaɪt] trotz II Unit 3, 53
destination [ˌdestɪˈneɪʃn] Reiseziel; Ziel I
to destroy [dɪˈstrɔɪ] zerstören II Unit 5, 88
*to be destroyed [bi dɪˈstrɔɪd] zerstört sein I
determination [dɪˌtɜːmɪˈneɪʃn] Entschlossenheit I
determined [dɪˈtɜːmɪnd] entschlossen; zielstrebig II Unit 3, 49
diagnosis (sg), diagnoses (pl) [ˌdaɪəgˈnəʊsɪs; ˌdaɪəgˈnəʊsiːz] Diagnose II Unit 4, 72
difference [ˈdɪfrəns] Unterschied I
digital [ˈdɪdʒɪtl] digital II Unit 4, 64
diner (AE) [ˈdaɪnə] einfaches Restaurant mit Theke und Tischen II Unit 5, 94
to direct [dɪˈrekt] den Weg zeigen II Unit 2, 30
natural disaster [ˌnætʃrl dɪˈzɑːstə] Naturkatastrophe I
discipline [ˈdɪsɪplɪn] Disziplin I
to discover [dɪˈskʌvə] entdecken I
display of affection [dɪˌspleɪ əv əˈfekʃn] hier: Austausch von Zärtlichkeiten I
disposable [dɪˈspəʊzəbl] Wegwerfartikel II Unit 5, 89
dissatisfaction [ˌdɪsˌsætɪsˈfækʃn] Unzufriedenheit II Unit 3, 51
to distract sb (from sth) [dɪˈstrækt (frəm)] jdn (von etw) ablenken II Unit 3, 55
district [ˈdɪstrɪkt] Bezirk; Distrikt II Unit 4, 64

diverse [daɪˈvɜːs] vielfältig; unterschiedlich II Unit 3, 46
division [dɪˈvɪʒn] Liga; Kategorie I
*to be divorced [bi dɪˈvɔːst] geschieden sein I
do you mind [du ju ˈmaɪnd] stört es dich/Sie, …; hast du/ haben Sie etwas dagegen, … II Unit 3, 58
dos and don'ts [ˌduːz ən ˈdəʊnts] Verhaltensregeln II Unit 2, 40
document [ˈdɒkjəmənt] Dokument; Unterlage II Unit 2, 30
to dominate [ˈdɒmɪneɪt] beherrschen; dominieren II Unit 5, 95
donation [dəˈneɪʃn] Spende I
to doubt [daʊt] bezweifeln II Unit 1, 15
*to break down [ˌbreɪk ˈdaʊn] abbauen; zerstören I
*to break down [ˌbreɪk ˈdaʊn] eine Panne haben II Unit 1, 16
drab [dræb] düster; eintönig II Unit 2, 36
dragon [ˈdrægn] Drache II Unit 4, 64
dramatic [drəˈmætɪk] dramatisch; spektakulär II Unit 3, 49
to dress [dres] sich kleiden; anziehen I
*to drink a pint [ˌdrɪŋk ə ˈpaɪnt] ein Bier trinken (gehen) II Unit 2, 28
driving licence [ˈdraɪvɪŋ ˌlaɪsns] Führerschein II Unit 1, 10
drought [draʊt] Dürre; Trockenheit II Unit 5, 82
to dump [dʌmp] wegwerfen; abladen II Unit 5, 88
dune [djuːn] Düne II Unit 5, 95
duration [djʊˈreɪʃn] Dauer I
duty [ˈdjuːti] Pflicht II Unit 2, 32

E

eager [ˈiːgə] eifrig; begierig II Unit 3, 50
earth [ɜːθ] die Erde; Boden I
earthquake [ˈɜːθkweɪk] Erdbeben I
economy [ɪˈkɒnəmi] Wirtschaft II Unit 5, 83
edge [edʒ] Rand II Unit 1, 21

V Vocabulary

effective [ɪˈfektɪv] wirksam; effektiv II Unit 5, 86
effort [ˈefət] Anstrengung; Bemühung II Unit 5, 85
to elect [ɪˈlekt] wählen I
emerald [ˈemərld] Smaragd; smaragdgrün II Unit 2, 28
carbon **emission** [ˈkɑːbn ˌɪmɪʃn] Kohlenstoffemission; Kohlenstoffausstoß I
to employ [ɪmˈplɔɪ] einstellen; anstellen; beschäftigen II Unit 5, 88
employee [ɪmˈplɔɪiː] Angestellte/-r; Mitarbeiter/-in; Arbeitnehmer/-in II Unit 1, 12
employer [ɪmˈplɔɪə] Arbeitgeber/-in II Unit 1, 10
empty [ˈemti] leer I
to end up [ˌend ˈʌp] enden; landen I
endangered [ɪnˈdeɪndʒəd] gefährdet I
endurance [ɪnˈdjʊərəns] Ausdauer I
energy-efficient [ˌenədʒi ɪˈfɪʃnt] energieeffizient I
energy-saving light bulb [ˌenədʒiseɪvɪŋ ˈlaɪt ˌbʌlb] Energiesparlampe I
*to get **engaged** [get ɪnˈgeɪdʒd] sich verloben I
environmental [ɪnˌvaɪərnˈmentl] ökologisch; Umwelt- II Unit 5, 84
racial **equality** [ˌreɪʃl ɪˈkwɒləti] Rassengleichheit II Unit 3, 55
eruption [ɪˈrʌpʃn] Ausbruch (Vulkan) I
especially [ɪˈspeʃli] besonders; vor allem I
estate [ɪˌsteɪt] Siedlung II Unit 2, 37
ethnic [ˈeθnɪk] ethnisch; Volks- II Unit 5, 82
ethnicity [eθˈnɪsəti] Ethnie; ethnische Zugehörigkeit II Unit 1, 19
to evacuate [ɪˈvækjueɪt] evakuieren I
eventually [ɪˈventʃuəli] schließlich; endlich; irgendwann II Unit 2, 37
evil [ˈiːvl] böse; schlecht I
*to set a good **example** [set ə ˌgʊd ɪgˈzɑːmpl] ein Vorbild sein I

to exclude [ɪkˈskluːd] ausschließen I
exhaust system [ɪgˈzɔːst ˌsɪstəm] Auspuffanlage; Abgasanlage II Unit 1, 17
exhibition [ˌeksɪˈbɪʃn] Ausstellung I
to exist [ɪgˈzɪst] existieren; bestehen I
exotic [ɪgˈzɒtɪk] exotisch I
to expand [ɪkˈspænd] ausdehnen; erweitern; vergrößern II Unit 5, 84
to experience [ɪkˈspɪəriəns] erfahren; erleben I
to express [ɪkˈspres] ausdrücken II Unit 5, 90
expression [ɪkˈspreʃn] Ausdruck; Äußerung I
novel **extract** [ˈnɒvel ˌekstrækt] Romanauszug II Unit 2, 36
eyewitness [ˈaɪwɪtnəs] Augenzeuge/Augenzeugin I

F

fabric [ˈfæbrɪk] Stoff II Unit 5, 88
factual [ˈfæktʃʊəl] sachlich; Sach- I
to fail [feɪl] versagen; scheitern II Unit 1, 12
failure [ˈfeɪljə] Versager; Scheitern II Unit 1, 12
fancy [ˈfænsi] modisch; ausgefallen I
farming [ˈfɑːmɪŋ] Landwirtschaft; Ackerbau I
fashionable [ˈfæʃnəbl] modisch II Unit 4, 73
It's my **fault.** [ɪts ˌmaɪ ˈfɔːlt] Es ist meine Schuld. I
feature [ˈfiːtʃə] Eigenschaft; Merkmal I
fee [fiː] (Studien)Gebühr II Unit 1, 20
feeling [ˈfiːlɪŋ] Gefühl I
fellow [ˈfeləʊ] Bursche; Kerl II Unit 2, 37
fibre [ˈfaɪbə] Ballaststoffe II Unit 5, 86
fictional [ˈfɪkʃnl] fiktiv I
fine [faɪn] Geldstrafe; Bußgeld II Unit 1, 10
fire brigade [ˈfaɪə brɪˌgeɪd] Feuerwehr I

to fire [faɪə] abfeuern; schießen II Unit 3, 54
to fire sb [faɪə] jdn feuern; jdn hinauswerfen I
firefighter [ˈfaɪəˌfaɪtə] Feuerwehrmann/-frau I
fishmonger [ˈfɪʃˌmʌŋgə] Fischhändler/-in II Unit 2, 29
to fix [fɪks] reparieren II Unit 2, 33
fixed-term [ˌfɪkst tɜːm] befristet II Unit 2, 30
flavour [ˈfleɪvə] Geschmacksrichtung; Geschmack; Sorte I
flight attendant [ˈflaɪt əˌtendnt] Flugbegleiter/-in II Unit 1, 17
to flow [fləʊ] fließen; strömen I
focus [ˈfəʊkəs] Schwerpunkt; Fokus II Unit 5, 91
to focus on sth [ˈfəʊkəs ɒn] sich auf etw konzentrieren I
food bank [ˈfuːd ˌbæŋk] Tafel (karitatative Essensausgabe) II Unit 5, 85
junk **food** [ˈdʒʌŋk ˌfuːd] ungesundes Essen I
carbon **footprint** [ˌkɑːbn ˈfʊtprɪnt] Kohlendioxid-Bilanz I
to form [fɔːm] formen; bilden II Unit 3, 51
formal [ˈfɔːml] förmlich; formell; formal II Unit 2, 30
freckles (pl) [ˈfreklz] Sommersprossen II Unit 2, 38
from the bottom up [frəm ðə ˌbɒtəm ˈʌp] von Grund auf; von unten nach oben I
to fry [fraɪ] braten; frittieren I
fuel [ˈfjuːəl] Treibstoff I
*to be **fulfilled** [bi fʊlˈfɪld] erfüllt werden II Unit 1, 11
*to have a sense of **fun** [hæv ə ˌsens əv ˈfʌn] Sinn für Spaß haben I
function [ˈfʌŋkʃn] Funktion; Aufgabe II Unit 4, 66
fundraising [ˈfʌndˌreɪzɪŋ] Spendenaktion I
furious [ˈfjʊəriəs] wütend I
furniture [ˈfɜːnɪtʃə] Möbel II Unit 1, 14
furthest [ˈfɜːðɪst] am weitesten I

G

to **gamble** [ˈgæmbl] spielen I
gambling [ˈgæmblɪŋ] Glücksspiel; Wetten I
gap [gæp] Lücke; Abstand I
garage [ˈgærɑːʒ] Werkstatt II Unit 1, 23
to **garden** [ˈgɑːdn] gärtnern II Unit 5, 92
clove of **garlic** [ˌkləʊv əv ˈgɑːlɪk] Knoblauchzehe I
tear **gas** [ˈtɪə ˌgæs] Tränengas II Unit 3, 51
gender [ˈdʒendə] Geschlecht (sozial) II Unit 1, 19
general [ˈdʒenrl] allgemein; Haupt- II Unit 2, 32
generous [ˈdʒenrəs] großzügig I
*to **get engaged** [get ɪnˈgeɪdʒd] sich verloben I
*to **get left behind** [get left bɪˈhaɪnd] liegen bleiben; zurückgelassen werden II Unit 5, 85
*to **get married** [get ˈmærɪd] heiraten I
*to **get on with sb** [get ˌɒn wɪð ˌsʌmbədi] mit jdm auskommen II Unit 2, 37
glacier [ˈglæsiə] Gletscher I
glasses (pl) [ˈglɑːsɪz] Brille I
Glaswegian [glæzˈwiːdʒn] Glasgower/-in I
glum [glʌm] bedrückt; deprimiert II Unit 2, 37
in one **go** [ɪn ˌwʌn ˈgəʊ] an einem Stück I
goalkeeper [ˈgəʊlˌkiːpə] Torwart/-in II Unit 3, 50
god [gɒd] Gott I
VR **goggles** [ˌviːˈɑː ˌgɒglz] Virtual-Reality-Brille II Unit 4, 64
golf club [ˈgɒlf ˌklʌb] Golfschläger I
(**golf**) **course** [ˈgɒlf ˌkɔːs] Golfplatz I
*to **set a good example** [set ə ˌgʊd ɪgˈzɑːmpl] ein Vorbild sein I
graphic novel [ˌgræfɪk ˈnɒvl] Bildergeschichte; Comic II Unit 1, 19
to **greet** [griːt] begrüßen II Unit 2, 30

grocery store [ˈgrəʊsri ˌstɔː] Lebensmittelladen I
guideline [ˈgaɪdlaɪn] Richtlinie II Unit 5, 84

H

habit [ˈhæbɪt] Gewohnheit II Unit 4, 66
hammer throwing [ˈhæmə ˌθrəʊɪŋ] Hammerwerfen I
to **hand out** [ˌhænd ˈaʊt] austeilen I
to **harvest** [ˈhɑːvɪst] ernten II Unit 5, 84
*to **have a sense of fun** [hæv ə ˌsens əv ˈfʌn] Sinn für Spaß haben I
*to **have in common** [ˌhæv ɪn ˈkɒmən] gemeinsam haben I
headquarters (pl) [ˌhedˈkwɔːtəz] Zentrale; Stammsitz II Unit 5, 83
healthy [ˈhelθi] gesund I
heat-absorbing [ˌhiːtəbˈzɔːbɪŋ] wärmeaufnehmend I
heaven [ˈhevn] Himmel I
heels (pl) [hiːlz] Stöckelschuhe I
height [haɪt] Höhe I
helpline [ˈhelplaɪn] telefonische Beratung; Notruf I
heptathlete [hepˈtæθliːt] Siebenkämpfer/-in I
herd [hɜːd] Herde; Rudel II Unit 3, 55
herewith [ˌhɪəˈwɪð] hiermit II Unit 4, 76
to **hike** [haɪk] wandern I
*to **hold** [həʊld] festhalten; halten I
home town [ˌhəʊm ˈtaʊn] Heimatstadt I
homeless [ˈhəʊmləs] Obdachlose/-r I
homelessness [ˈhəʊmləsnəs] Obdachlosigkeit I
hopeful [ˈhəʊpfl] hoffnungsvoll I
hopeless [ˈhəʊpləs] hoffnungslos I
to **host** [həʊst] ausrichten (Veranstaltung) II Unit 3, 47
household [ˈhaʊshəʊld] Haushalt II Unit 3, 58
hug [hʌg] Umarmung I

human [ˈhjuːmən] Mensch II Unit 5, 88
humble [ˈhʌmbl] bescheiden; einfach II Unit 1, 21
hygiene [ˈhaɪdʒiːn] Hygiene; Sauberkeit II Unit 5, 88

I

I'm afraid … [ˌaɪm əˈfreɪd] Leider … II Unit 5, 90
iconic [aɪˈkɒnɪk] ikonisch; mit Kultcharakter II Unit 3, 49
to **identify with** [aɪˈdentɪfaɪ wɪð] sich identifizieren mit II Unit 4, 66
illegal [ɪˈliːgl] illegal; unrechtmäßig; rechtswidrig I
illness [ˈɪlnəs] Krankheit II Unit 4, 71
to **illustrate** [ˈɪləstreɪt] veranschaulichen; darstellen; illustrieren II Unit 2, 33
immediately [ɪˈmiːdiətli] sofort; gleich I
imported [ɪmˈpɔːtɪd] importiert; eingeführt I
impression [ɪmˈpreʃn] Eindruck I
impressive [ɪmˈpresɪv] beeindruckend II Unit 3, 55
imprisoned [ɪmˈprɪznd] eingesperrt; inhaftiert II Unit 1, 12
in case (of) [ɪn ˈkeɪs] im Falle (von); falls I
in contrast to [ɪn ˈkɒntrɑːst tə] im Gegensatz zu II Unit 3, 53
in fact [ɪn ˈfækt] tatsächlich; eigentlich II Unit 4, 74
in one go [ɪn ˌwʌn ˈgəʊ] an einem Stück I
in order to [ɪn ˈɔːdə tə] um … zu; mit der Absicht II Unit 3, 51
to **include** [ɪnˈkluːd] umfassen; enthalten; einschließen I
income [ˈɪnkʌm] Einkommen II Unit 2, 37
info terminal [ˈɪnfəʊ ˌtɜːmɪnl] Infosäule I
ingredient [ɪnˈgriːdiənt] Zutat I
*to be **inhabited** [bi ɪnˈhæbɪtɪd] bewohnt sein I
injured [ˈɪndʒəd] verletzt I
ink [ɪŋk] Tinte I

V Vocabulary

innovation [ˌɪnəˈveɪʃn] Innovation; Neuerung II Unit 5, 83
*to be **inspired** by sth/sb [bi ɪnˈspaɪəd baɪ] inspiriert werden von jdm/etw I
installation [ˌɪnstəˈleɪʃn] Montage; Einbau II Unit 2, 32
to **interact** [ˌɪntəˈæk] zusammenspielen; zusammenwirken II Unit 3, 57
intern [ˈɪntɜːn] Praktikant/-in II Unit 2, 32
internship [ˈɪntɜːnʃɪp] Praktikum II Unit 1, 14
to **interrupt** [ˌɪntəˈrʌpt] unterbrechen I
to **intimidate** [ɪnˈtɪmɪdeɪt] einschüchtern II Unit 3, 51
to **introduce** [ˌɪntrəˈdjuːs] einführen; einleiten I
to **invest** [ɪnˈvest] investieren I
It's my **fault**. [ɪts maɪ ˈfɔːlt] Es ist meine Schuld. I

J
job agency [ˈdʒɒb ˌeɪdʒnsi] Arbeitsagentur; Stellenbörse II Unit 2, 31
to **judge** [dʒʌdʒ] beurteilen; bewerten I
junk food [ˈdʒʌŋk ˌfuːd] ungesundes Essen I

K
kilt [kɪlt] Schottenrock; Kilt I
kind [kaɪnd] liebenswürdig; nett; freundlich I
know-how [ˈnəʊhaʊ] Erfahrung; Fachwissen II Unit 1, 17
knowledge (no pl) [ˈnɒlɪdʒ] Wissen; Kenntnisse II Unit 3, 54

L
landfill [ˈlænfɪl] Mülldeponie II Unit 5, 88
traffic **lane** [ˈtræfɪk ˌleɪn] Fahrspur II Unit 2, 36
native **language** [ˌneɪtɪv ˈlæŋgwɪdʒ] Muttersprache II Unit 3, 47
official **language** [əˌfɪʃl ˈlæŋgwɪdʒ] Amtssprache I

to **last** [lɑːst] dauern I
Latino [ləˈtiːnəʊ] Lateinamerikaner/-in; lateinamerikanisch II Unit 5, 82
lawyer [ˈlɔɪə] Anwalt/Anwältin I
*to **lay** a cable [leɪ ə ˈkeɪbl] ein Kabel verlegen II Unit 1, 23
leaf (sg), **leaves** (pl) [liːf, liːvz] Blatt II Unit 5, 84
at **least** [ət ˈliːst] mindestens; wenigstens II Unit 2, 30
*to get **left** behind [get ˌleft bɪˈhaɪnd] liegen bleiben; zurückgelassen werden II Unit 5, 85
leftovers [ˈleftˌəʊvəz] Speisereste; Überbleibsel II Unit 5, 86
legal [ˈliːgl] legal; rechtlich; Rechts- I
length [leŋθ] Länge I
to **liberate** [ˈlɪbreɪt] befreien I
driving **licence** [ˈdraɪvɪŋ ˌlaɪsns] Führerschein II Unit 1, 10
to **lie** [laɪ] lügen I
once in a **lifetime** [ˌwʌns ɪn ə ˈlaɪftaɪm] einmalig; einmal im Leben I
traffic **light** [ˈtræfɪk ˌlaɪt] (Verkehrs-)Ampel II Unit 2, 36
energy-saving **light bulb** [ˌenədʒiseɪvɪŋ ˈlaɪt ˌbʌlb] Energiesparlampe I
lime [laɪm] Limette I
to **limit** to [ˈlɪmɪt tə] limitieren auf; begrenzen auf; beschränken auf II Unit 4, 66
assembly **line** [əˈsembli ˌlaɪn] Fließband I
local [ˈləʊkl] hiesig; örtlich; lokal I
*to be **located** [bi ləʊˈkeɪtɪd] sich befinden; liegen I
lodge [lɒdʒ] Ferienhotel; Lodge II Unit 3, 54
logistics coordinator [ləˈdʒɪstɪks kəʊˌɔːdɪneɪtə] Logistikkoordinator/-in II Unit 2, 29
*to be **lost** [bi ˈlɒst] sich verirrt haben II Unit 4, 68
parking **lot** (AE) [ˈpɑːkɪŋ ˌlɒt] Parkplatz I
lush [lʌʃ] üppig; saftig II Unit 2, 28

M
sewing **machine** [ˈsəʊɪŋ məˌʃiːn] Nähmaschine I
you've **made** my day [juv ˌmeɪd maɪ ˈdeɪ] Du hast meinen Tag gerettet! II Unit 4, 76
magic [ˈmædʒɪk] Magie; Zauberei; Zauber- I
main [meɪn] Haupt- II Unit 3, 59
*to be **made** up of [bi ˌmeɪd ˈʌp əv] bestehen aus II Unit 3, 46
to **manage** [ˈmænɪdʒ] organisieren II Unit 4, 67
manufacturing [ˌmænjəˈfæktʃrɪŋ] Produktion; Produktionsbetrieb I
march [mɑːtʃ] Marsch; Kundgebung II Unit 3, 51
mark [mɑːk] Note; Zensur II Unit 1, 18
arranged **marriage** [əˌreɪndʒd ˈmærɪdʒ] arrangierte Ehe I
*to get **married** [ˌget ˈmærɪd] heiraten I
mass production [ˌmæs prəˈdʌkʃn] Massenfertigung I
match [mætʃ] Paar; Verbindung I
no **matter** [nəʊ ˈmætə] egal; ganz gleich II Unit 1, 19
meadow [ˈmedəʊ] Wiese II Unit 5, 95
measure [ˈmeʒə] Maßnahme I
medal [ˈmedl] Medaille II Unit 3, 46
medicine [ˈmedsn] Medikamente; Medizin II Unit 1, 17
member [ˈmembə] Mitglied I
mental [ˈmentl] geistig II Unit 4, 71
to **mention** [ˈmenʃn] erwähnen II Unit 1, 17
merchandise [ˈmɜːtʃndaɪz] Fanartikel I
military base [ˌmɪlɪtri ˈbeɪs] Militärbasis; -stützpunkt II Unit 3, 48
mind [maɪnd] Geist; Verstand II Unit 3, 55
do you **mind** [ˌdu ju ˈmaɪnd] stört es dich/Sie, …; hast du/haben Sie etwas dagegen, … II Unit 3, 58

to not mind [ˌnɒt ˈmaɪnd] nichts dagegen haben; nichts ausmachen II Unit 1, 17
prime minister [ˌpraɪm ˈmɪnɪstə] Premierminister/-in I
misery [ˈmɪzri] Elend; Armseligkeit II Unit 1, 19
mole [məʊl] Maulwurf I
to raise money [ˌreɪz ˈmʌni] Geld sammeln I
mood [muːd] Stimmung; Laune II Unit 4, 72
to motivate [ˈməʊtɪveɪt] motivieren I
Mumbaiker [mʌmˈbaɪkə] Einwohner/-in von Mumbai I
musical scale [ˌmjuːzɪkl ˈskeɪl] Tonleiter II Unit 5, 92

N

naked [ˈneɪkɪd] nackt I
narrow [ˈnærəʊ] eng; schmal II Unit 2, 30
native language [ˌneɪtɪv ˈlæŋgwɪdʒ] Muttersprache II Unit 3, 47
natural disaster [ˌnætʃrl dɪˈzɑːstə] Naturkatastrophe I
nearly [ˈnɪəli] fast; annähernd II Unit 5, 88
necessary [ˈnesəsri] nötig; erforderlich I
needle [ˈniːdl] Nadel I
neighbourhood [ˈneɪbəhʊd] Nachbarschaft; Viertel I
nevertheless [ˌnevəðəˈles] trotzdem; dennoch II Unit 3, 51
no matter [ˌnəʊ ˈmætə] egal; ganz gleich II Unit 1, 19
non-violent [ˌnɒnˈvaɪələnt] friedlich; gewaltfrei I
to not mind [ˌnɒt ˈmaɪnd] nichts dagegen haben; nichts ausmachen II Unit 1, 17
graphic novel [ˌgræfɪk ˈnɒvl] Bildergeschichte; Comic II Unit 1, 19
novel extract [ˈnɒvel ˌekstrækt] Romanauszug II Unit 2, 36
nursery assistant [ˈnɜːsri əˌsɪstnt] Kindergartenhelfer/-in II Unit 2, 32

O

to obey [əˈbeɪ] gehorchen; befolgen II Unit 1, 11
obligation [ˌɒblɪˈgeɪʃn] Pflicht; Verpflichtung II Unit 1, 10
obstacle [ˈɒbstəkl] Hürde; Hindernis II Unit 3, 55
to turn off [ˌtɜːn ˈɒf] abschalten; ausschalten II Unit 2, 40
offensive [əˈfensɪv] beleidigend; anstößig I
official language [əˌfɪʃl ˈlæŋgwɪdʒ] Amtssprache I
once in a lifetime [ˌwʌns ɪn ə ˈlaɪftaɪm] einmalig; einmal im Leben I
open-minded [ˌəʊpnˈmaɪndɪd] aufgeschlossen II Unit 2, 29
optional [ˈɒpʃnl] optional; wahlweise I
in order to [ɪn ˈɔːdə tə] um … zu; mit der Absicht II Unit 3, 51
organic [ɔːˈgænɪk] Bio- I
origin [ˈɒrɪdʒɪn] Herkunft; Abstammung II Unit 1, 19
*to overcome [ˌəʊvəˈkʌm] überwinden II Unit 3, 55
overloaded [ˌəʊvəˈləʊdɪd] überladen I
to overlook [ˌəʊvəˈlʊk] übersehen II Unit 5, 86
shop owner [ˈʃɒp ˌəʊnə] Ladenbesitzer/-in I

P

travel package [ˈtrævl ˌpækɪdʒ] Pauschalreise I
packaging [ˈpækɪdʒɪŋ] Verpackung; Verpackungsmaterial II Unit 5, 88
to paddle [ˈpædl] paddeln I
pain [peɪn] Schmerz II Unit 3, 49
painful [ˈpeɪnfl] schmerzhaft I
paint [peɪnt] Farbe I
painting [ˈpeɪntɪŋ] Gemälde; Malerei II Unit 1, 14
panel [ˈpænl] Bild (eines Comics) II Unit 1, 19
paramedic [ˌpærəˈmedɪk] Sanitäter/-in I
theme park [ˈθiːm ˌpɑːk] Freizeitpark I
parking lot (AE) [ˈpɑːkɪŋ ˌlɒt] Parkplatz I
participation [pɑːˌtɪsɪˈpeɪʃn] Teilnahme I
party [ˈpɑːti] Partei II Unit 3, 48
to pass [pɑːs] zuspielen; passen I
to pass on [ˌpɑːs ˈɒn] weitergeben II Unit 2, 33
passion [ˈpæʃn] Leidenschaft II Unit 2, 30
patient [ˈpeɪʃnt] geduldig II Unit 1, 16
percent [pəˈsent] Prozent (%) I
to perform [pəˈfɔːm] auftreten; aufführen I
performance [pəˈfɔːməns] Aufführung; Leistung II Unit 2, 33 II Unit 4, 67
permission [pəˈmɪʃn] Erlaubnis; Genehmigung II Unit 1, 10
to permit [pəˈmɪt] erlauben II Unit 1, 11
personal data [ˌpɜːsnl ˈdeɪtə] persönliche Daten; persönliche Angaben II Unit 2, 34
personality [ˌpɜːsnˈæləti] Persönlichkeit I
phase [feɪz] Phase; Abschnitt I
physical [ˈfɪzɪkl] körperlich II Unit 4, 71
to pick [pɪk] pflücken; ernten II Unit 1, 13
pickup [ˈpɪkʌp] Hochnehmen; Aufnahme II Unit 4, 66
picturesque [ˌpɪktʃrˈesk] malerisch II Unit 3, 55
pile of rubble [ˌpaɪl əv ˈrʌbl] Schutthaufen I
pin [pɪn] Stecknadel I
*to drink a pint [ˌdrɪŋk ə ˈpaɪnt] ein Bier trinken (gehen) II Unit 2, 28
pitch [pɪtʃ] Spielfeld; Platz I
retirement plan [rɪˈtaɪəmənt ˌplæn] Altersvorsorge II Unit 2, 30
tectonic plate [tekˌtɒnɪk ˈpleɪt] tektonische Platte I
plumber [ˈplʌmə] Installateur/-in; Klempner/-in II Unit 1, 13
poisonous [ˈpɔɪznəs] giftig I

V Vocabulary

politician [ˌpɒlɪˈtɪʃn] Politiker/-in II Unit 4, 73
polluted [pəˈluːtɪd] verschmutzt I
popularity [ˌpɒpjəˈlærəti] Beliebtheit II Unit 4, 75
to **pose** [pəʊz] Modell stehen; posieren II Unit 3, 50
position [pəˈzɪʃn] Position; Stelle II Unit 3, 59
possible [ˈpɒsəbl] möglich I
to **pour** [pɔː] schütten; einschenken; eingießen I
powder [ˈpaʊdə] Pulver I
power [ˈpaʊə] Energie; Kraft; Macht I
prank [præŋk] Streich II Unit 4, 75
prediction [prɪˈdɪkʃn] Vorhersage; Voraussage I
preference [ˈprefrns] Vorliebe II Unit 1, 22
present [ˈpreznt] Gegenwart II Unit 2, 31
to **present** [prɪˈzent] darstellen II Unit 4, 68
to **pretend** [prɪˈtend] so tun als ob; vorgeben; vortäuschen I
primary school [ˈpraɪmri ˌskuːl] Grundschule II Unit 2, 31
prime minister [ˌpraɪm ˈmɪnɪstə] Premierminister/-in I
probation [prəˈbeɪʃn] Probezeit II Unit 2, 32
produce [ˈprɒdjuːs] landwirtschaftliche Erzeugnisse I
record **producer** [ˈrekɔːd prəˌdjuːsə] Schallplattenproduzent/-in I
mass **production** [ˌmæs prəˈdʌkʃn] Massenfertigung I
productive [prəˈdʌktɪv] produktiv II Unit 5, 82
profession [prəˈfeʃn] Beruf I
professional [prəˈfeʃnl] Profi-; professionell; berufsmäßig I
profit [ˈprɒfɪt] Gewinn I
profitability [ˌprɒfɪtəˈbɪləti] Rentabilität II Unit 5, 85
progressive [prəˈɡresɪv] fortschrittlich II Unit 5, 83
to **promote** [prəˈməʊt] fördern; werben für I

property [ˈprɒpəti] Eigentum II Unit 1, 11
to **prove** to be [pruːv] sich erweisen als II Unit 4, 74
to **provoke** [prəˈvəʊk] provozieren; hervorrufen I
public [ˈpʌblɪk] öffentlich I
public bathroom [ˌpʌblɪk ˈbɑːθruːm] öffentliche Toilette I
to **publish** [ˈpʌblɪʃ] veröffentlichen; publizieren I
pulp [pʌlp] Fruchtfleisch; Mus II Unit 5, 86
pumpkin [ˈpʌmpkɪn] Kürbis; Kürbis- I
to **punish** [ˈpʌnɪʃ] bestrafen I
push [pʊʃ] Vorstoß; Druck II Unit 4, 74

Q

qualification [ˌkwɒlɪfɪˈkeɪʃn] Qualifikation; Abschluss II Unit 2, 31
to **qualify** for sth [ˈkwɒlɪfaɪ fɔː] für etw geeignet sein; sich für etw qualifizieren II Unit 2, 33
to **question** [ˈkwestʃən] hinterfragen; fragen II Unit 5, 92

R

racial equality [ˌreɪʃl ɪˈkwɒləti] Rassengleichheit II Unit 3, 55
railway [ˈreɪlweɪ] Eisenbahn I
to **raise** [reɪz] anheben; heben II Unit 3, 49
to **raise** money [ˌreɪz ˈmʌni] Geld sammeln I
to **rank** [ræŋk] einstufen; in eine Rangfolge bringen II Unit 1, 13
rate [reɪt] Preis; Anteil I
to **reach** [riːtʃ] erreichen I
virtual **reality** (VR) [ˌvɜːtjuəl rɪˈæləti (ˌviːˈɑː)] virtuelle Realität II Unit 4, 64
to **rebel** against sb [rɪˈbel] gegen jdn rebellieren; sich auflehnen I
*to **rebuild** [ˌriːˈbɪld] wieder aufbauen I
reception [rɪˈsepʃn] Rezeption; Empfang II Unit 2, 32
to **recommend** [ˌrekəˈmend] empfehlen I

recommendation [ˌrekəmenˈdeɪʃn] Empfehlung II Unit 2, 29
record producer [ˈrekɔːd prəˌdjuːsə] Schallplattenproduzent/-in I
to **refer** to sth [rɪˈfɜː tə ˌsʌmθɪŋ] sich auf etw beziehen II Unit 2, 35
reference [ˈrefrns] Empfehlung; Arbeitszeugnis; Referenzschreiben II Unit 2, 34
to **reflect** [rɪˈflekt] widerspiegeln II Unit 3, 46
regulation [ˌreɡjəˈleɪʃn] Vorschrift; Regelung II Unit 4, 68
to **reject** [rɪˈdʒekt] zurückweisen; ablehnen I
relationship [rɪˈleɪʃnʃɪp] Beziehung I
to **remove** [rɪˈmuːv] entfernen II Unit 4, 70
to **renovate** [ˈrenəveɪt] renovieren I
rent [rent] Miete I
reparation [ˌrepəˈreɪʃn] Entschädigung I
to **report** [rɪˈpɔːt] anzeigen I
to **represent** [ˌreprɪˈzent] stehen für; darstellen I
upon **request** [əpɒn rɪˈkwest] auf Anfrage II Unit 2, 34
*to be **required** to [bi rɪˈkwaɪəd tə] müssen; verpflichtet sein II Unit 1, 11
requirement [rɪˈkwaɪəmənt] Voraussetzung II Unit 2, 30
to **rescue** [ˈreskjuː] retten I
reserve [rɪˌzɜːv] Naturschutzgebiet II Unit 3, 54
to **resist** [rɪˈzɪst] sich widersetzen; widerstehen I
resource [rɪˈzɔːs] Ressource; Mittel I
responsibility [rɪˌspɒnsəˈbɪləti] Verantwortung; Aufgabe II Unit 1, 12
retail (no pl) [ˈriːteɪl] Einzelhandel II Unit 2, 30
retirement plan [rɪˈtaɪəmənt ˌplæn] Altersvorsorge II Unit 2, 30

Vocabulary

reusable [ˌriːˈjuːzəbl] wiederverwendbar; Mehrweg- II Unit 5, 88
*to **rise** [raɪz] steigen I
risk [rɪsk] Risiko I
ritual [ˈrɪtjuəl] Ritual I
robotics [rəˈbɒtɪks] Robotertechnik II Unit 5, 92
rocky [ˈrɒki] felsig; steinig II Unit 2, 28
rooftop [ˈruːftɒp] Hausdach I
pile of **rubble** [ˌpaɪl ˌəv ˈrʌbl] Schutthaufen I
*to **set the rules** [ˌset ðə ˈruːlz] Regeln aufstellen; Regeln vorgeben II Unit 4, 68
to **rule** [ruːl] herrschen; regieren I
runaway [ˈrʌnəweɪ] entlaufen I
runner [ˈrʌnə] Läufer/-in I
rural [ˈrʊərl] ländlich II Unit 4, 73

S

salesperson [ˈseɪlzˌpɜːsn] Verkäufer/-in I
salon [ˈsælɒn] Geschäft; Salon II Unit 1, 17
salt-flat [ˈsɒlt ˌflæt] Salzwüste II Unit 5, 95
satisfaction *(no pl)* [ˌsætɪsˈfækʃn] Zufriedenheit; Erfüllung II Unit 4, 72
savings *(pl)* [ˈseɪvɪŋz] Ersparnisse I
musical **scale** [ˌmjuːzɪkl ˈskeɪl] Tonleiter II Unit 5, 92
primary **school** [ˈpraɪmri ˌskuːl] Grundschule II Unit 2, 31
to **score** [skɔː] Tor schießen; Punkte erzielen I
screen [ˌskriːn] Bildschirm II Unit 4, 66
screenplay [ˈskriːnpleɪ] Drehbuch I
to **search** [sɜːtʃ] durchsuchen I
to **season** [ˈsiːzn] würzen I
seasonal [ˈsiːznl] saisonal; jahreszeitlich bedingt II Unit 4, 73
secondary school [ˈsekəndri ˌskuːl] weiterführende Schule II Unit 2, 31
section [ˈsekʃn] Abteilung II Unit 2, 30
segregated [ˈseɡrɪɡeɪtɪd] getrennt II Unit 3, 48

self-confidence [ˌselfˈkɒnfɪdns] Selbstvertrauen II Unit 4, 72
self-esteem [ˌselfɪsˈtiːm] Selbstwertgefühl; Selbstachtung II Unit 4, 67
selfish [ˈselfɪʃ] selbstsüchtig; egoistisch II Unit 1, 21
*to have a **sense** of fun [hæv ə ˌsens əv ˈfʌn] Sinn für Spaß haben I
series [ˈsɪəriːz] Serie; Reihe II Unit 3, 54
a **set** of [ə ˈset əv] eine Liste von II Unit 5, 86
*to be **set** (in) [bi ˈset ɪn] spielen (in); seinen Schauplatz haben (in) I
*to **set** a good example [ˌset ə ˌɡʊd ɪɡˈzɑːmpl] ein Vorbild sein I
*to **set the rules** [ˌset ðə ˈruːlz] Regeln aufstellen; Regeln vorgeben II Unit 4, 68
several [ˈsevrl] einige; mehrere; verschiedene I
*to **sew** [səʊ] nähen I
sewing machine [ˈsəʊɪŋ məˌʃiːn] Nähmaschine I
shame [ʃeɪm] Schande; Schmach I
shape [ʃeɪp] Form I
shift [ʃɪft] Schicht II Unit 2, 30
cruise **ship** [ˈkruːz ˌʃɪp] Kreuzfahrtschiff II Unit 1, 23
shocking [ˈʃɒkɪŋ] entsetzlich; schrecklich; schockierend I
shop owner [ˈʃɒp ˌəʊnə] Ladenbesitzer/-in I
to **sigh** [saɪ] seufzen I
similar [ˈsɪmɪlə] ähnlich II Unit 3, 47
similarity [ˌsɪmɪˈlærəti] Ähnlichkeit; Gemeinsamkeit II Unit 2, 39
sin [sɪn] Sünde I
construction **site** [kənˈstrʌkʃn ˌsaɪt] Baustelle II Unit 1, 20
*to be **situated** [bi ˈsɪtʃueɪtɪd] gelegen sein II Unit 3, 59
skin [skɪn] Haut I
slavery [ˈsleɪvri] Sklaverei I
slide [slaɪd] Folie II Unit 5, 95
to **slip away** [ˌslɪp əˈweɪ] wegrutschen; entgleiten II Unit 3, 49

slot machine [ˈslɒt məˌʃiːn] Glücksspielautomat I
smooth [smuːð] glatt I
to **snore** [snɔː] schnarchen I
so far [ˌsəʊ ˈfɑː] bisher; bis jetzt II Unit 1, 23
so that [ˌsəʊ ˈðæt] damit; so dass II Unit 3, 52
to **solve** [sɒlv] lösen II Unit 5, 84
soul [səʊl] Seele I
space [speɪs] Raum; Platz I
attention **span** [əˈtenʃn ˌspæn] Aufmerksamkeitsspanne II Unit 5, 91
specialist [ˈspeʃlɪst] Spezialist/in II Unit 2, 29
spicy [ˈspaɪsi] würzig; pikant I
sponsorship [ˈspɒnsəʃɪp] Förderung; Unterstützung I
spontaneous [spɒnˈteɪniəs] spontan I
spot [spɒt] Punkt I
*to **spread** [spred] (sich) verbreiten II Unit 3, 52
spring [sprɪŋ] Quelle I
staff [stɑːf] Mitarbeiter; Personal II Unit 5, 88
*to **stand up for sb/sth** [ˌstænd ˈʌp fə] sich für jdn/etw einsetzen I
to **stay in touch (with)** [ˌsteɪ ɪn ˈtʌtʃ wɪð] in Kontakt bleiben (mit) I
steam [stiːm] Dampf I
steel [stiːl] Stahl I
stick [stɪk] Schläger (Hockey); Stock I
to **stir** [stɜː] rühren; umrühren I
grocery **store** [ˈɡrəʊsri ˌstɔː] Lebensmittelladen I
stranded [ˈstrændɪd] gestrandet I
straw [strɔː] Trinkhalm II Unit 5, 88
strength [streŋθ] Stärke II Unit 2, 35
stressful [ˈstresfl] stressig; anstrengend II Unit 1, 22
stuff [stʌf] Zeug I
subject [ˈsʌbdʒɪkt] Betreff; Thema I
suburb [ˈsʌbɜːb] Vorort I
to **succeed** [səkˈsiːd] Erfolg haben II Unit 1, 12
to **suggest** [səˈdʒest] hinweisen auf; vorschlagen I

V Vocabulary

suitable ['suːtəbl] passend; geeignet II Unit 2, 32
sunrise [ˌsʌnraɪz] Sonnenaufgang II Unit 3, 54
sunset ['sʌnset] Sonnenuntergang I
to **supply** with [səˈplaɪ wɪð] zur Verfügung stellen; liefern II Unit 1, 16
support [səˈpɔːt] Unterstützung; Hilfe II Unit 4, 68
to **support** [səˈpɔːt] unterstützen; helfen I
surface ['sɜːfɪs] Oberfläche I
surrounded by [səˈraʊndɪd baɪ] umgeben von I
surrounding [səˈraʊndɪŋ] umgebend II Unit 3, 57
suspenseful [səˈspensfl] spannend II Unit 3, 53
sustainability [səˌsteɪnəˈbɪləti] Nachhaltigkeit I
*to **swear** [sweə] schwören I
to **switch** on [ˌswɪtʃ ˈɒn] einschalten II Unit 4, 71
exhaust **system** [ɪgˈzɔːst ˌsɪstəm] Auspuffanlage; Abgasanlage II Unit 1, 17

T

to clear the **table** [ˌklɪə ðə ˈteɪbl] den Tisch abräumen II Unit 1, 23
to **tackle** sb ['tækl] jdn zu Boden bringen (Rugby); jdn anpacken; jdn angreifen (im Zweikampf) I
*to **take** a deep breath [ˌteɪk ə ˌdiːp ˈbreθ] tief einatmen; tief Luft holen II Unit 3, 54
*to **take** care of sb [ˌteɪk ˈkeər əv] sich um jdn kümmern; für jdn sorgen II Unit 1, 13
task [tɑːsk] Aufgabe; Auftrag II Unit 2, 30
taste [teɪst] Geschmack I
tax [tæks] Steuer II Unit 1, 10
*to **teach** [tiːtʃ] unterrichten; lehren; beibringen I
teammate ['tiːmmeɪt] Mannschaftskamerad/-in I
tear gas [ˈtɪə ˌgæs] Tränengas II Unit 3, 51

technical ['teknɪkl] technisch; handwerklich II Unit 2, 30
technological [ˌteknəˈlɒdʒɪkl] technologisch I
tectonic plate [tekˌtɒnɪk ˈpleɪt] tektonische Platte I
info **terminal** [ˈɪnfəʊ ˌtɜːmɪnl] Infosäule I
so **that** [səʊ ˈðæt] damit; so dass II Unit 3, 52
theme park [ˈθiːm ˌpɑːk] Freizeitpark I
therefore [ˈðeəfɔː] deshalb; deswegen I
thought bubble [ˈθɔːt ˌbʌbl] Denkblase; Gedankenblase II Unit 1, 19
hammer **throwing** [ˈhæmə ˌθrəʊɪŋ] Hammerwerfen I
to **tie** [taɪ] binden; zubinden II Unit 5, 84
tonight [təˈnaɪt] heute Abend; heute Nacht I
tool [tuːl] Werkzeug; Gerät II Unit 1, 16
to stay in **touch** (with) [ˌsteɪ ɪn ˈtʌtʃ wɪð] in Kontakt bleiben (mit) I
to **touch** [tʌtʃ] berühren I
home **town** [ˌhəʊm ˈtaʊn] Heimatstadt I
to **track** [træk] verfolgen; nachverfolgen II Unit 4, 66
trade [treɪd] Handel I
trader [ˈtreɪdə] Händler/-in II Unit 3, 48
traditional [trəˈdɪʃnl] traditionell I
traffic light [ˈtræfɪk ˌlaɪt] (Verkehrs-)Ampel II Unit 2, 36
traffic lane [ˈtræfɪk ˌleɪn] Fahrspur II Unit 2, 36
to **train** [treɪn] trainieren; ausbilden I
traineeship [ˌtreɪˈniːʃɪp] Ausbildung; Praktikum II Unit 2, 40
transportation (AE) [ˌtrænspɔːˈteɪʃn] Transport I
*to be **trapped** [bi ˈtræpt] eingeschlossen sein; in der Falle sitzen I
trash (AE) [træʃ] Abfall; Müll II Unit 5, 84

travel agency [ˈtrævl ˌeɪdʒnsi] Reisebüro I
travel package [ˈtrævl ˌpækɪdʒ] Pauschalreise I
to **treat** [triːt] behandeln I
to **tremble** [ˈtrembl] zittern; beben I
tribal [ˈtraɪbl] Stammes- I
*to be **true** to oneself [bi ˈtruː tə wʌnˌself] sich selbst treu bleiben I
*to come **true** [ˌkʌm ˈtruː] wahr werden; in Erfüllung gehen I
to **turn** (18) [tɜːn] (18 Jahre alt) werden II Unit 1, 10
to **turn** off [ˌtɜːn ˈɒf] abschalten; ausschalten II Unit 2, 40
typically [ˈtɪpɪkli] typisch I

U

ugly [ˈʌgli] hässlich I
uncomfortable [ʌnˈkʌmftəbl] unwohl; unangenehm I
underground [ˌʌndəˈgraʊnd] unter der Erde; unterirdisch I
*to be **unemployed** [ˌʌnɪmˈplɔɪd] arbeitslos sein I
unfortunately [ʌnˈfɔːtʃnətli] leider; unglücklicherweise I
unique [juːˈniːk] einzigartig II Unit 3, 54
universal [ˌjuːnɪˈvɜːsl] allgemein II Unit 3, 48
to **unpack** [ʌnˈpæk] auspacken II Unit 1, 17
unskilled [ʌnˈskɪld] ungelernt II Unit 1, 13
unused [ʌnˈjuːzd] unbenutzt I
upon request [əpɒn rɪˈkwest] auf Anfrage II Unit 2, 34
uprising [ˈʌpˌraɪzɪŋ] Aufstand II Unit 3, 48
urban [ˈɜːbn] (inner)städtisch II Unit 4, 64

V

vacant [ˈveɪknt] frei; unbesetzt II Unit 2, 30
valley [ˈvæli] Tal II Unit 5, 95
valuable [ˈvæljuəbl] wertvoll II Unit 4, 74
value [ˈvæljuː] Wert I

V Vocabulary

variety (of) [vəˈraɪəti əv] Vielzahl (an); Vielfalt (von) I
vehicle [ˈvɪəkl] Fahrzeug I
via [vaɪə] per; über II Unit 2, 31
victory [ˈvɪktri] Sieg II Unit 3, 50
viewer [ˈvjuːə] Zuschauer/-in II Unit 3, 49
virtual reality (VR) [ˌvɜːtjuəl riˈæləti (ˌviːˈɑː)] virtuelle Realität II Unit 4, 64
vision [ˈvɪʒn] Vorstellung; Vision II Unit 3, 55
visual [ˈvɪʒuəl] Bild II Unit 1, 21
vocational [vəˈkeɪʃnl] beruflich; Berufs- II Unit 2, 40
volunteer work [ˌvɒlənˈtɪə ˌwɜːk] Freiwilligendienst I
to volunteer [ˌvɒlənˈtɪə] ehrenamtlich arbeiten I
vote [vəʊt] Abstimmung; Stimme; Wahl II Unit 5, 89
VR goggles [ˌviːˈɑː ˌɡɒɡlz] Virtual-Reality-Brille II Unit 4, 64

W

waste [weɪst] Verschwendung II Unit 1, 16
to waste [weɪst] verschwenden II Unit 5, 84
waterfront [ˈwɔːtəfrʌnt] Hafenviertel; Ufer II Unit 4, 64
weight [weɪt] Gewicht I
What else …? [ˌwɒt ˈels] Was sonst …?; Was noch …? I
whether [ˈweðə] ob II Unit 4, 73
wilderness [ˈwɪldənəs] Wildnis II Unit 5, 95
wildfire [ˈwaɪldfaɪə] Flächenbrand II Unit 5, 82
*to be **willing** to do sth [bi ˌwɪlɪŋ tə ˈduː ˌsʌmθɪŋ] bereit sein etw zu tun II Unit 1, 19
to wonder [ˈwʌndə] sich fragen II Unit 4, 64
volunteer work [ˌvɒlənˈtɪə ˌwɜːk] Freiwilligendienst I
to work out (well) [ˌwɜːk aʊt ˈwel] gut ausgehen; klappen I
workplace [ˈwɜːkpleɪs] Arbeitsplatz II Unit 1, 17
worrying [ˈwʌriɪŋ] beunruhigend; besorgniserregend II Unit 4, 67

Y

to yell [jel] brüllen; laut schreien I
You've made my day! [juv ˌmeɪd maɪ ˈdeɪ] Du hast meinen Tag gerettet! II Unit 4, 76
Yum! [jʌm] Lecker! I

Quellennachweis

Umschlagbild 1 Getty Images Plus, München; E+/Rocky89; **Umschlagbild 2** stock.adobe.com, Dublin; by-studio; **10.1** ShutterStock.com RF, New York; Benny Marty; **10.2** ShutterStock.com RF, New York; Michael Major; **10.3** Getty Images Plus, München; iStock Editorial/Lux_D; **10.4** ShutterStock.com RF, New York; ChameleonsEye; **10.5** ShutterStock.com RF, New York; Rich Carey; **12.1** iStockphoto, Calgary, Alberta; stocknroll; **12.2** stock.adobe.com, Dublin; VAKSMANV; **12.3** stock.adobe.com, Dublin; Wayhome Studio; **13.1** ShutterStock.com RF, New York; Billion Photos; **13.2** Getty Images Plus, München; E+/SolStock; **16** plainpicture GmbH & Co. KG, Hamburg; plainpicture; **17.1** ShutterStock.com RF, New York; Olena Yakobchuk; **17.2** ShutterStock.com RF, New York; Dmitry Kalinovsky; **17.3** stock.adobe.com, Dublin; WavebreakmediaMicro; **17.4** stock.adobe.com, Dublin; Kzenon; **17.5** Getty Images Plus, München; E+/Adene Sanchez; **17.6** ShutterStock.com RF, New York; sirtravelalot; **19.1** Bernhard, Julia - Illustratorin, Mainz; **20.1** Bernhard, Julia - Illustratorin, Mainz; **22.1** ShutterStock.com RF, New York; fizkes; **22.2** ShutterStock.com RF, New York; Joshua Resnick; **22.3** ShutterStock.com RF, New York; GaudiLab; **22.4** ShutterStock.com RF, New York; Tawatchai chaimongkon; **22.5** ShutterStock.com RF, New York; LightField Studios; **22.6** ShutterStock.com RF, New York; hedgehog94; **23.1** Franconia Films, Selb; Moritz Weiß, Marktredwitz; **23.2** Getty Images Plus, München; franckreporter; **23.3** Getty Images Plus, München; kali9; **24** ShutterStock.com RF, New York; Alex Bascuas; **25** ShutterStock.com RF, New York; **26** ShutterStock.com RF, New York; Anurat Imaree; **28.1** ShutterStock.com RF, New York; Stefano_Valeri; **28.2** ShutterStock.com RF, New York; David Ardura; **28.3** Alamy stock photo, Abingdon; Cultura Creative RF/George Karbus Photography; **28.4** Getty Images Plus, München; iStock/Susanne Neumann; **28.5** Alamy stock photo, Abingdon; ilpo musto; **29.1** ShutterStock.com RF, New York; Josep Suria; **29.2** Alamy stock photo, Abingdon; Arterra Picture Library/De Meester Johan; **29.3** ShutterStock.com RF, New York; M2020; **29.4** stock.adobe.com, Dublin; goodluz; **33** www.CartoonStock.com, Bath; Bandura, Dmitry; **35** ShutterStock.com RF, New York; Photographee.eu; **36.1** Getty Images, München; Corbis Historical/George Rinhart; **36.2** Alamy stock photo, Abingdon; Vitalli; **36.3** From: Evening Class © 1996 Maeve Binchy; **38.1** Kramer, Peer, Düsseldorf; **38.2** Kramer, Peer, Düsseldorf; **40** Franconia Films, Selb; Moritz Weiß; **42** ShutterStock.com RF, New York; fizkes; **43** ShutterStock.com RF, New York; AJR_photo; **44** ShutterStock.com RF, New York; Rolf G Wackenberg; **46.1** ShutterStock.com RF, New York; SteffenTravel; **46.2** Getty Images Plus, München; iStock/180705510; **46.3** dreamstime.com, Brentwood, TN; Andrea Basile; **46.4** ShutterStock.com RF, New York; Finn stock; **46.5** ShutterStock.com RF, New York; Moobatto; **48.1** ShutterStock.com RF, New York; Carlo Kaminski; **48.2** Getty Images, München; Rodger Shagam; **48.3** ShutterStock.com RF, New York; Creative Photo Corner; **48.4** Getty Images, München; Corbis Historical; **49** imago images, Berlin; ZUMA Press; **50.1** Getty Images, München; AFP/BORIS HORVAT; **50.2** ShutterStock.com RF, New York; WildSnap; **50.3** Getty Images, München; AFP/MARCO LONGARI; **50.4** Getty Images Plus, München; E+/Rocky89; **51** Alamy stock photo, Abingdon; Andy Myatt; **53** Getty Images Plus, München; E+/Rocky89; **54** ShutterStock.com RF, New York; Martin Prochazkacz; **55** ShutterStock.com RF, New York; JonathanJonesCreate; **57** stock.adobe.com, Dublin; Franz Pfluegl; **58.1** Getty Images Plus, München; iStock/monkeybusinessimages; **58.2** ShutterStock.com RF, New York; Dean Drobot; **58.3** ShutterStock.com RF, New York; Leonid Andronov; **58.4** ShutterStock.com RF, New York; Mangostar; **58.5** ShutterStock.com RF, New York; MilanMarkovic78; **58.6** Getty Images Plus, München; E+/izusek; **59** Dekelver, Christian Illustration, Weinstadt; **61** ShutterStock.com RF, New York; Michal Hornicky; **62.1** ShutterStock.com RF, New York; Sandra Mori; **62.2** ShutterStock.com RF, New York; Debbie Aird Designs; **63.1** Alamy stock photo, Abingdon; Paul Gregg /Travel Africa; **63.2** ShutterStock.com RF, New York; goran_safarek; **64.1** ShutterStock.com RF, New York; FS11; **64.2** ShutterStock.com RF, New York; Daniel Fung; **64.3** ShutterStock.com RF, New York; URAIWONS; **64.4** ShutterStock.com RF, New York; JoeyCheung; **64.5** ShutterStock.com RF, New York; valeriy eydlin; **65** Getty Images Plus, München; DigitalVision/Luis Alvarez; **67.1** nach: GlobalWebIndex 2018; **67.2** ShutterStock.com RF, New York; Rawpixel.com; **67.3** ShutterStock.com RF, New York; Ebichan; **68** ShutterStock.com RF, New York; Ebichan; **70.1** ShutterStock.com RF, New York; elwynn; **70.2** ShutterStock.com RF, New York; Joshua Davenport; **70.3** ShutterStock.com RF, New York; Siam Vector; **70.4** ShutterStock.com RF, New York; Pelikh Alexey; **70.5** ShutterStock.com RF, New York; HikoPhotography; **70.6** ShutterStock.com RF, New York; Jimmy Siu; **72** ShutterStock.com RF, New York; Peshkova; **73** ShutterStock.com RF, New York; Mumemories; **75** ShutterStock.com RF, New York; Chokniti Khongchum; **76** Franconia Films, Selb; Tom Körner; **77** CartoonStock Ltd, Bath; Baldwin, Mike; **78.1** ShutterStock.com RF, New York; Atstock Productions; **78.2** ShutterStock.com RF, New York; William Perugini; **78.3** ShutterStock.com RF, New York; RossHelen; **78.4** ShutterStock.com RF, New York; Hadrian; **78.5** ShutterStock.com RF, New York; Jacob Lund; **80** ShutterStock.com RF, New York; SAHACHATZ; **82.1** ShutterStock.com RF, New York; Sean Pavone; **82.2** Alamy stock photo, Abingdon; inga spence; **82.3** Getty Images Plus, München; iStock Editorial/Austin Nooe; **82.4** ShutterStock.com RF, New York; littlenySTOCK; **82.5** Getty Images Plus, München; iStock/Toa55; **84** © 2019 CBS Interactive Inc. All Rights Reserved.; **84** ShutterStock.com RF, New York; acidmit; **85** ShutterStock.com RF, New York; Carol Mellema; **86** ShutterStock.com RF, New York; iuliia_n; **88** ShutterStock.com RF, New York; Monkey Business Images; **89** CartoonStock Ltd, Bath; Keet, Keren; **90** ShutterStock.com RF, New York; stock_photo_world; **91** ShutterStock.com RF, New York; Lapina; **92** ShutterStock.com RF, New York; Lightcube; **92** Getty Images, München; Joe Amon/Denver Post; **94.1** ShutterStock.com RF, New York; ONYXprj; **94.2** ShutterStock.com RF, New York; galunga.art; **95.1** ShutterStock.com RF, New York; agap; **95.2** ShutterStock.com RF, New York; Bill Perry; **95.3** ShutterStock.com RF, New York; Mikhail Kolesnikov; **96.1** ShutterStock.com RF, New York; Francesco Carucci; **96.2** ShutterStock.com RF, New York; Toa55; **96.3** ShutterStock.com RF, New York; Katrina Brown; **96.4** ShutterStock.com RF, New York; Gleb Tarro; **96.5** ShutterStock.com RF, New York; randy andy; **96.6** ShutterStock.com RF, New York; pablopicasso; **97** iStockphoto, Calgary, Alberta; Scott Vickers; **98** ShutterStock.com RF, New York; anna42f; **98** ShutterStock.com RF, New York; anna42f; **100** Toni O'Loughlin, © 2009 Guardian News & Media Ltd.; **100.1** ShutterStock.com RF, New York; Studio Lucky; **100.2** Getty Images, München; Getty Images Entertainment/Getty Images AsiaPac; **102** © 2019 Guardian News & Media Ltd.; **102.1** ShutterStock.com RF, New York; Andrey_Popov; **103** www.CartoonStock.com, Bath; Kincaid, Kelly; **104** Marianne Thamm, 2016 Guardian News & Media Ltd.; **104** Getty Images, München; Getty Images North America/Theo Wargo; **105** From: Born a Crime ©2016 Trevor Noah; **106** Press Association, 5th Oct 2017; **106** ShutterStock.com RF, New York; Jacob Lund; **108** Susie Cagle © 2020 Guardian News & Media Ltd.; **108** ShutterStock.com RF, New York; emattil; **113.1** Getty Images, München; Corbis Historical/George Rinhart; **113.2** Alamy stock photo, Abingdon; Vitalli; **115.1** ullstein bild, Berlin; C. T. Fotostudio; **115.2** Alamy stock photo, Abingdon; Granger Historical Picture Archive; **115.3** Alamy stock photo, Abingdon; kolvenbach; **115.4** Picture-Alliance, Frankfurt/M.; RAINER JENSEN; **116.1** Getty Images, München; AFP/BORIS HORVAT; **116.2**